SIX AMERICAN POETS

from Emily Dickinson

to the Present:

An Introduction

Edited by ALLEN TATE

UNIVERSITY OF MINNESOTA PRESS · MINNEAPOLIS

Library of Congress Catalog Card Number: 70-172932

ISBN 0-8166-0630-7

The sources of quoted passages in this volume are as follows:

EMILY DICKINSON: Lines from poems 305, 341, 642, 838, 1445, 1551, 1714 are reprinted by permission of the publishers and the Trustees of Amherst College from Thomas H. Johnson, Editor, *The Poems of Emily Dickinson*, Cambridge, Mass.: The Belknap Press of Harvard University Press, Copyright 1951, 1955 by The President and Fellows of Harvard College. Lines from poems 305, 341, and 642 are reprinted by permission of Little, Brown and Co. from Thomas H. Johnson, Editor, *The Complete Poems of Emily Dickinson* (no. 341 and no. 642 Copyright 1929, © 1957 by Mary L. Hampson; no. 305 Copyright 1914, 1942 by Martha Dickinson Bianchi).

EDWIN ARLINGTON ROBINSON: Excerpts from *Collected Poems of Edwin Arlington Robinson* (1937) are quoted by permission of The Macmillan Company.

MARIANNE MOORE: Excerpts from poems in the following volumes by Marianne Moore are reprinted with the permission of The Macmillan Company: *Selected Poems* (copyright 1935 by Marianne Moore; renewed 1963 by Marianne Moore and T. S. Eliot); *What Are Years* (copyright 1941 by Marianne Moore); *Nevertheless* (copyright 1941 by Marianne Moore); *Collected Poems* (copyright 1951 by Marianne Moore). Faber and Faber, Ltd., and Miss Moore also granted permission for the use of excerpts from *Collected Poems*.

CONRAD AIKEN: Permission to use the excerpts from *Collected Poems* (published by Oxford University Press, copyright 1953) and *Selected Poems* (published by Oxford University Press, copyright 1961) was granted by Conrad Aiken.

E. E. CUMMINGS: "nonsun blob a," Copyright, 1944, by E. E. Cummings. Reprinted from his volume *Poems 1923–1954* by permission of Harcourt Brace Jovanovich, Inc. "mortals)," Copyright, 1940, by E. E. Cummings; renewed 1968 by Marion Morehouse Cummings. Reprinted from his volume *Poems 1923–1954* by permission of Harcourt Brace Jovanovich, Inc. "1 (a," from *95 Poems*, © 1958 by E. E. Cummings. Reprinted by permission of Harcourt Brace Jovanovich, Inc.

HART CRANE: Excerpts from *Complete Poems and Selected Letters and Prose* by Hart Crane used by permission of Liveright Publishers, New York. Copyright 1933, 1958, 1966 by Liveright Publishing Corp.

THE MINNESOTA

LIBRARY

ON AMERICAN WRITERS

THE six essays which appear in this book were first published separately in the series of University of Minnesota Pamphlets on American Writers and, together with the other pamphlets in the series, are intended as introductions to authors who have helped to shape American culture over the years of our colonial and national existence. The editors of the pamphlet series have been Richard Foster, William Van O'Connor, Allen Tate, Leonard Unger, Robert Penn Warren, and George T. Wright. Many pamphlets, in addition to the six represented here, are available, and others are scheduled for publication by the University of Minnesota Press.

Contents

SIX AMERICAN POETS

FROM EMILY DICKINSON

TO THE PRESENT

Introduction

O F THE six poets discussed in this volume only two are living, and they are both past eighty: Marianne Moore and Conrad Aiken. Miss Moore and Mr. Aiken are poets of great vitality and staying power, but one can scarcely believe that they still have their most important work to do. Here, in this collection, we begin with Emily Dickinson who died in 1886, a year before Miss Moore was born and three before Mr. Aiken. Robinson was seventeen in 1886; he could have known some of Emily Dickinson's poems and been influenced by them, though this possible influence is not obvious. Robinson was exactly thirty years older than Hart Crane, and outlived him by three years: Crane committed suicide in 1932 and Robinson died in 1935. Crane is the youngest poet to be considered here, Robinson next to Dickinson the oldest. To belabor this chronology is not wholly irrelevant, for the overlap in ages from Dickinson to Moore, Aiken, and Crane gives a somewhat longer perspective to modern American poetry than the rise of modernism around 1912 has led us to look for. All six of our poets were born in the nineteenth century: I state this obvious fact in order to state another, equally obvious: the nineteenth century is seven decades in the past. The impressive

3

variety and versatility of contemporary American poetry, includ-
ing its "modernist" development, has been the achievement of
men and women born before 1901.

The poets who are usually credited with bringing about the
twentieth-century revolution — Pound and Eliot — could well be
dropped from the literary history of our age, and we should still
have one of the great epochs of poetry in English. They cannot,
of course be dropped out, except insofar as we must consider in
the top rank Robinson and Frost; for all the others, certainly
four of the poets now under consideration either were influenced
by Pound and Eliot or would at any rate be different had Pound
and Eliot not preceded them. Crane, for example, had to fight
his way through Eliot in order to develop his own style — a not
unusual situation in the history of poetry as well as of the novel.
But with Robinson and Frost one must also remember two other
older poets, who are generally "placed" with the innovators, but
who were not influenced by them: Marianne Moore and Wallace
Stevens, neither of whom owes anything to Pound and Eliot, for
they developed independently of the modernist revolution, though
both represent a radical break with their nineteenth-century prede-
cessors. Miss Moore, as Jean Garrigue demonstrates, owes nothing
to anybody, except perhaps to T. S. Eliot for encouragement;
Stevens knew the Imagists, but any contemporaneous influence
stopped with them. And yet the "programmatic" criticism of
Pound and Eliot undoubtedly created an atmosphere in which
the later work of these two poets could be written and appreci-
ated. Eliot's *The Sacred Wood* and Pound's *Pavannes and Divi-
sions* made it possible for the small audience for poetry to accept
poets who were, like Miss Moore, unlike either Pound or Eliot.
Stevens frequently told people that he didn't want to risk being
influenced by Eliot and therefore refused to read him; and Eliot
once told me that he admired Stevens but felt that he repeated
himself too often, a negative fault that he might have avoided
had he asked his friends to read his poems before they were pub-
lished. Stevens of all the first-rate poets of our time was the most
complete "loner." Eliot himself always sought the criticism of

his friends — Aiken and Pound in the early days and, later, in the period of the *Quartets,* John Hayward.

E. E. Cummings (1894–1962), a poet of whom I was immensely fond as a friend for almost forty years, was a "loner" too, but in all other qualities different from Wallace Stevens. (As a footnote, or perhaps as an item for literary sub-history, I can report that Stevens told me he thought Cummings a disciple of Guillaume Apollinaire, and therefore did not like his poems.) Estlin Cummings's genius developed from romantic lyricism into a genre that may be described as lyrical satire: his modernist poetry was a violent protest against everything modern. Most modern poets have been conservatives, politically and socially; among those of my acquaintance Cummings was the only "reactionary." He is the great satirist among modernist poets. His typographical tricks are not important: his poems, read aloud, especially by himself — for he had a beautiful voice — were quite as effective as when read with the eye. His "My father moved through dooms of love" is one of the finest modern elegies, good enough to stand with Yeats's "In Memory of Major Robert Gregory." Mrs. Triem's essay is useful descriptive criticism.

Of the six poets under consideration here, three are in the strict sense "modernist": Aiken, Cummings, and Crane. Miss Moore, who in no other sense is like Emily Dickinson, is, like her, unique. Robinson, like Robert Frost, is pre-modernist, a late Victorian agnostic and formalist, who in retrospect reminds one of the impenetrable mysteries of the history of literary reputations. William Vaughn Moody was his exact contemporary (born in 1869) and George Edward Woodberry was only slightly older: both overshadowed Robinson as the leading poets of the period 1890–1918 and were no doubt the American poets Eliot had in mind when he wrote, in 1945, that Americans of his generation had no immediate tradition to take off from and develop. Pound and Eliot might have admired Robinson (is it recorded anywhere that they did?), but they could not have "used" him. I myself tried in the early twenties to write Robinsonian verse, but it was imitation at a low pitch; it could only have been Robinson warmed over had I continued it. Robinson, as Mr. Coxe shows us, brought to an end a great mode of Anglo-American poetry, not inferior to that of his older Victorian contemporaries; for as Radcliffe Squires has observed of another American poet, it takes as much talent to end a period as to begin one. One would like to explore the anomaly offered us by the independent, extra-revolutionary pre-modernists, Frost along with Robinson; but Leonard Unger, in his Introduction to *Seven Modern American Poets*, has deprived me of the privilege of discussing Frost by making the most judicious observations that I have seen. The only American poet of my own generation who assimilated Robinson without imitating him was Phelps Putnam (1894–1948), a first-rate poet now forgotten; but Putnam "used" him in one poem only, a long narrative masterpiece, based upon a classical myth, called "Ballad of a Strange Thing."

Like Gerard Manley Hopkins, Miss Dickinson had to wait many years after her death to receive the recognition that was her due. It was not until the publication of *The Single Hound* in 1914, a collection edited and in many instances revised and "improved" by her niece, Martha Dickinson Bianchi, that she began to be recognized as a great poet. In 1924, Madame Bianchi, with the aid of her secretary Alfred Leete Hampson, published *The Complete Poems of Emily Dickinson*. The title is misleading: there were literally hundreds of poems yet to be discovered. This is not the place to enter the dark, tangled wood of Dickinson scholarship. Suffice it to say that not until the research of Thomas H. Johnson, published in three volumes, 1955, 1960, and 1961, could we be certain of having anything like a definitive collection. In my opinion the crucial essay on Miss Dickinson, to which all future critics are indebted, is the Introduction to *Selected Poems of Emily Dickinson* by Conrad Aiken. This was published in London in 1924, but not, I believe, in the United States. The essays by R. P. Blackmur and myself, who discovered Aiken's essay at about the same time, would not have been possible without Aiken's pioneer work: it was the first serious critical reading of Dickinson and it remains one of the best. Miss Dickinson's admirers should also read Austin Warren's "Emily Dickinson," a review-essay of Mr. Johnson's three-volume edition of 1955. Aiken, Blackmur, Warren, and now Denis Donoghue are the most perceptive readers' guides to the difficult spinster of Amherst.

Over the years I have written so much about Hart Crane that I hesitate to attempt further critical comment. Crane criticism proliferates like a tropical jungle: much of it is useless, but there is a great deal that the reader will find rewarding. Philip Horton's *Hart Crane: The Life of an American Poet*, published in 1937, five years after Crane's death, is an indispensable book, even though Horton could not have known as much about Crane as John Unterecker gives us, in an almost day-by-day chronology, in his recent biography. Crane was a great lyric poet whose "problem," complicated by the quasi-epic *The Bridge*, will never be solved; in this he resembles all other great poets: the work remains inexhaustible. In my opinion, the best essay on Crane, up to 1957, is R. P. Blackmur's, in *Form and Value in Modern Poetry*. And now Mr. Spears does for Crane, on a smaller scale, what he did at length for the poetry of W. H. Auden: he has written the most sensible, the most perceptive, and the most astute criticism of Crane that we have. If the reader is interested in Crane's place in the larger context of "modernist" poetry, he would do well to read Mr. Spears's recent book, *Dionysus and the City*, which is to date the definitive historical criticism of twentieth-century poetry.

I come last to Conrad Aiken, and in doing so I am aware of a certain irony. Aiken is one of the great poets of a great period, and he usually brings up the rear in a procession led by Pound and Eliot. He is now past eighty, and one almost despairs of seeing justice done him in his lifetime. He is the most versatile man of letters of the century: he has excelled in criticism, in fiction, and in poetry. Why has he been underestimated in all three categories? The answer is not far to seek. In criticism, he has not written a theoretical essay, like Eliot's "Tradition and the Individual Talent," which formulated a program for an entire generation of poets (among whom I include myself). His criticism consists of reviews almost exclusively; I submit that without exception they

are as valid today as they were the day they were written; and I
cite as a brilliant example the review of *The Waste Land*, writ-
ten a few months after the poem appeared. (Matthiessen am-
plified Aiken's insights but did not exceed them.) Among his
five novels there is no *The Sun Also Rises*, no *The Great Gatsby*,
and (let us be thankful) no *Ulysses*. But *Blue Voyage* (1927) is the
equal of if not superior to all the novels of Virginia Woolf, with
the possible exception to *Mrs. Dalloway*. And the poetry? What
poet of this century has written as many sustained masterpieces
as Conrad Aiken? I will list a few of them: *Senlin, Punch: The
Immortal Liar, Prelude* and *Preludes for Memnon, John Deth,*
"Tetélestai," *Time in the Rock, The Morning Song of Lord Zero,*
and last but not least, and out of chronological order, *Brownstone
Eclogues*. This series of "city" poems is far superior to Eliot's
Preludes. Why are they not better known? One answer to this
question and to the question of the general neglect is that, al-
though Aiken is as modernist as anybody, he is the most tradi-
tional of the modernists. He has never gone in for the fragmenta-
tion and distortion of traditional forms, such as gave *The Waste
Land* its sensational influence. He is a master of traditional
prosody, of a great variety of scanned versification. He is modern-
ist in his critical introspection, his subtle psychological search into
the Freudian ego and id; and this exploration of the modern
consciousness is subtler and more profound than anything Wal-
lace Stevens achieved. I put him above Pound (the innovator and
gadfly is not always the greater poet) and at the top with Eliot.
When posterity reshuffles the cards, three other poets of that
generation, not directly related to the innovators, will, I predict,
come out aces: Van Doren and Wheelock, and Ransom, the only
one of the three to have had, while living, his just fame. Jay
Martin's *Conrad Aiken: A Life of His Art* (1962) is now bril-
liantly supplemented by Reuel Denney's essay in the present vol-
ume. One hopes that this publication will bring it to the attention
of an even larger public than it has had as a pamphlet in the
Minnesota series on American writers.

Emily Dickinson

O<small>N</small> T<small>UESDAY</small>, August 16, 1870, Thomas Wentworth Higginson visited Emily Dickinson at her home in Amherst, Massachusetts. It was their first meeting, although they had been in correspondence since April 1862 when the poet addressed herself to the well-known critic "to say if my Verse is alive." Higginson's account of this first meeting is given in a letter to his wife. "A step like a pattering child's in entry," he reported, "& in glided a little plain woman with two smooth bands of reddish hair & a face a little like Belle Dove's; not plainer — with no good feature — in a very plain & exquisitely clean white pique & a blue net worsted shawl. She came to me with two day lilies which she put in a sort of childlike way into my hand & said 'These are my introduction' in a soft frightened breathless childlike voice — & added under her breath Forgive me if I am frightened; I never see strangers & hardly know what I say . . ." Perhaps Emily Dickinson protested her shyness too much. When she chose to speak, she had no difficulty in finding voice. On this occasion, indeed, "she talked soon & thenceforward continuously — & deferentially — sometimes stopping to ask me to talk instead of her — but readily recommencing." Higginson thought some parts of the conversation worth quoting. "If I read a book," Emily Dickinson said, and if "it makes my whole body so

9

cold no fire ever can warm me I know *that* is poetry. If I feel physically as if the top of my head were taken off, I know *that* is poetry." She spoke of finding "ecstasy in living." When Higginson asked "if she never felt want of employment, never going off the place & never seeing any visitor," she answered, "I never thought of conceiving that I could ever have the slightest approach to such a want in all future time," adding, "I feel that I have not expressed myself strongly enough." In Emily Dickinson the tokens of frailty are genuine, but they do not deny a certain independence of spirit.

Emily Elizabeth Dickinson was born in Amherst on December 10, 1830, the second child of Edward and Emily Dickinson. Her brother William Austin Dickinson was born on April 16, 1829, her sister Lavinia Norcross Dickinson on February 28, 1833. The Dickinsons were an important family in Amherst. Emily's father was a prominent man in public life, treasurer of Amherst College from 1835, a member of the state legislature for several terms, a member of Congress for one term. He was a dedicated Whig, and a resolute defender of temperance. As a parent, he was somewhat harsh, or at best remote: "thin dry & speechless," he appeared to Higginson; "I saw what her life has been." Emily Dickinson told Higginson, "My father only reads on Sunday — he reads *lonely* & *rigorous* books." " 'I say unto you,' Father would read at Prayers, with a militant Accent that would startle one." "Could you tell me what home is," Emily Dickinson asked Higginson; "I never had a mother. I suppose a mother is one to whom you hurry when you are troubled." In 1862 she wrote, "I have a Brother and Sister — My Mother does not care for thought — and Father, too busy with his Briefs — to notice what we do — He buys me many Books — but begs me not to read them — because he fears they joggle the Mind." When her father died, however, in June 1874, Emily was deeply distressed: "Though it is many nights, my mind never comes home." A year later, her mother suffered paralysis and became an invalid for the rest of her life. During those years Emily attended her mother and came to love her. "We were never intimate Mother and Children while she was our Mother — but Mines in the same Ground meet by tunneling and when she became our Child, the

Affection came." Mrs. Dickinson died in November 1882: "We hope that Our Sparrow has ceased to fall, though at first we believe nothing."

But "Childhood's citadel" was a somber place. The three children were devoted to one another, but their home did not provoke gaiety. When Austin Dickinson married Susan Gilbert in 1856 and set up house next door, gaiety began to find its natural home. One visitor, Kate Anthon, later recalled happy days to Susan. "Those happy visits at your house! Those celestial evenings in the Library — The blazing *wood* fire — *Emily* — *Austin*, — The music — The rampant fun — The inextinguishable laughter, The uproarious spirits of our chosen — our most congenial circle." But that was next door. Edward Dickinson's house was an upright place, indeed perpendicular, in some respects like Mr. Wentworth's house in Henry James's *The Europeans*, where responsibilities are taken hard. "Where are our moral grounds?" Mr. Wentworth demands on an occasion of great stress in that novel, challenged by moral ambiguities painfully French. Emily Dickinson read the novel and quoted Mr. Wentworth's question in a letter to her friend Mrs. Holland. There is a certain propriety in the question, as Emily Dickinson recalled it, since she herself grew up in a place and time of such questions. To her, in that setting, conscience was "Childhood's nurse." Father might be remote, but he was an inescapable moral fact, God but more than God. "I see — New Englandly," Emily Dickinson said in a poem (numbered 285 in the Johnson edition; the numbers in parentheses hereafter refer to that edition). She sees New Englandly for the same reason that, in the same poem, she takes the robin as her "Criterion for Tune," because "I grow — where Robins do."

She went to school at Amherst Academy, studying Latin, French, history, rhetoric, botany, geology, and mental philosophy. In 1847 she entered Mount Holyoke Female Seminary at South Hadley, a lively school where she confronted the large religious questions and engaged in the more tangible study of history, chemistry, Latin, physiology, and English grammar. But her official education was often interrupted by debility and poor health.

With the exception of brief visits to Boston, Philadelphia, and
Washington, her life was lived entirely in a small New England
circle of which Amherst was the center. Even in Amherst her
life was not omnivorous. In October 1856 she won the second
prize and seventy-five cents for her rye and Indian bread at the lo-
cal cattle show, and the following year she was a member of the
committee in that category. But she did not roam the hills; she saw
what could be seen from her window, from her garden, from next
door, occasionally from the church. She chose to live in that way, as
if to do so were then to live New Englandly. There is no reason to
assume that her choice was morbid. Rather, it was conscientious.

In 1881 she wrote to Higginson. "We dwell as when you saw
us — the mighty dying of my Father made no external change —
Mother and Sister are with me, and my Brother and pseudo Sister,
in the nearest House — When Father lived I remained with him
because he would miss me — Now, Mother is helpless — a holier
demand — I do not go away, but the Grounds are ample — al-
most travel — to me, and the few that I knew — came — since
my Father died." As a young girl she took her seclusion more
lightly. From Mount Holyoke she wrote to her brother, asking,
"Has the Mexican war terminated yet & how? Are we beat? Do you
know of any nation about to besiege South Hadley?" Years later,
she told Mrs. Holland that her notion of politics was accurately
represented by the sentence "George Washington was the Father
of his Country," qualified by the rejoinder "George Who?" But
in fact she kept up with current events, mainly because of her de-
votion to the *Springfield Daily Republican*. A letter to Susan
in September 1882 makes a literary joke of the capture of Ahmed
Arabi Pasha at Tel-el-Kebir. Gordon and the British garrison at
Khartoum are fodder for a witty letter to Theodore Holland in
1884. True, she was not interested in "the stale inflation of the
minor News." She was odd, reticent, private. In Amherst she was
considered a mythological being. Children longed to see her, since
the sight would constitute a vision. When the doorbell rang, she
ran away, deeper into the house. "All men say 'What' to me," she
told Higginson; so she restricted the number of questioners.

If she was a lonely girl, by common standards, loneliness was her choice. Company did not flee her. Some requirement of her sensibility was fulfilled by seclusion which could not have been fulfilled by company. It is clear in the poems that loneliness was one of the conditions she chose to know. Sometimes she thought of isolation as her fate, "circumstance of Lot" (1116), and in the love poems absence of the beloved constitutes a terrible kind of loneliness, "The Horror not to be surveyed" (777). But in one poem (1695) she speaks of "That polar privacy/ A soul admitted to itself," calling it "Finite Infinity." This was the solitude she chose to know; it was like the solitudes of space, sea, and death, but greater than these, because deeper. It occupied a "profounder site" than any other solitude. It is evoked again in another poem (1116) as "another Loneliness/ That many die without." This loneliness is the consequence of "nature," sometimes, and sometimes of "thought," "And whoso it befall/ Is richer than could be revealed/ By mortal numeral." Emily Dickinson elected to be "rich" in this sense, at whatever common cost. Higginson said that the Dickinson home in Amherst was "a house where each member runs his or her own selves." This was especially true of Emily Dickinson's life; she ran her own life, she conducted her own "self." Her sufferings were of the common kind, abrasions of feeling, the pain of loss, partings, deaths; the experiences were not extraordinary, only the particular character of their reception. Loneliness was one of those experiences, remarkable only in the intensity of its reception. It might almost be said that Emily Dickinson did not suffer loneliness; she commanded it. She commanded everything she needed. When she needed a relationship, she commanded it.

The pattern of these relationships is exemplified in Emily Dickinson's friendship with Benjamin Franklin Newton, a law student who spent two years in her father's office in Amherst. Newton was nine years older than Emily Dickinson; he "became to me," she said, "a gentle, yet grave Preceptor, teaching me what to read, what authors to admire, what was most grand or beautiful in nature, and that sublimer lesson, a faith in things unseen, and in a life again, nobler, and much more blessed." He died on March 24, 1853. "When a little Girl, I had a friend," Emily Dickinson later wrote to Higginson, "who taught me Immortality — but venturing too near, himself — he never returned." For the rest of her life, Emily Dickinson sought gentle yet grave preceptors, men older than herself, more accomplished in the ways of the world. It may be said that she sought a father, a more benign father than her own. But this does not say much. The men she found were diverse in character and temper; further differences were prescribed in the terms of each relationship. Rev. Charles Wadsworth was Emily Dickinson's spiritual preceptor for several years. Samuel Bowles, editor of the *Springfield Daily Republican*, was important as an object of feeling: "We miss your vivid Face and the besetting Accents, you bring from your Numidian Haunts." Higginson was Emily Dickinson's literary guide, critic, surgeon. "And for this, Preceptor, I shall bring you — Obedience — the Blossom from my Garden, and every gratitude I know." Her most impassioned relationship was with Judge Otis P. Lord: it appears that Emily Dickinson was in love with him for the last six years of his life, from 1878 to 1884. And there is the unknown man, unless he is Bowles, addressed as "Master": "I want to see you more — Sir — than all I wish for in this world — and the wish — altered a little — will be my only one — for the skies."

These relationships were important to Emily Dickinson, in different ways and in different degrees. It is impossible to be precise; not enough is known. Where a friendship was crucial to her, she commanded it even beyond the grave, writing to Bowles's widow, for instance, as if to retain the affection by reciting it. Some of her greatest poems were provoked by moments in the drama of these relationships. "He fumbles at your Soul" (315) may be a poem about God, or about some less celestial power; whatever its ostensible subject, it is totally dependent upon the experience of one soul "mastering" another. That experience may be real, or imaginatively conceived; but that it came, however deviously, from Emily Dickinson's sense of master and pupil, there can be no doubt. The least that may be said of these relationships is that they tested, extended, and sometimes tormented her sensibility, with results good in the poems if hard in the life.

Some of the relationships were easy enough. Higginson never quite decided whether his Amherst correspondent was a genius or merely crazed, but it is clear that, within his limits, he helped her. He thought her poems wayward and disorderly, he protested that he could not understand. She promised to do better, next time. But there is no evidence that he damaged the work or disabled the genius. When he published, with Mabel Loomis Todd, Emily Dickinson's *Poems*, the second series, in 1891, one of the first readers was Alice James, sister of Henry James and William James. In her *Diary* for January 6, 1892, she wrote: "It is reassuring to hear the English pronouncement that Emily Dickinson is fifth-rate — they have such a capacity for missing quality; the robust evades them equally with the subtle." Then she continued: "Her being sicklied o'er with T. W. Higginson makes one quake lest there be a latent flaw which escapes one's vision." There were, indeed, latent flaws in Emily Dickinson: a tendency to play up problems as if they were mysteries, a disposition to cultivate the breathless note, a certain coyness disfiguring the charm. But there are no grounds for assuming that Higginson was responsible for these flaws; they were in Emily Dickinson long before she knew her mentor. He is blameless. If he had understood her more profoundly, he would have been, in addition, angelic.

So Emily Dickinson ran her life at Amherst, moving between the kitchen, the garden, her room. She baked bread, made puddings, attended to her knitting, sent messages next door, wrote hundreds of poems and hundreds of letters as pointed as poems. She played the piano. In the garden she had green fingers, succeeding where others failed with Daphne odora, violet, and the day lily. She walked with her dog Carlo, "large as myself, that my Father bought me." From her window, she saw the circus pass. "I saw the sunrise on the Alps since I saw you," she wrote to Mrs. Holland. "Travel why to Nature, when she dwells with us? Those who lift their hats shall see her, as devout do God." Her dreams were bountiful, as in a poem (646) she invoked "Certainties of

Sun" and "Midsummer — in the Mind." In the same mood she
identified Nature with "what we know," in her own case with the
hill, the afternoon, the squirrel, the bumble bee, the bobolink,
thunder, the cricket — the unquestionable things. "Nature —
the Gentlest Mother is,/ Impatient of no Child" (790). But there
were other moods; as Emerson wrote in the essay "Circles," our
moods do not believe in each other. In one of those moods (364)
nature seemed to Emily Dickinson rude, uttering jubilee the morn-
ing after woe; and in another (1624) "an Approving God" sets his
minions to work, making pain, sorrow, and death. There is no
contradiction. Emily Dickinson is a moody poet, giving herself to
the moment.

Perhaps she trusted that, at some level, everything would co-
here; one moment would not disown another. "All her life," R. P.
Blackmur wrote of her, "she was looking for a subject, and the
looking *was* her subject, in life as in poetry." Perhaps she knew
this, or hoped against hope that it might be so. In a blunt para-
phrase, many of her poems would contradict one another; but her
answers are always provisional. Only her questions are definitive.
She spent, but did not waste or consume, her life in looking for a
subject. Looking for one thing, she nevertheless lived by taking
whatever each occasion offered; if it was not the definitive thing,
it would serve, for the present, instead of finality. "Forever — is
composed of Nows" (624). So she trusted in the significance of
Now, and in the search conducted under present auspices. Many
poems speak of the "exultation" of search, the thrill of voyaging,
"the going/ Of an inland soul to sea" (76). "Our lives are Swiss"
(80), she says, except that the imagination discloses to us the Alps
and Italy beyond. Let us say that her imagination was Alpine,
ascribing to the poet a corresponding urge to scale the heights of
experience. "I would go, to know!" (114). In a letter to Higginson
she wrote, "Nature is a Haunted House — but Art — a House that
tries to be haunted." This does not demean art; rather, it gives the
terms of its challenge. To Emily Dickinson, art is the place of ex-
periment and risk, to write is to dare, the imagination sends up
strange words as trial balloons. The greatest risks are taken by the

inland soul. "To fight aloud, is very brave," she concedes. "But *gallanter,* I know/ Who charge within the bosom/ The Cavalry of Wo" (126). For ignorance, there is nothing to be said. "At least, to know the worst, is sweet!" (172). No wonder Emily Dickinson was content to stay in her room, her garden; with an imagination as challenging as hers, practical experience was bound to appear dull, predictable, banal. She was already far beyond anything life could give as event or experience, because she had already imagined it. She had haunted every house.

This was her way. She tested everything, whether it was given by experience or by imagination. Every house had to be searched for ghosts. Many of her poems apply to the great religious doctrines the same interrogative pressure. Of her own religious faith, virtually anything may be said, with some show of evidence. She may be represented as an agnostic, a heretic, a skeptic, a Christian. She grew up in a Christian family, but she was not devout. She did not possess a talent for conviction. In 1873 her father, his own faith recently renewed, arranged that the local Congregational minister, J. L. Jenkins, would offer Emily some spiritual guidance. The interview took place. The minister's son later wrote, "All that is really known is that my father reported to the perplexed parent that Miss Emily was 'sound,' and let it go at that." The report was generous. At about the same time as her spiritual interview, Emily Dickinson wrote to her cousins Louise and Frances Norcross: "There is that which is called an 'awakening' in the church, and I know of no choicer ecstasy than to see Mrs. [Sweetser] roll out in crape every morning, I suppose to intimidate antichrist; at least it would have that effect on me." But, in fact, Emily Dickinson's Christianity was never a firm conviction. As a schoolgirl, she resisted the religious stirrings of her circle; the Amherst revival in 1844 did not succeed with her. In January 1846 she reported to a former schoolmate, Abiah Root, "I was almost persuaded to be a christian," but the strongest emphasis was on the word "almost."

Throughout her life, there were moments in which she longed for faith. In a late poem she wrote:

Those — dying then,
Knew where they went —
They went to God's Right Hand —
That Hand is amputated now
And God cannot be found —

The abdication of Belief
Makes the Behavior small —
Better an ignis fatuus
Than no illume at all —   (1551)

But this was one moment among many different moments. Emily
Dickinson seems to have thought of religious faith as an enforced
choice: one must choose between God and man, between eternity
and time. In 1846 she wrote: "I have perfect confidence in God &
his promises & yet I know not why, I feel that the world
holds a predominant place in my affections." The question of
faith was the question of affection, and in the Calvinist idiom one
affection canceled another. In 1848 she wrote: "There is a great
deal of religious interest here and many are flocking to the ark of
safety. I have not yet given up to the claims of Christ, but trust I
am not entirely thoughtless on so important & serious a subject."
But within a short time, she declared herself "standing alone in
rebellion, and growing very careless." She quarreled with Susan
about religion: "and though in that last day, the Jesus Christ you
love, remark he does not know me — there is a darker spirit will
not disown it's child." Again, it is momentary bravado, one rhet-
oric incited by another. A more urbane version appears some
months later: "I went to church all day in second dress, and boots.
We had such precious sermons from Mr Dwight. One about un-
belief, and another Esau. Sermons on unbelief ever did attract me."
Sermons on Christian doctrine did not attract her. When Mr.
Steele preached upon "predestination," she refused to listen; "I
do not respect 'doctrines.'" She wrote to Higginson of her family:
"They are religious — except me — and address an Eclipse, every
morning — whom they call their 'Father.'"

While Emily Dickinson's early emotions often took a religious
turn, she was never willing to have them curbed by the discipline

of belief. Doctrine was discipline, and therefore alien to a sensibility always somewhat willful. She would have believed, if she had been allowed to believe anything she liked. In later years her emotions took several different turns, as if her will were the wind. Now, for the most part, she was content to think of the "Supernatural" as "the Natural, disclosed." Of course, many of her pronouncements upon first and last things are more occasional than definitive. She was sincere, but her idea of sincerity was to say whatever, on the given occasion, would help. One of her poems, "How brittle are the Piers" (1433), urges that we may still believe in God and His promises, the evidence being Christ's word. But the poem was enclosed in a letter to Higginson, consoling him after the death of his wife. Another occasion supplied another need, perhaps a different note of consolation; as she wrote, again to Higginson, "To be human is more than to be divine, for when Christ was divine, he was uncontented till he had been human." Reading *Middlemarch*, she was convinced that "the mysteries of human nature surpass the 'mysteries of redemption,' for the infinite we only suppose, while we see the finite." When a neighbor, Mrs. Stearns, called to inquire if the Dickinsons did not think it shocking for Benjamin Butler to "liken himself to his Redeemer," Emily's answer was "we thought Darwin had thrown 'the Redeemer' away." But in one of her most ardent letters to Judge Lord, Emily Dickinson, reciting a high ethic, ascribed it to God: "The 'Stile' is God's — My Sweet One — for your great sake — not mine — I will not let you cross — but it is all your's, and when it is right I will lift the Bars." In the same letter: "It may surprise you I speak of God — I know him but a little, but Cupid taught Jehovah to many an untutored Mind — Witchcraft is wiser than we."

Again it is fair to say that Emily Dickinson would have been a Christian if she had been permitted to ascribe to Christ the same status which she ascribed, in that ardent moment, to Cupid and Jehovah; the same, but no more. Clearly, that Christianity would have been merely a function of self, Emily Dickinson's aspiration in one of her many moods. Indeed, it is arguable that religion was never more to her than a book of metaphors. She did not be-

lieve in a Mosaic religion, though the figure of Moses was espe-
cially vivid to her. What she wanted, when she wanted anything
in this way, was an Orphic religion, in which dogma and doctrines
would penetrate her sensibility, like music. Truth would suggest
itself as harmony, unassertive because unquestionable, audible
to instinct. "Orpheus' Sermon captivated —/ It did not condemn"
(1545). But to be entranced by Orpheus' song was one thing; to
follow Christ, obeying his word, was another. Christianity offered
itself as truth, embodied with whatever degree of divergence in
doctrine, but it had to reckon with Emily Dickinson's sensibility.
It was the mark of that sensibility either to discard what was of-
fered or to translate it, imperiously, into her own terms.

So she took her Christianity not as she found it but as she altered
it. She read her Bible as a rhetorical manual. Her poems and let-
ters are full of references to Genesis, Revelation, the Psalms, and
the Gospels, but the references are invariably rhetorical. Nothing
is necessarily to be believed, only entertained as a trope. There
are several poems in which Gabriel is invoked, but Emily Dickin-
son's Gabriel is merely an idealized version of Samuel Bowles or
another wise preceptor, bringing glad tidings and praise. "Get
Gabriel — to tell — the royal syllable" (195); but the syllable in
question is part of the earthly lover's vocabulary. In "The face I
carry with me — last" (336) Gabriel is again assimilated to an
earthly function, endorsing the idiom of love and compliment.
In "Where Thou art — that — is Home" (725) Emily Dickinson is
featured as Mary in Gabriel's praise, but the purpose is hyperbole;
the sacred moment is invoked only to be transcended by the
earthly love declared. In a love letter to Judge Lord she writes,
"Dont you know you have taken my will away and I 'know not
where' you 'have laid' it?"; Mary Magdalene's words give the lover's
complaint its appropriate style.

Emily Dickinson used her hymnbooks in the same way. They
are metaphorical and tropical. She owned three hymnbooks:
The Psalms, Hymns, and Spiritual Songs of the Rev. Isaac Watts,
edited by Samuel Worcester; *Church Psalmody, Selected from Dr.
Watts and Other Authors,* edited by Lowell Mason and David

Greene; and *Village Hymns, a Supplement to Dr. Watts's Psalms and Hymns,* edited by Asahel Nettleton. The letters and poems often depend upon the recollection of a hymn or of phrases from a hymn. A letter of September 1877 to Mrs. Holland recalls, somewhat loosely, a phrase from Watts's hymn "Were the Whole Realm of Nature Mine." But again the hymn is recalled for the phrase. "How precious Thought and Speech are! 'A present so divine,' was in a Hymn they used to sing when I went to Church." For Emily Dickinson, the estate of the hymns is ablative; rhythms and phrases are retained, but not their endorsing faith. What she took from the hymns, beyond that need, was a prosody; like other English and American poets she wrote secular poems in the meters of the Psalms, particularly the common measure.

The pattern persists in her reading. She took what her sensibility needed, from whatever source. Her motive in reading other writers, great and small, was not to discover the variety and potentiality of the art she shared with them, but rather to find there a provocation for her own imagination. Sometimes a phrase was enough. She was deeply engaged by the Brontës, but on the other hand the abiding interest of Emily Brontë largely resolved itself in a magical line, "Every existence would exist in Thee," from "No Coward Soul Is Mine." The line is quoted three times in letters. A few writers were deeply pondered. "After long disuse of her eyes," Higginson said, "she read Shakespeare & thought why is any other book needed." But even with Shakespeare her needs were exclusive. Sometimes a line moved her because of its associations: "'An envious Sliver broke' was a passage your Uncle peculiarly loved in the drowning Ophelia," she told Abbie Farley, niece of Judge Lord. The same phrase occurs in a letter, nearly five years earlier, to Mrs. Holland. The reading of Longfellow's *Kavanagh* caused a domestic flurry, so it lodged inordinately in her imagination. Reading novels, she often compared the relationships with her own, playing personal games with *David Copperfield* and *The Old Curiosity Shop.* She read the American writers, notably Bryant, Emerson, Hawthorne, and Lowell, when their current work appeared in the *Atlantic Monthly* or

when it was announced in a current periodical, *Scribner's Monthly*
or another. She was assiduous in reading Higginson. Often, as in
that case, her interest in the work was primarily an interest in the
writer. She was enchanted by the Brownings, Elizabeth "that
Foreign Lady" and Robert "the consummate Browning." She
read virtually everything by George Eliot, and admired her
greatly, but she never chose to say anything of critical significance
about the works, except that *Daniel Deronda* was a "wise and ten-
der Book." But she was fascinated by the news of George Eliot's
life, and pursued every biographical detail. When she read of
the novelist's death, she wrote to the Norcrosses: "The look of the
words as they lay in the print I shall never forget. Not their face
in the casket could have had the eternity to me. Now, *my* George
Eliot." Clearly, Emily Dickinson's interest in George Eliot as a
romantic and heroic figure transcended her critical concern with
the novels; she was moved by George Eliot's representative char-
acter, the aura surrounding her. The books merely provided evi-
dence that the personal interest was not grossly misplaced.

This may help to explain the vagaries of Emily Dickinson's
literary taste. Sometimes the explanation is simple; if a writer
reached her under Higginson's auspices, he was sure of approval.
There were exceptions. Higginson appears to have suggested that
she read Joaquin Miller's *Songs of the Sierras*, but she declined.
"I did not read Mr Miller because I could not care about him —
Transport is not urged." On the other hand she read Helen Hunt
Jackson's poems, recommended by Higginson, and echoed his
praise. "Mrs Hunt's Poems are stronger than any written by
Women since Mrs — Browning, with the exception of Mrs Lewes."
Later, she went further. When Higginson's *Short Studies of
American Authors* appeared in 1879, she wrote to him: "Mrs
Jackson soars to your estimate lawfully as a Bird, but of Howells
and James, one hesitates — Your relentless Music dooms as it re-
deems." But the real difference between Mrs. Jackson and her
male competitors was that Emily Dickinson had already met and
approved the authoress; she never met James or Howells. Her
critical standards were largely determined by the local require-

ments of her sensibility. A multitude of poetic defects might readily be covered by her friendship and affection. In any case, her reading was casual. Books came to her, and she read them, but she never allowed her mind to be intimidated by anything she read. Indeed, she was easily put off by a personal consideration. It is not certain that she ever read Poe: "Of Poe, I know too little to think." "You speak of Mr Whitman," she wrote to Higginson: "I never read his Book — but was told that he was disgraceful."

That her sensibility was strange is clear enough. It often appears, in the relation between her imagination and reality, that very little reality was required, her imagination being what it was, exorbitantly acute. Reading her poems, one is surprised to find that they have any base in reality or fact, since a base in that element is what they seem least to need. Philosophers have sometimes wondered what would happen if our senses were to be, for some inordinate reason, acutely intensified, the first conclusion being that the victim would inhabit a different universe of relationships. There is a passage in *Middlemarch* (chapter xx) where George Eliot considers how little reality the human frame can bear. "If we had a keen vision and feeling of all ordinary human life," she says, "it would be like hearing the grass grow and the squirrel's heart beat, and we should die of that roar which lies on the other side of silence." It often seems as if Emily Dickinson's senses were of this order. But there is a difference. The sensory power, as George Eliot conceives it, is still a power of response to reality, and it serves reality as its first and last object. It claims nothing for itself; it is willing to lose itself in the grass of ordinary human life. But the intensity of Emily Dickinson's imagination has a different object. She is not, after all, one of the great celebrants of life, the proof being how little of life, in the common sense, she chose to live. It is the peculiar nature of her sensibility that it deals with experience by exacerbating it, as if prompted by a conscience for which nothing less would do. No wonder she restricted the amount of life she was prepared to live, since the living had to be so intense, so relentlessly acute.

Santayana has written of the "Poetry of Barbarism," meaning

in the given cases Browning and Whitman; in general, the barbar-
ian "is the man who regards his passions as their own excuse for
being." So far as this goes, Emily Dickinson is a barbarian, and
her barbarism arises from the same source, the rejection of classic
and Christian ideals of discipline. But there is a crucial distinction.
To Emily Dickinson, the passions required no excuse because they
were the life and form of her sensibility; and sensibility was one
guise of her conscience. In this way and from this direction, the
exercise of sensibility became the exercise of conscience and duty.
She saw and heard the grass grow, but she saw and heard New
Englandly; so she wore the rue of her barbarism with a differ-
ence. This is why she gives the impression, contrasted with Whit-
man and Browning, of living upon her nerves; in this contrast,
Whitman and Browning appear even more nonchalant than they
are.

Think, for instance, how she goes out of her way to culti-
vate what others go out of their way to avoid, the intensities of
apprehension made possible by pain. "A *Wounded* Deer — leaps
highest" (165), so wounds are sought. The "scant degree/ Of Life's
penurious Round" (313) can only be raised by leaps of percep-
tion, magic, witchcraft. The leaps are facilitated by "Opposites,"
which therefore "entice" as "Water, is taught by thirst" (135). "I
like a look of Agony," she says, "Because I know it's true" (241).
In a later poem (963) "A nearness to Tremendousness —/ An
Agony procures," and the agony is its own justification. This is, in
other poems, the idiom of awe, an epic grandeur of spirit which
shames the petty difference between happiness and misery. One
of her most powerful poems (281) begins, " 'Tis so appalling — it
exhilirates." This is not a melodramatic indulgence, a self-regard-
ing exercise in Gothic horror; it is, for this New England poet, the
conscientious imagination at its sworn task. Emily Dickinson's
special way of feeling is to drive apprehension to the pitch of awe;
at that pitch, the discrimination of subject and object in the act
of perception is dissolved, and a new state strains to be released.
This is the moment at which "Perception of an object costs/ Pre-
cise the Object's loss" (1071). The object does not detach itself

from the subject; rather, the dualism of subject and object is, in a flash, consumed. What occupies the scene then is a new state of consciousness. The given object, like experience itself in Emily Dickinson, must take the risk of losing itself to a new state, becoming something else which is not the sum of experience and sensibility but their product. Consciousness is X, an unknown quantity, unknown because its limits have never been reached. Free of limits, it can enter into majestic equations with other quantities, known by name if not yet measured. In a poem on the free soul (384) Emily Dickinson says, "Captivity is Consciousness —/ So's Liberty."

Her word for this unknown quantity, when she does not call it consciousness, is circumference. In one poem (1620) it is "Circumference thou Bride of Awe." In "Circles" Emerson says: "The life of man is a self-evolving circle, which, from a ring imperceptibly small, rushes on all sides outwards to new and larger circles, and that without end." These circles are always deemed to be known, because divinely allowed and consistent with the human mind. The circles, in another version, are concentric, with man at the center, so they can be verified at any moment. But circumference, as Emily Dickinson uses the word, marks an area, on all sides, where consciousness ranges beyond enclosure. It is her version of the sublime. Circles define what they enclose; since an expanding circle depends upon the force of soul, in Emerson's terms, it may be held at any point. But circumference marks the end of definition and the beginning of risk. As Emily Dickinson put it (633), "When Cogs — stop — that's Circumference —/ The Ultimate — of Wheels," using Emerson's words with her own inflection. Another kindred word is impossibility: in one poem (838), "Impossibility, like Wine/ Exhilirates the Man/ Who tastes it; Possibility/ Is flavorless." And there is, in forty poems, immortality; which, nearly enough, is the spiritual form of impossibility. They are all sublime terms, as Emily Dickinson uses them, outrunning nature. "I worried Nature with my Wheels/ When Her's had ceased to run" (786).

But the key word is consciousness. Sometimes it is equated with

God. "The Brain — is wider than the Sky"; it is "deeper than the sea." Finally, it is "just the weight of God"; if it differs from God, it is only as "Syllable from Sound" (632). In another poem it is equated with life itself. "No Drug for Consciousness — can be" (786); if this is the form of "Being's Malady," the only escape is to die. The justification of consciousness is the justification of will; given the power, one must use it. "What are the sinews of such cordage for/ Except to bear" (1113). But there is another justification. Samuel Beckett has ascribed to Proust some thoughts on habit. "If Habit is a second nature, it keeps us in ignorance of the first, and is free of its cruelties and its enchantments." To Emily Dickinson, it appears, the common part of experience was a habit. She seems to have thought of religious belief, for instance, as a habit, perhaps a good habit, but open to the same disability, that, congealed as second nature, it prevents us from seeing our first. Institutions were dedicated to the formation of habit. But the chief means of defeating or circumventing habit was the imagination, consciousness. The imagination insists upon penetrating to the cruelties and enchantments of our first nature; that is its particular glory, and from thence it acquires its heroic note. This perhaps explains why Emily Dickinson is constantly forcing her mind beyond or beneath the familiar marks of the senses, the easy gifts. If she sees something, she never rests content with sight or even with possession of what it sees; she always goes further, further back or further forward, in her own directions. Very often her mind, in a typical cadence, starts with the sense, or with the declared failure of sense, only to run from it, above or below:

> Not seeing, still we know —
> Not knowing, guess —
> Not guessing, smile and hide
> And half caress —
>
> And quake — and turn away . . .   (1518)

Or, more urbanely: "To see is perhaps never quite the sorcery that it is to surmise, though the obligation to enchantment is always binding." It is as if the senses themselves, for all their merit, merely beguiled one into habit, and something else was needed, a sixth sense, critical and subversive, to correct the happy five. The sixth sense is the imagination.

There is another way of putting it. In the Preface to *The Portrait of a Lady* Henry James, explaining the special light in which he saw his heroine Isabel Archer, says that he conceived of the center of the subject as Isabel's consciousness, with one particular qualification. Shakespeare's heroines, George Eliot's heroines, are mainly revealed in their relations to other characters. Isabel Archer is mainly revealed in her relation to herself. This is, preeminently, the main direction of her consciousness. We think of Emily Dickinson in this character, without forcing the comparison. Emily's relations to other people were sufficiently numerous and sufficiently engrossing for her particular purposes, but they were all, in varying measure, as James says of Isabel's relations to other people, "contributive only to the greater one," her relation to herself. Some of Emily Dickinson's most daring poems turn the speaker into a haunted house, where she is at once the house, the ghost, and the haunted inhabitant:

> Ourself behind ourself, concealed —
> Should startle most —
> Assassin hid in our Apartment
> Be Horror's least.   (670)

In another poem, the mind's quarrel with itself is conducted in terms of banishment, monarchy, and abdication:

> But since Myself — assault Me —
> How have I peace
> Except by subjugating
> Consciousness?   (642)

Indeed, when we speak of Emily Dickinson's relation to herself, we should think of it rather as a relation to her many selves, the different ghosts haunting her house.

So the "charm of the actual," which James recites in his *Autobiography*, had to meet, in Emily Dickinson, the resistance of a demanding sensibility. There are several poems in which the charm, like Orpheus, overcomes the resistance, but the defeat of resistance was never final. Emily Dickinson seems to have a scrupulous objection, a qualm of conscience, whenever any charm comes too easily. To lie in Abraham's bosom seems a guilty indulgence. Certainly, her imagination is more often animated by the feeling which flows toward its object, and then flows away, than by the feeling which rests there. There are several poems on expectation, which qualify the common estimate of the relation between expectation and fulfillment. "Expectation — is Contentment —/ Gain — Satiety" (807); the reason is that there must be "an Austere trait in Pleasure." "Danger — deepens Sum," partly because the sense of danger, like fear, may be exhilarating, and partly because, at such moments, the will is exercised. But the will is exercised even more dramatically in Emily Dickinson's afterwords. Indeed, there is a special rhythm in her sensibility which is heard when the chosen estate is ablative.

There is an extraordinary letter to the Norcrosses, August 1876, in which Emily Dickinson speaks of cats, and especially of her sister Vinnie's new cat, "the color of Branwell Brontë's hair." Then she says: "You remember my ideal cat has always a huge rat in its mouth, just going out of sight — though going out of sight in itself has a peculiar charm. It is true that the unknown is the largest need of the intellect, though for it, no one thinks to thank God." But if the unknown has this status among needs of the intellect, equal status must be given to that which has been known and is now gone. To Emily Dickinson, a peculiar charm resides in "going out of sight," when the object, lost or consumed, becomes a part of memory, loss, and need. "By a departing light/ We see acuter, quite,/ Than by a wick that stays" (1714). In Emily Dickinson generally, experiences are more intensely apprehended just after their loss. Wallace Stevens wrote of "credences of Summer," but Emily Dickinson believed in summer more profoundly when it was just gone. "Summer has two Beginnings —/ Beginning once in June —/ Beginning in October/ Affectingly again" (1422). Indeed, she owned an October imagination, with June for experience. To apprehend June in June is of course a joy, called "Riot," but the October sense of June is "graphicer for Grace," presumably because Grace is a mode of the imagination. For the same reason, "finer is a going/ Than a remaining Face"; a remaining face is merely entertained, the other is recovered by a strain of will. "That it will never come again/ Is what makes life so sweet" (1741). This is why Emily Dickinson's imagination so often moves along "a route of evanescence," as if on one side everything were premonition, and on the other the fatality of loss. In one of her most majestic poems, "As imperceptibly as Grief," when the summer has "lapsed away,"

> The Dusk drew earlier in —
> The Morning foreign shone —
> A courteous, yet harrowing Grace,
> As Guest, that would be gone —   (1540)

The morning sunshine is foreign because alien, intractable in its resistance to the rhythm of lapse and departure.

There are many variants in the rhythm of evanescence. Some are easy, like the "dear retrospect" (1742) in which the dead are recalled. When evanescence is positively sought, it is called renunciation, "The letting go/ A Presence — for an Expectation." A few lines later, "Renunciation — is the Choosing/ Against itself —/ Itself to justify/ Unto itself" (745). This is another version of Emily Dickinson's scruple, where evanescence is felt New Englandly. In the love poems, evanescence is absence of the lover, where absence recalls and enforces presence so vividly that both states are transformed to something else, for which the poem is the only name. The transformation is achieved by writing the poem. "To lose thee — sweeter than to gain/ All other hearts I knew" (1754). And there is a consolatory poem, sent to Higginson when Emily Dickinson read of his infant daughter's death: "The Face in evanescence lain/ Is more distinct than our's" (1490). Indeed, it almost appears that Emily Dickinson welcomed pain and loss for the intensity they provoked; or, if that is excessive, that she was extraordinarily resourceful in finding power where common eyes see only pain.

If this sounds somewhat Emersonian, the association may be allowed and pursued. In the fifth chapter of the long essay *Nature*, there is a beautiful passage of evanescence. "When much intercourse with a friend has supplied us with a standard of excellence, and has increased our respect for the resources of God who thus sends a real person to outgo our ideal; when he has, moreover, become an object of thought, and, whilst his character retains all its unconscious effect, is converted in the mind into solid and sweet wisdom, it is a sign to us that his office is closing, and he is commonly withdrawn from our sight in a short time." This goes beyond acceptance to a deep assent, an Emersonian "yea." The equivalent in Emily Dickinson is more resistant, less urbane; or the urbanity may be presumed to reach the words much later. Emerson's posture is one of assent, even before the circumstances arrive to request assent. Emily Dickinson takes up no position at all, makes no promises, until the occasion demands an answer. There is a passage in *The Spoils of Poynton* which is closer to her spirit. In chapter xxi of James's novel Fleda Vetch goes to visit Mrs. Gereth at her house, Ricks. Fleda is enchanted with the place, and particularly with what Mrs. Gereth has made of it. The house declares a sense of loss, but this is part of its distinction — "the impression somehow of something dreamed and missed, something reduced, relinquished, resigned: the poetry, as it were, of something sensibly *gone.*" She conceives of the house as haunted by its characteristic ghosts. Ricks has been owned by Mrs. Gereth's old maiden aunt, to whom Fleda now ascribes "a great accepted pain." This is something like the pain of Emily Dickinson's world, great and accepted but still pain. It is the note of tragedy where Emerson's is the note of romance or, finally, the note of comedy. We hear Emily Dickinson's note in a poem (910) about the incrimination of mind and experience; the discipline of man forces him to choose "His Preappointed Pain."

This is Emily Dickinson's special area of feeling: the preappointed pain, how we choose it, the consequences of the choice. If her poems had titles, the names would fix themselves upon the great abstractions, the large words which range the individual acts and sufferings of man in categories, as pain, love, self, will, desire, expectation, and death. From these grand categories the particular experience issues, moving toward the sensibility; there the drama begins, if it has not already begun in the mind's engagement with itself. For the poem, it does not matter; great poems have been written according to both prescriptions. With Emily Dickinson's poems in view it is only a minor extravagance to say that nearly everything is sensibility. "Tell me what the artist is," James said in the Preface to *The Portrait of a Lady*, "and I will tell you of what he has *been* conscious."

So we come, by a long way round, to the definitive poems; or to a sample, barely enough to suggest what the extraordinary enterprise of Emily Dickinson's vision came to.

> After great pain, a formal feeling comes —
> The Nerves sit ceremonious, like Tombs —
> The stiff Heart questions was it He, that bore,
> And Yesterday, or Centuries before?
>
> The Feet, mechanical, go round —
> Of Ground, or Air, or Ought —
> A Wooden way
> Regardless grown,
> A Quartz contentment, like a stone —
>
> This is the Hour of Lead —
> Remembered, if outlived,
> As Freezing persons, recollect the Snow —
> First — Chill — then Stupor — then the letting go —   (341)

In a letter to Higginson, April 25, 1862, Emily Dickinson wrote: "I had a terror — since September — I could tell to none — and so I sing, as the Boy does by the Burying Ground — because I am afraid." It is agreed that this poem issued from the September terror, whatever other form that terror took, including "a funeral in my brain" (280). But the reverberation of the poem comes not from one historical crisis but from a classic situation, "felt in the blood" and exacerbated till it released itself in this form. The situation, as given in another poem (396), is "Pain's Successor — When the Soul / Has suffered all it can." So the poem is a ritual, imaginatively conducted from the great accepted pain to the "letting go." But the ritual has been practiced in many other poems, which we may call afterpoems to indicate a characteristic figure already glossed. Indeed, it may have been necessary for Emily Dickinson to practice her ritual in twenty more or less preparatory poems, all devoted to the same figure, so that she might employ the ritual in this great poem once for all.

The poem allows the experience whatever latitude it needs to impose its own nature, as the nerves, the heart, and the feet maintain the disjunct semblance of life, everything but its animating principle — the formula, without the spiritual form. This is what experience brings to sensibility. What sensibility has done to the experience is exacerbation, but in a peculiar kind. The experience is all intensity, and in an exactly equal and opposite measure the sensibility is all resistance. Discipline is the enabling form of resistance, in this poem and for this occasion. What seems like numbness in the poem is ostensible; it is really the effect of resistance offered by sensibility to the experience. Set off against the terror and the pain there are the strict sentences, severe, formal, ascetic. That is to say, the sensibility is operative preeminently in the syntax. The wilder the experience, the more decorous the sentence. In another poem (735), giving the same principle, Emily Dickinson speaks of "Life's sweet Calculations" imposed upon "Concluded Lives"; music played at a funeral "Makes Lacerating Tune": "To Ears the Dying Side — / 'Tis Coronal — and Funeral — / Saluting — in the Road."

Of the demanding passions in Emily Dickinson, the first is love. "Till it has loved — no man or woman can become itself — Of our first Creation we are unconscious," she wrote to Higginson. Is there more than love and death, she asked Mrs. Holland. It often seems as if, for the good of her poems, nothing more was required. "I cannot live with You" (640) is one of her grand love poems, one to remind the reader of many; and "Unable are the Loved to die" (809) will serve to hold the two motifs together, as they so often come together in this poet. "Born — Bridalled — Shrouded — / In a Day," she exclaims in a famous poem (1072). The love lyrics, naturally enough, are subject to exacerbation. If she writes of desire, there is the demand for fulfillment, but the demand is hardly spoken until it is almost retracted, "lest the Actual — / Should disenthrall thy soul" (1430), a characteristic sequence. Do not, she says in another poem (1434), try to "climb the Bars of Ecstasy," since "In insecurity to lie/ Is Joy's insuring quality." Love, indeed, is one of the two great absolutes in Emily Dickinson's world, the other being death. Many of her poems enact certain moments on the way toward love, including desire, expectation, premonition, fear. But more poems still dispose certain moments on the other side of love, as loss, despair, terror, then death.

For despair, there are several poems, and those among her finest achievements. In "There's a certain Slant of light" (258) despair is absolute, beyond question or argument:

> There's a certain Slant of light,
> Winter Afternoons —
> That oppresses, like the Heft
> Of Cathedral Tunes —

Heft means weight, with a further note of heaving, strain, oppression. The cathedral tunes oppress because of the sullen weight of faith which they ask the listener to receive and to lift. These intimations course back through "oppresses" to the slant of light, which would be neutral and innocent, even with the addition of winter afternoons. This is one of Emily Dickinson's common procedures, to start a poem with a first line which is neutral, or as neutral as the barest narrative can be; and then to expose the line to alien associations, until it, too, is tainted and there is nothing but the alien. On the face of it, the slant of light is innocent, but its innocence cannot survive the accretion of oppressive effects. The sinister element is not visible, in the nature of the case cannot be visible, light being merely light; so the sinister element is within. By the beginning of the second stanza, the light brings "Heavenly Hurt," again invisible, making only an internal difference, "Where the Meanings, are." Now its absolute nature appears, alien like the cathedral tunes, an absolute music, malign and in that nature heavenly. Emily Dickinson now gathers these intimations together, calling them despair, "An imperial affliction/ Sent us of the air"; so the air, too, like the wintry light, is tainted, slave of Heaven:

> When it comes, the Landscape listens —
> Shadows — hold their breath —
> When it goes, 'tis like the Distance
> On the look of Death —

It is as if the landscape were on the poet's side, sharing the terror;
there is enmity even between the light and nature, alien premoni-
tions. But the poet does not call upon the landscape to receive her,
hiding her feeling from the light. She merely notes a further en-
mity, another figure, oppressed in its own way. Perhaps the dis-
tance between the poet and her landscape is narrowed somewhat
by the shadows; but again there is no kinship. When the despair
goes, it leaves behind not its opposite but a memory of itself, look-
ing now like the face of death. Distance and death are cousins in
many of Emily Dickinson's poems, especially in the love poems,
where the absence of the lover, his distance, is indeed like death.
Here the despair has defined its "seal" or sign as the personifica-
tion of death; when the seal is defined in this final sense, the poem
is finished.

The same association of despair merging in death is made in
another poem (305):

> The difference between Despair
> And Fear — is like the One
> Between the instant of a Wreck —
> And when the Wreck has been —

Fear is not further described, it is absolute in its way. But despair
is given as an image in the second and last stanza; it is transformed
to death:

> The Mind is smooth — no Motion —
> Contented as the Eye
> Upon the Forehead of a Bust
> That knows — it cannot see —

It is a quartz contentment. Emily Dickinson often uses words like
"contented" and "content" in a special sense. When something is,
once for all, what it is; when it is the "perfection" of itself, with
all its possibilities embodied in one figure, it may be fancied to be
content, whatever its nature or character. Good or bad is indiffer-

ent. If one is thinking of existence, merely, then all things which equally exist are equal. In another poem (756) she describes an inordinate blessing she had, "A perfect — paralyzing Bliss," definitive, ultimate. Then she says, "Contented as Despair," meaning that both the bliss and the despair were absolute. They may decorously be compared with each other, or with anything else similarly perfect. This is one of the marks of Emily Dickinson's sensibility, that it takes particular note of a thing's perfection, whatever its nature; takes note, and allows to the perfection of pain the same credence as to the perfection of joy. Both are definitive, therefore contented. In Emily Dickinson, everything is allowed to become itself, whatever the character of that self; it will not be deprived of its possibilities. This is why we think of her as preeminently associated not with pain, joy, or loneliness, but with accepted pain, accepted joy, accepted loneliness. Her ministry does not end with acceptance, but it never begins without acceptance. To accept that something is what it is, and that its character is its own, is the first act of her sensibility. What the later acts are, only the poems can say. "It might be lonelier/ Without the Loneliness" (405), because the loneliness has become a character, almost a person, in Emily Dickinson's life, a member of the house. Darkness and a room have been prepared for his reception; even such a person might be missed. "Not seeing, still we know" (1518), the statues may say; but if all they know is that they cannot see, that is despair, fear's afterword.

It is evident that there is an apocalyptic element in Emily Dickinson's imagination. We think of it when we advert to its rage for completeness, perfection; it insists upon conceiving what lesser imaginations, or more genial imaginations, are content to hint. It forces itself to the end of the line. Mostly, in Emily Dickinson's poems, the end of the line is death; so her imagination insists upon conceiving that, too. There is a passage in one of George Eliot's letters, July 1, 1874: "Your picture of Mr. and Mrs. Stirling, and what you say of the reasons why one may wish even for the anguish of being *left* for the sake of waiting on the beloved one to the end — all that goes to my heart of hearts. It is what I think of almost daily.

For death seems to me now a close, real experience, like the approach of autumn or winter, and I am glad to find that advancing life brings this power of imagining the nearness of death I never had till of late years." This is very much in Emily Dickinson's spirit. Among perfections, death is hardly to be challenged. "To be alive — is Power" (677); true enough, and especially true in Emily Dickinson's poems, but if all absolutes are, in this respect, equal, an apocalyptic imagination attends most upon death. Or rather, upon dying, since this slight change in the character of the word makes the conceit more approachable.

A motto for these death poems is provided in a poem (412) in which Emily Dickinson says, "I made my soul familiar — with her extremity —/ That at the last, it should not be a novel Agony." As always, she exacerbates what is domestic, domesticates the apocalypse; either way, the imagination asserts itself. Death and the soul are to be "acquainted —/ Meet tranquilly, as friends," or if not as friends, then as neighbors, to whom courtesy is due. In "The last Night that She lived" (1100) Emily Dickinson notes that "It was a Common Night/ Except the Dying — this to Us/ Made Nature different." The tone is properly judicious; the mourners are, to an unusual degree, aware of things, but we are not to hear the grass grow. Ordinary things are "Italicized — as 'twere." The feelings are ordinary, too, the common resentment that the dead child has been chosen and others less worthy left:

> We waited while She passed —
> It was a narrow time —
> Too jostled were Our Souls to speak . . .

The mourners merely wait while the dying one goes; because the waiting is oppressive, the time is narrow; even in the hours and minutes before the death, friends are already conceived as attending the funeral, sitting around the corpse, congested. The language of soul is taken from the language of body, as the language of eternity is derived from the language of time, because there is no other language. All language is, in this sense, domestic. Death poems are life poems. Emily Dickinson's death poems accept this condition; acceptance gives them their extraordinary resilience. It is as if she had only to assent to the temporal nature of language, cooperating with its domestic bias, to write death poems which are among the greatest short poems in the language. "Too jostled were Our Souls to speak": here the imagination is going about its proper business, not by trying to do the whole work but by co-operating with the language. "Jostled" is the product of a dramatic imagination in league with a domestically inclined language; knowing, too, that what is beyond experience must accept a finite language, or remain silent. At the end of the poem the mourners are released to their own lives: "And then an awful leisure was/ Belief to regulate." To regulate; to govern, direct, or control, a discipline domestic in its language, esoteric in its particular application. The strongest link in Emily Dickinson's chain is invariably the common word, taken from a domestic language and applied, with the force of courtesy, where ostensibly it does not belong. This is why her triumphs so often appear, on first reading, to be wrong; and then we understand them to be incalculably right: "I died for Beauty—but was scarce/ Adjusted in the Tomb . . ." (449).

This is to say that Emily Dickinson uses a plebeian language with a patrician imagination; willingly, with the commitment of knowledge. That the words are plebeian has perhaps already appeared; that the imagination is patrician appears in its independence, its pride, its *sprezzatura*. Where both forces are fully engaged, the result is a classic poem, as near perfection as the association allows. "I heard a Fly buzz—when I died" (465) is such an occasion. The speaker is the dying one, the "post of observation" her deathbed. The mourners are given as eyes and breaths, the breaths "gathering firm/ For that last Onset—when the King/ Be witnessed—in the Room." Then the dying one sees a fly interposed "Between the light—and me"; "And then the Windows failed—and then/ I could not see to see." Death is imagined, in the last stanza, as the end of a sequence in which the first parts are played by things not yet to die. In the victim's failing life the buzzing fly is there, but "With Blue—uncertain stumbling Buzz," then the windows fail, two failures prefiguring a third, "I could

not see to see." Allen Tate has recalled the last scene in Dosto-
evski's *The Idiot,* where Prince Myshkin and Rogozhin stand, in
the dark, over the corpse of the murdered Nastasya. A fly appears,
out of nowhere, and settles upon Nastasya's pillow. Mr. Tate says
of the fly that it "comes to stand in its sinister and abundant life
for the privation of life, the body of the young woman on the bed."
In Emily Dickinson's poem the fly hovers to represent all the
remaining things, alien because resistant, which detach themselves
from the dying; privation, yes, but perhaps in greater measure,
alienation. The imagination, when it is dramatic, seeks to establish
relations between perceiver and the thing perceived, as here the
dying speaker draws fly and window to herself, to her own lapse
and failure. The effort fails when, with death, detachment is com-
plete. There is a passage in Wordsworth's Preface to his *Poems* of
1815 where the poet describes this tendency of the imagination;
he speaks of "images independent of each other, and immediately
endowed by the mind with properties that do not inhere in them,
upon an incitement from properties and qualities the existence
of which is inherent and obvious." In Emily Dickinson's poem the
imagination, conceiving of the mourners, the fly, the air in the
room, and the windows, draws everything into the circle of lapse
and failure until the last line, when the center fails, and there is
nothing.

For the same reason, in "Because I could not stop for Death"
(712) the imagination represents the grain as "Gazing." The gaze
is transferred from the speaker; or rather, the speaker draws the
grain toward herself, to share in the nature of her vision. Indeed,
this imaginative principle is active in the structure of the poem.
Grim death is domesticated, fitted to the common sequences of
life, a gentleman of Amherst come to call upon a lady. Yeats speaks
of "that discourtesy of death"; Emily Dickinson enacts its civility.
The gentleman caller arrives and conveys his lady to the carriage.
The poem has been compared with Browning's "The Last Ride
Together," partly on the strength of Browning's lines

> What if we still ride on, we two
> With life for ever old yet new,

> Changed not in kind but in degree,
> The instant made eternity . . .

It is a nice conjunction, especially when we recall that Emily Dickinson, reading Browning's poem several years later, was struck by the line "So, one day more am I deified" in the second stanza. But Browning's poem has nothing of Emily Dickinson's civility. A comparison nearer home is feasible, a later poem by Emily Dickinson herself (1445) in which death is personified as "the supple Suitor/ That wins at last"; a comparison the more attractive because both poems stroke death with the melody of love. In the later poem death's "stealthy Wooing" is first conducted by "pallid innuendoes":

> But brave at last with Bugles
> And a bisected Coach
> It bears away in triumph
> To Troth unknown
> And Kinsmen as divulgeless
> As throngs of Down —

It is a different pageantry, of course. The pageantry of "Because I could not stop for Death" is a more equable courtship, featured in the slow drive into the country, the courtesy with which the gentleman pauses so that they may look at the old house. So the conclusion is quieter, there are no bugles:

> Since then — 'tis Centuries — and yet
> Feels shorter than the Day
> I first surmised the Horses Heads
> Were toward Eternity —

Surmise; meaning, to go somewhat beyond the evidence. Evidence gives the direction, but not the distance or the end. It is as if the whole enterprise, death's designs upon the soul, were conducted by "stealthy Wooing," without the bravery of bugles and triumph. In "surmised" one stealth is quietly answered by another.

What is remarkable in the poem is the power of an imagination which can live, apparently, upon so little. We feel that a poem which aspires to do so much might reasonably claim, for its essential materials, pretty nearly everything. But this poem does more

with poverty than other poems with wealth; or so it is permissible
to feel. A few common words, a simple plot, almost nothing in
the way of description, no thoughts, no ideas; and the extraor-
dinary work is done. There is something of this seeming ease in
another poem about death (1078), or rather about the morning
after a death:

> The Bustle in a House
> The Morning after Death
> Is solemnest of industries
> Enacted upon Earth —
>
> The Sweeping up the Heart
> And putting Love away
> We shall not want to use again
> Until Eternity.

William Dean Howells quoted the last lines in his review of *Poems
of Emily Dickinson* in January 1891, and he recalled them, several
years later, when he visited his daughter's grave in Boston. "What
an indescribable experience!" he wrote to Mark Twain, October 23,
1898; "I thought I could tell you about it, but I can't. Do you
know those awful lines of Emily Dickinson?" And he quoted
them. Deaths were many in Amherst, as Emily Dickinson's poems
and letters show; and, to her, the only really accredited rituals
were domestic, the daily industries. It is typical of her imagination
to see the solemnity of death yield, as a matter of domestic fact,
to the sense of continuing life, while the accepted loss persists. So
the domestic rituals are the serious endgames, played when one
season yields to another, but there is no attempt to assuage the loss
by invoking the rhythms of seasonal time to transcend it. Loss is
absolute, too.

In October 1883, Emily Dickinson's nephew Gilbert died, the
youngest child of Austin and Susan, eight years old, from typhoid
fever. "Dawn and Meridian in one," she wrote to Susan, enclosing
an elegy, "Pass to thy Rendezvous of Light, / Pangless except for us"
(1564). To Emily herself, sorrow was inexpressible. Within a few
weeks she was ill. "The Physician says I have 'Nervous prostration.'
Possibly I have — I do not know the Names of Sickness. The Crisis

of the sorrow of so many years is all that tires me." In March 1884, Judge Lord died. "I hardly dare to know that I have lost another friend, but anguish finds it out." In June, she herself suffered a nervous collapse. "I have not been strong for the last year," she told her friend Mrs. Mack; she was never to be strong again. The last letters tell the story, often in single lines. There are occasional spurts of energy, and the result is a longer letter, or a few lines of verse. In August 1885, Helen Jackson died. During the following months Emily Dickinson's letters are necessities of condolence, often picking up fragments of the dead lives and sharing them with friends. Her health improved a little in the spring of 1886: "The velocity of the ill, however, is like that of the snail," she told Charles Clark, Wadsworth's friend. In May, she became ill again. On the thirteenth she passed into a coma, paralysis as a consequence of Bright's disease. She died on Saturday evening, May 15, 1886.

Some time after her death, her sister Lavinia found a locked box containing about seven hundred short poems. The pages were bound together in fascicles of four or five sheets. Emily had been averse to publication. It was as foreign to her thought, she told Higginson, "as Firmament to Fin." Publication, she wrote in a poem (709), is "the Auction/ Of the Mind of Man." In a letter to Higginson in 1862 she wrote: "If fame belonged to me, I could not escape her — if she did not, the longest day would pass me on the chase." But Lavinia determined to show that fame belonged to her sister. Susan Dickinson was approached, without success; then Higginson was asked to edit the material; finally Mabel Loomis Todd, wife of a professor at Amherst College, agreed to work on the manuscripts. Higginson had undertaken to look over the poems if they could be shown to him in fair copies; Mrs. Todd would do the heavy work first. Collaborating, they eventually published *Poems by Emily Dickinson* (1890), a selection of 116 poems. By herself, Mrs. Todd edited a selection of Emily Dickinson's letters in 1894. In 1896, however, a quarrel broke out between Lavinia and Mrs. Todd; the first result was that Emily Dickinson's manuscripts were divided. The papers in Lavinia's possession passed to

Susan Dickinson, and subsequently to Martha Dickinson Bianchi, Emily's niece. From 1914 until her death in 1943, Mrs. Bianchi issued several volumes of Emily Dickinson's poems. But Mrs. Todd's share of the manuscripts remained under lock until her daughter, Millicent Todd Bingham, published about 650 unpublished poems as *Bolts of Melody* (1945). Finally, Thomas H. Johnson brought all the known poems together in *The Poems of Emily Dickinson* (1955), in three volumes, giving all the available poems and their variant readings. *The Letters of Emily Dickinson*, edited by Mr. Johnson and Theodora Ward, was published in three volumes in 1958. Mr. Johnson has also published *The Complete Poems of Emily Dickinson* in one volume (1960) and a rich sample called *Final Harvest: Emily Dickinson's Poems* (1961), a selection in paperback of her choice work, 576 poems from the 1775 of the variorum edition.

Appropriately, Mr. Johnson's work on the manuscripts has been greatly praised. Before 1955, it was impossible to know precisely what authority the printed volumes had. It was feared that the early editors had been more zealous than scrupulous; they had a difficult, angular poet on their hands, so perhaps they had smoothed the rough patches. In fact, they compromised, retaining the exact text when it was tolerably lucid and altering a word or two when the poet ran beyond that mark. Not very many poems are seriously affected. "Further in Summer than the Birds" (1068) was smoothed by Higginson's hand, the third stanza made to follow a more conventional grammar than that given in the original version. There are some readers, including Yvor Winters, who prefer the smooth version; they met Emily Dickinson's poems for the first time in the old editions, and they resent the modern scholar's insistence upon textual fidelity, if it means revising old affections. The same readers, long accustomed to the conventional punctuation of the old editions, cannot welcome the dashes, Emily Dickinson's favorite gesture, reproduced in the Johnson edition. It has been argued that the dashes are rhetorical rather than grammatical notes, hints to the reading voice rather than to the silent eye. There is also the problem of the capitals: not every noun in the manuscripts is awarded a capital, but a method is dimly visible. In most cases the capitalized words are those upon which the fate of the line largely depends, so it is natural that the poet should wish to give them a mark of special favor, "italicized, as 'twere." The words thus appraised begin to look and sound like moral universals; as if they were more than nouns. Again, many of the best poems exist in different versions; the poet often incorporated them in letters, and she felt inclined to tinker with them, perhaps in deference to their recipients. Mr. Johnson is reasonably sure, in the crucial poems, how the sequence of the manuscripts goes. In some instances the versions are sufficiently distinct to make separate poems. Where choice is obligatory, Mr. Johnson has nearly always chosen well. But the procedure is doubtful in one respect; as a general policy, later texts are preferred, but in some cases the later version spoils the poem. There are two copies of "I Years had been from Home" (609) and it is possible to think the earlier version of 1862 the better poem, more powerful than the official version of 1872. Logically, Mr. Johnson's policy gives preference to the later poem, so this is the only one offered in *Final Harvest*. On the other hand, Mr. Johnson has chosen the earlier version of "The Moon upon her fluent Route" (1528) for sound poetic reasons. The result is a certain confusion between editorial principle in the selection of copy texts and a natural desire to see Emily Dickinson represented by her best poems. In some cases a satisfactory choice cannot be made. "Essential Oils — are wrung" (675) exists in two versions, their implications mutually incompatible, one hopeful, one despairing. Both were written about the same time. Mr. Johnson has given the hopeful one his preference, so it stands in *Final Harvest*; the despairing voice can only be heard in small print in the variorum edition.

But these are minor troubles, hardly to be counted at all in the great satisfaction: the extraordinary body of poetry is available. Readers make their own anthologies, the choice poems brought to memory. There are readers who love the comic poems, which I have not mentioned; Emily Dickinson's wit was not continuous, but it was strong when it appeared. There are other readers who care for the quirky poems, sardonic glances at eternal verities. Emily Dickinson was often irreverent; some readers are attracted by her boldness. In "God is a distant — stately Lover" (357) Christ's coming on earth in behalf of the Father is compared to John Alden's service in behalf of Miles Standish in Longfellow's poem. Rev. Brooke Herford read the verses in the Boston *Christian Register* and thought them "one of the most offensive bits of contemptuous Unitarianism that I have met with." The editor of the *Register* disagreed, and wrote an editorial to defend the poet. But Emily Dickinson's transaction with God is a longer story.

If I admit a bias, it is in favor of those poems in which Emily Dickinson's sensibility encounters the great moral universals: love, pain, loss, doubt, death. What happens to the universals, what happens to the sensibility: the poems which give this double drama are among the greatest poems in the language. R. P. Blackmur said that in Emily Dickinson "direct experience (often invented, sometimes originally contingent) was always for the sake of something else which would replace the habit and the destructive gusto (but not the need) of experience in the world, and become an experience of its own on its own warrant and across a safe or forbidding gap." The gap is visible, or nearly visible, in the letters. The "something else" for which Emily Dickinson lived is in the poems, unless we say, with no more ado, that it is the poems themselves, poetry. The something else may be fulfilled in the poetry, with no remainder; or the poetry may be an instrument, means to a further end on the other side of silence. Between such alternatives it is hardly necessary to make a choice.

Edwin Arlington Robinson

G RANTED a real talent and an access to experience, a poet deserves the name and earns it chiefly by his honesty. It is never enough that he be up with or beyond the times; who knows what those are? Technical feats rise, shine, evaporate, and fall, and there are unread poets who could have taught Shakespeare lessons in prosody. The sources from which poets "steal" metaphors and ideas often show the difference between knowing all about poetry and being a poet: it is not a matter of know-how, for if it were, Abraham Cowley would be greater than John Milton and Edward Young than Samuel Johnson. What is necessary is to see and to say with that direct honesty of vision that is apparently accessible only to genius and is therefore to the ordinary critic the least readily detectable of poetic qualities. A passion torn to tatters, a fit of the vapors, or a commitment to slogans of whatever degree of sophistication does not argue a true poetic vision; what counts supremely is the double commitment to the Muse and to the view of things the Muse inspires. In many cases, poets take years to find the vision, to see it for what it is, and that seeing may be only momentary and fleeting, but we know ultimately whether the poet has seen indeed or whether he has merely faked and trumped up. Larger or smaller, deeper or shallower, vision truly seen and honestly shown marks

45

the poet, and it may be said fairly enough that in few instances have the contemporary critics shared enough of the visionary power or the honesty to see the poet's for what they are.

Edwin Arlington Robinson is a poet of true vision and unimpeachable honesty. Lest that sound forbidding — suggestive of something crabbed, angular, and inept — one should add that he had a consummate mastery of versification and rhetoric, that he could pile on the colors with the best of them, and that he had the inventiveness to tease the mind with symbol and intellectual puzzle. He indulged these capacities from time to time, the latter most frequently, but not until his later years did he allow them to assume the upper hand. All of Robinson's best work is the product of a sensibility that was on guard against fraud, that concerned itself with making into form what vision had discovered. The word "seeing" occurs frequently in Robinson, on various levels of seriousness and relevance; for this poet honesty is not so much what one has as what one tries to achieve after however much time spent among deceptions, lies, illusions. He knew a great many people, including members of his own family, who perished by such chimeras. He was born into, and grew to full maturity in, a time that is a kind of *locus classicus* for all lies on whatever scale. See Henry Adams, the later works of Mark Twain, and any history of the years just before the Great War and of that war itself. The era marked Robinson, for good and for ill. It disillusioned him with democracy and with the classic New England liberalism, and it "dated" him hopelessly in the eyes of the later generation of poets and literary folk.

To an older friend he wrote from his deathbed in the New York Hospital: "I doubt if you would care much for Auden and Spender. They are for the youngsters." It is not untypical of the man that he should have read these poets and be in a position to speak of them, yet give the impression of being the old fogy; ironically he puts himself in the position of his correspondent, who was twenty years his senior, and sees perfectly the faults of that rigidity of taste and habit likely to come with age. The diffidence, the hesitancy, with which he always expressed and qualified opinions stayed with him all his life, even in the era of his apparent preeminence after achieving both fame and something like fortune. His fine poem "Hillcrest," written at the artists' summer colony in Peterborough, New Hampshire, which was founded and maintained by the widow of the musician Edward MacDowell, expresses his acute sense of the insignificance of human achievement and the ephemeral nature of any one man's claim to rightness. He was a considerable "lion" at the MacDowell Colony during his latter years and he enjoyed being lionized, yet he never forgot that ". . . great oaks return / To acorns out of which they grew." In 1925, with a Pulitzer prize and other awards to his credit (if that is the phrase!), he wrote thus to a friend asking for a *Blue Guide* to London: "I'm not going to London, but sometimes I like to take up that book. It is almost as exciting as an illustrated seed catalogue, and far more reliable."

Small wonder that the generation of Pound and Eliot did not find Robinson's work and aesthetic congenial, chiefly because they never took the trouble to read him, but also, and understandably, because the era of which Robinson was inevitably part had finally ended in the hitherto unknown destructiveness of World War I. The period between the American Civil War and the War to End War may seem to us in retrospect not to lack appeal; to those who lived in it, like Henry Adams and Mark Twain, it seemed the shabbiest, most degrading of times. We can read their separate records of it: *The Education of Henry Adams* and *The Gilded Age*; in the latter, Twain created the most memorable of all fictional persons representative of the promoter in that raucous era, Colonel Beriah Sellers, the immortal speculator and harebrained proponent of get-rich-quick. He might well have been the spiritual godfather of Robinson and of his entire generation.

Robinson's youth and young manhood, the years leading up to to *The Torrent and the Night Before* (1896), seem to have been lived in a barren time indeed. He was born in the tiny village of Head Tide, Maine, in 1869, at the very dawn of the Gilded Age, and though the family moved very shortly thereafter to the larger town of Gardiner, Maine, on the Kennebec River, we today can see both the provinciality on the one hand and the national craze for speculation and wealth on the other which equally marked the Robinson family and many others of the period. Despite all that might be said of Maine's natural beauty, its classical New England heritage, its abiding interest in learning and literature, and its tough moral legacy of Puritanism (rather less severe in Maine than elsewhere in New England), the fact remains that the Gardiner of 1870–1900 was a typical American boom town with its trade in lumber, ice, and shipping as well as certain manufactures. The more substantial capitalists of the town had interests in western properties and speculative enterprises: lumber, land, railroads, mines. And just as the depredation of the land of Maine and other parts of the country typified the attitude of the exploiters, so did their driving, piratical Philistinism in the arts and culture generally set the tone of public and private taste. Poetry, real poetry, had to go underground. From the death of Emily Dickinson (and who had ever heard of her?) in 1886, and of Whitman in 1892, until the renascence at the time of World War I, there is almost literally nothing in the poetry of America. Stephen Crane died young and inchoate; all the early promise of Vachel Lindsay and Edgar Lee Masters turned to little or nothing much, and the one truly impressive, salient figure of this lonely time is that of the lonely, dedicated, self-deprecating man for whom, if ever for any poet, the time was out of joint.

Robinson's father had moved to Gardiner in anticipation of a boom in his business; he was concerned in the lumber trade and had ventured into speculation in western property. He was a man of a not insensitive nature and in different circumstances might have shown his oldest and youngest boys more sympathy. The poet's mother was a woman of some literary taste, though perhaps we may feel free to be skeptical of the quality of such taste as it impinged upon the sensibility of her son. It should be said that in Robinson's early years he read as poets usually do: widely, omnivorously, wholly without discrimination, and it may be that much that was bad had as strong an effect upon him as the good. Be that as it may, the good was not entirely lacking, in literature, education, and recreation. There was a literary set in Gardiner and notable among its members was Dr. Alanson Tucker Schumann, a physician and poet whose infatuation with poetry led him to Robinson when the latter was a boy in high school. Perhaps Robinson may have had him partly in mind when he spoke in "The Wandering Jew" of a "fealty that presents/ The tribute of a tempered ear/ To an untempered eloquence." But the boy learned a great deal from Schumann, particularly verse forms and a respect for them. Under that kindly tutelage Robinson wrote ballades, villanelles, rondeaus, and other forms so dear to the post-Pre-Raphaelite heart. Nor was the regimen anything but beneficial: Schumann was a taskmaster and Robinson learned a respect for scrupulous workmanship the results of which may be seen not only all through his work, but more directly in such early poems as the villanelle "The House on the Hill," which exhibits the typically Robinsonian merging of the old, traditional form with the laconic, sinewy plain diction that was both new and typical of the region, and "The Ballade of Broken Flutes," Robinson's statement of his mission as the bringer of a new kind of poetry. Is it mere coincidence that the poet's mother was descended from the family of America's first poet, Anne Bradstreet?

And of course Gardiner was the home of Laura E. Richards, the daughter of Julia Ward Howe who wrote "The Battle Hymn of the Republic." Mrs. Richards was an author and the friend of authors; whatever one may think of her taste and her own literary work, one must acknowledge both her great humanity and her insight. She practically dragged the young, shy poet out of hiding and into her ebullient, charming family where Robinson found another home after his own had disintegrated. Here he found stimulation of various kinds: the companionship of Mrs. Richards, her architect husband, and their sons and daughters, and simple recognition as a poet. True, we may see in the influence of the family certain limiting factors, of taste and of ideas, but Mrs. Richards was certainly on sure ground in preferring and encouraging the lyrical rather than the philosophical Robinson. It would seem that Robinson himself took little advice from anyone throughout his career, but he took from the Richardses affection and a sense of

identity as poet. Perhaps Miss Rosalind Richards is the woman of
Hagedorn's hints (in his biography) and perhaps we shall know
one day when the documents pertaining to the poet deposited in
the Houghton Library at Harvard are made available.

Love and marriage were not to be for Robinson. Gardiner, the
Tilbury Town of the poems, left a mark on him, in part because of
its very nature as a town of its time and place and in part because
of the personal tragedies and wounds he knew there. So many of
the portraits of his early volumes seem drawn from the life, his
own or another's, that the reader never forgets what Gardiner
meant to him always. For years the young man was to all intents
and purposes an idler and a failure; the consciousness that he was
so considered embittered him far beyond anything the actual opin-
ion of his fellow townsmen seems to have warranted. Many ad-
mired and liked him, but it was not a merely parochial matter with
Robinson: his response to the realization that he was indeed a poet
is characteristically American. If art is considered trivial and idle in
America, he might have said, then I can justify my life and work
only by success. And success means publication and profits, money
and position. After all, Gardiner, along with all America, strove
mightily with Roscoe Conkling, the Stalwart Republican from
New York, and President U. S. Grant for the power and the money
that are success, and when in their turn Robinson's father and both
brothers failed in the scramble, the young man might well have
felt in his heart that he was doomed with the rest of his kin. He
saw, in any event, a vision of American life that marked him per-
manently. The moral collapse of his brothers, on top of the hor-
rible death by diphtheria of his mother and the disintegration of
his father, could scarcely be accounted for by the philosophies
and theologies of a century of New England storekeepers. After all,
Puritanism no longer worked as a creed; Unitarianism had given
way to Mrs. Eddy's gospel of Christian Science, and the sages of
Concord provided pretty thin gruel to the hungry poet of the
Grant-McKinley dispensation.

The young Robinson, classically, was a sensitive youth — he was
born with his skin inside out as he said himself — and though he

had friends (friends were his passion) and loved his years at the Gardiner High School, he was always an enigma to his associates and to his family, who let him go his dreamy way, but scarcely thought that he would ever outshine the brilliant, handsome Dean, the oldest, or the driving, vital Herman, next in order. To a Freudian, all things are Oedipal and there is indeed a case for seeing in Robinson's life the familiar pattern of the unwanted third son, rejected, kindly enough, by the father and kept at a distance by a too-beloved mother. In his later years, Robinson seems to have gained help from a psychiatrist who was also a poet, Dr. Merrill Moore. Gardiner in the eighties and nineties knew no such amenities, and one may perhaps be permitted to feel a callous relief since if Robinson had the anguish, we have the poetry. Yet we must feel pity as well, for the years following Robinson's graduation from high school, with the exception of two at Harvard, must have been an almost unrelieved agony of soul. Dean, the star of the family, was breaking up under the influence of drugs; he contracted the habit while trying to force himself into the exhausting routine of a country doctor. The father, Edward Robinson, decayed physically while his investments vanished; Herman, now married and with two small daughters, somehow seemed to have lost his way. Colonel Beriah Sellers like a proper godfather had vowed things in Herman's name. Yet before the smash became total, E. A. R. had his two years as a special student at Harvard. Following a period of isolation and near-despair after his graduation from high school, Cambridge, Boston, and Harvard came as deliverers and saviors. The young poet learned something of languages and literatures, of taverns and aesthetics, of the theater and above all of opera, particularly Wagner. When the money gave out and he had to leave, he even then knew he had been saved, though Barrett Wendell, the critic and Harvard professor, years later, when Robinson told him he had to leave Harvard after two years, growled, "You were damn lucky." Perhaps he was.

Try as one will, one cannot help the conviction that throughout his life Robinson was the victim of the classic strategy of America with its artists, poets in particular, perhaps. It would seem that

the formative years provide a diet too thin, too miserly and defi-
cient in nutriment, the last years a regimen of indigestible fats:
success, when and if it comes, comes with a vengeance, frequently
confirming the artist in his worst faults and conferring on him
both an authority of opinion beyond his competence and oppor-
tunities to sell not just his work but himself to commercial inter-
ests. But before Robinson could have reached any such position,
he knew fully what neglect and unsuccess could be. His was for a
time the world of the down-and-out, the panhandlers and outcasts.
Abject poverty and slavery to alcohol went hand in hand. In later
years he himself said that the only thing that saved him was that
he never took a drink before six in the evening.

Yet the worst was isolation, isolation from the best minds of his
time and from those whose work and thought might have been
useful and encouraging to him. Kind, understanding, and helpful
as Robinson's friends were (and indeed they kept him alive and in
health for years with simple charity), they do not seem to us today
men and women who could have helped him in his struggle to
learn and to grow as a poet; in all humility, we must call them sec-
ond-rate. Of the poets with whom he was well acquainted, three
names stand out: William Vaughn Moody, Josephine Preston Pea-
body, and Ridgely Torrence, of whom the first two were far better
known in their time than Robinson. There were literary figures of
various shades of distinction among his friends and associates,
notably Mrs. Richards, yet again there was none who seemed to
have the insight into the true quality of his best work that would
have helped the poet to grow. For all the voluminous correspond-
ence with the literary and near literary which carried Robinson on
through many years, there can be no escaping the conclusion that
time, place, and circumstance conspired to deprive him of incen-
tives toward development, growth, and change. His first book sets
a pattern which will not be broken, and in his beginning is his end.

Robinson is a nineteenth-century product, a Romantic, and a
scion of the New England stock. Did he not say himself that had
he lived in the time of Brook Farm he would have been strongly
tempted to go along? One can see in him the qualities that made a

Jones Very, and although he repudiated both Thoreau and Emerson, as philosophers or thinkers, he admired Emerson's poetry, saturated himself in nineteenth-century prose and poetry, and generally conformed to the canons of taste of the sensitive, provincial, cultivated New Englander. It was some old atavistic urge that led him to Poe and to Hawthorne, to the darker side. He seems to have known nothing of Melville, though he liked Whitman and Twain, particularly the former, but it should be said that like most New Englanders of the age, his eyes were on England rather than his own country — for literature at least — and surely his love of Cowper and Crabbe shows how much more comfortable he was with traditional English verse than with that of the Decadents. He dismissed the *Yellow Book* as mere sensation. He seemed to feel kinship among poets of the nineties only with Kipling and Hardy. And all his tastes, like his ideas and convictions, came early and came to stay. In this as in so much else he is typical of his race and milieu, the New England eccentric with the eccentricity raised to genius and the right to his crotchets confirmed and made great by virtue of his earning and living that right to the end and with the utmost rigor. It is not too much to say that Robinson worked out to its conclusion and at large what Emily Dickinson, tentatively, found and named in the decay of the New England sensibility. The tradition still lives, and strongly, in the work of Robert Lowell, in whose dramatic soliloquies or monologues one may find the plain, vital influence of Robinson and his peculiar, involute syntax. *The Mills of the Kavanaughs* is Lowell's obeisance — and perhaps farewell — to his master.

After the destruction of family ties, for the most part, with Gardiner, Robinson went to live in New York, where he stayed almost without intermission, except for long summers at the MacDowell Colony, until his death in 1935. He knew poverty so great that he was often without proper food and clothing and lived on the charity of his friends. His first books made no impression on the "little sonnet men" who reviewed for magazines, nor did any periodicals think it worthwhile to publish this unknown when after all Clinton Scollard and George Edward Woodberry and many another sweetsinger were the acknowledged masters. Robinson's first two books were published at his own expense and that of friends, and the manuscript of *Captain Craig* (1902) languished in a brothel until the editor who had left it there came back, not presumably for the manuscript. He turned it down in any case. In 1905, President Theodore Roosevelt, who had heard of Robinson's work through his son Kermit, found a place, a sinecure, in the New York Custom House for the poet, and for four years Robinson knew financial independence. He also knew bondage to drink. At any rate, he did not write much in these years at the Custom House; it was an extended period of frustration which finally disappeared, and in 1910 he published *The Town Down the River*.

In this volume we may see the typically Robinsonian themes and approaches, but with possibly three exceptions, none of the poems represents the finest he could do. "For a Dead Lady" surely shows him at his best in one of his veins, and to a lesser extent and in a less formidable vein, "Two Gardens in Linndale." And "Momus" has a terse, bitter strength that characterizes the epigrammatic strain that is one of his most pungent. It would appear that in these years Robinson was looking for a stance, a position from which to view his own experience and his ideas. As he grew older and took to writing the long narrative poems, his tendency to become oracular, cryptic, and philosophical by turns overcame the achieved starkness of his view; moreover in his letters one may find evidence that Robinson, when he was at his best as poet, had no thoroughgoing idea of his own best qualities. At one time a young lady who was writing a graduate thesis on the philosophy in his work wrote to ask him certain questions. In his reply he told her that he wished she could concern herself less with the philosophy and more with the poetry, a recommendation we may properly wish the poet himself had adopted. For the fatal New England fascination with cloudy abstractions miscalled thought or profundity overcame Robinson and he never broke the spell, except as it would seem almost inadvertently. Even in as interesting a long narrative as *Amaranth* (1934) the nightmare atmosphere, the very real subject, the grim humor, and the subdued lyricism frequently get lost in the interminable rehashing of Favorite Transcendental-isms: what is Truth? or Reality? In the Arthurian trilogy of a few years before we can see much the same tendency.

Robinson is a late Romantic, a Victorian, a transcendentalist whose lust after the abstract was inveterate and nearly always, when indulged, destructive. The moment of stasis, of balance, when he treats the Vast with steady eye and nerve, is to be found in "The Man against the Sky" in the volume of that title (1916); he met the subject with all its imponderables and impalpables head on in that poem, and never fully recovered. Although "The Man against the Sky" solves nothing — and it is of course unfashionable to do other than dismiss it — it nonetheless seems to be almost the last time in literature (Western) when a poet singlehanded calls down the Eter-nal Verities and Cosmic Powers and asks them to declare them-selves. It is an altogether remarkable performance and would have been wholly impossible for a more "sophisticated" poet; one knows why Mr. Eliot characterized Robinson as "negligible"; the direct attack is hardly the Eliot strategy.

Yet there are times and poems that put real questions and often imply real answers. Essentially, like any good poet, Robinson is less the philosopher than the metaphysician, and the question for him is the old ontological one. "The Man against the Sky" sums up the essence of Robinson's thought and feeling on the subject, thought and feeling which when they are working poetically prompt most of his best work, in both shorter lyrics and the poems of middle length. How does a man reconcile the idea of a beneficent, om-nipotent God with the naked and frightening facts of existence? "What inexorable cause/ Makes time so vicious in his reaping"? God or no God, for Robinson the true question is this: Is there a life after this one? If so, then it is all worth it, the suffering and the terror. If not, then why live? Yet in fact men do not often com-mit suicide, a phenomenon which Robinson seizes upon as a kind of proof that man does not end with the grave. Again and again, he will assert his belief in immortality and the ultimate importance of this life, while he utterly rejects materialism. Everywhere, in the poems, letters, and reported comment, such a deliberate choice of belief crops up, implied or stated. For all their polarities of style and rhetoric, "The Man against the Sky" and Wallace Stevens' "Sunday Morning" are complementary and classical views of the single question, and clearly emerge less from differing philosophies than from opposed temperaments. There is a will to doubt as well as to belief, and the existentialists' answer is not the only possible one. If truly philosophical influence on Robinson's views can be found, it seems clear, from Mr. Stevick's essay mentioned in the bibliography at the end of this volume, that William James played the leading part in such influence. Yet even here it should be noted that James himself emphasizes that in dealing with such matters, he has entered the realm of metaphysics, and Robinson's discomfort under the rubric "philosopher" ought to be taken at least as seriously as any quasi-philosophical propositions he may seem to enunciate.

Robinson was a poet and poems are made with words, yet as a man so conspicuously of his century and heritage he was often at war with mere language and all unknowingly. By his own testimony it was words that fascinated him, that made and kept him a poet and a fine one, though the New Englander and the Victorian in him insisted that he must be the Seer, the Prophet, the Unacknowledged Legislator. Small wonder that in the direct conflict of these tendencies poetry is sometimes annihilated, and grist to the Ph.D. mill accumulates. This is not to say that Robinson had no mind and no ideas; it is simply that he mistook speculation in verse for poetic thought, as did unnumbered nineteenth-century writers before him. Still, each time he got a long poem out of his system and had as it were satisfied the Transcendental Philosopher in him, he could turn to real poetry again, and in *The Three Taverns* (1920) and *Avon's Harvest* (1921) he published some half-dozen of his best poems; even in the volume *Dionysius in Doubt* (1925), the last of his books containing short lyrics, there are two of his best sonnets, "New England" and "The Sheaves," and one or two others of real quality. But after that, there are only the long narratives, for the most part one each year up to his death. Of these, only

Amaranth would seem to bear repeated reading, and that in part for reasons not wholly artistic.

He had in a sense become a Man of Letters in the solid nineteenth-century sense of the term and the punctual appearance of a new volume seemed necessary to him — not, one supposes, because he needed the money as he himself claimed, but because publication, so long denied him, was both compensatory and reassuring. It made him as poet real to himself; when there was no book, there was no poet and no man, for rarely has an American poet lived in and for his work as did Robinson. One might say that apart from it, he had no life at all, at least after he went to New York to live. "If only they had said something about me! It would not have mattered what. They could have called me stupid or crazy if they liked. But they said nothing. Nobody devoted as much as an inch to me. I did not exist." If this, Robinson's own statement, is not absolutely true, it is near enough to full accuracy to convey the near-despair the poet must have felt during the years of total neglect. Friends helped, as did alcohol until it interfered with the poetry and then it was alcohol that had to go. But the lean years made a permanent and damaging mark on Robinson as poet, though they seem to have deepened his capacity as a man for the understanding of suffering, loneliness, and despair, as many of his letters testify. Deliberately reticent for fear of damaging self-exposure, he seems to have become more and more committed to one of his less attractive poetic characteristics, that of overqualification. Even in his letters, as apparently in conversation, his statements are frequently qualified by a deprecatory admission that the exact opposite may well be the case. Eventually this not unattractive personal quality is to become a stylistic tic and finally almost a major poetic device. In "Eros Turannos" we can note the modifying, qualifying lines and phrases. By the time of the long narratives, the tendency has solidified and we observe the not uncommon phenomenon of a poet's self-parody: his complication of the simple and his propensity for giving to us for complex what is merely complicated and obscured, in other words, overqualified. These lines from *Cavender's House* (1929) illustrate the point:

He knew there was a woman with two hands
Watching him, but he saw no more of her
Than would assure him she was there. He feared
To see her face, and he feared not to see it;
And then he found it as it was before,
Languid and unrevealing. Her eyes closed,
And her lips moved as if repeating words
That had no meaning. . . .

Robinson tried, over a period of years, to write drama and fiction
that would make some money — to no avail — and one suspects that
in this case failure derived from a shortcoming he himself pointed
out: he had no real subject. He later destroyed all his manuscripts
of fiction, but two Ibsenite plays were published which leave no
doubt that what is a bore in the poems is equally so in the plays.
The truth is that the lack of a real subject in his later years, coupled
with a growing inaptitude for straightforward storytelling, finally
rendered narrative for the most part unavailable to him. The lines
just quoted show how far he has come from the concrete and the
sensuous and he will go even farther. Yet up until the last ten years
of his life he was capable of first-rate work in various stanza forms,
notably the sonnet.

Neglect, near-despair, and poverty had formed him and they
worked themselves out to the bitter end even in the days of success.
"Why don't they *read* me?" he would ask in mock despair. It was,
and is, a good question and one surely that many a poet would like
a fit answer to. They didn't read him because they did not like his
tone of voice. For all that has been written of Robinson's original-
ity, one is hard put to it to say precisely where the innovations lie.
He is simple. Yet his vocabulary is frequently polysyllabic and his
metric jingly and derived. He seems rarely to be aware of the nat-
ural world or of the city, or if he does use the city as locale it is
only in the vaguest, most perfunctory way as a stylized background.
None of the qualities we associate with the Imagists, with Pound
or Eliot, or with the ferment of the period is here, nor is there a
trace of Frost's feeling for and against nature and rural New Eng-
land. Even as serenely autumnal and lovely a poem as "Isaac and
Archibald" lacks the specific and the minutely noted detail we

think of as central to "nature poetry," whatever that may be. It is far closer to Wordsworth than to Frost and perhaps to Cowper than to either of the others in feeling. But one cannot read Robinson expecting certain things and find what he has to tell. If in his own time editors and others dismissed him because they thought his work grim and "pessimistic" they were at least nearer the right track than those who, enamored of the Great Rebellion, thought of him as a stuffy, mindless Yankee who had failed to get the word. The fact is, of course, that Robinson, between two movements and two worlds, could not be accepted by either. When triumph and commercial success came, they came late and for the most part in response to relatively inferior work.

Robinson loved words. Shy and almost wholly inarticulate in company, he wrote with great labor and with total absorption; not unexpectedly, therefore, he frequently confused best and worst in his work and failed to see where the logic of his own poetic intelligence took him. In his love of the involute and the tangential, he is kin to Henry James; in his fascination with language and metric, to Tennyson. But in his penetrating, naked vision of the reality that underlies human predicaments he seems close to the French novelists of the late nineteenth century and to Ibsen. He professed dislike of Flaubert and he sometimes inveighed against the sexual concern of many of the naturalists, yet Zola and Whitman cast a spell on him, however briefly. Kipling's capacity to make poetry out of the commonplace interested and excited him, but more than all of these there was a Yankee eclecticism of language that made him go anywhere for words that would when pressed together make something hard, curious, and impenetrable. Milton, Shakespeare, Browning, Crabbe, Tennyson, Cowper, and a host of Romantics supply part of the vocabulary and the subject matter a vocabulary discovers for itself.

And what is the subject? the temper of it and the tone in which it comes to us? "When the stars are shining blue / There will yet be left a few / Themes availing — / And these failing, / Momus, there'll be you." Here is one of the faces of his Muse, and another was Pity; not tenderness or really what we would call sympathy, but pity for poor souls caught in the trap that their own weakness and fate have combined to spring. Viewed from the modern point of view, many of the best poems lack what is called compassion, as witness the destruction of Pink, Miss Watchman, and Atlas in *Amaranth*. We somehow demand that the poet express a feeling for the fates of his doomed victims. Robinson will not gratify the common expectations, for he is concerned to show the plight and to imply the terror and the rigor of the doom — a doom, one sees, both merited and gratuitous. When this fate is a secretion from the poem and not its nominal subject, the poem is likely to be terse, packed, and utterly objective: the poet presents certain people in certain predicaments and tells what happened. In nearly every case we can see that the issue is one of illusion overcoming the sense of reality. At times illusion is shown as something a character wills and achieves; a state which the person deliberately chooses as preferable to actuality or as providing the only alternative to suicide. Job's wife, Robinson implies, is the stern realist and recommends to Job that he "curse God and die." She has seized "the swift logic of a woman." But though many of Robinson's fated creatures do indeed doom themselves by failing to "see," as he puts it, there are occasionally those who, staking their lives and honors on "illusions," come through triumphantly.

Conrad might have understood these poems had he known them. For Robinson as for Conrad, illusion is the very stuff of living and the naked realist is either the complete and successful Romantic, or a suicide. Illusion is willed and forced into some kind of reality, or it is escape. And in the latter case, it will eventually destroy its slave. The mother in "The Gift of God" forces her wholly inaccurate dream of her son's worth into what is for her the realm of fact which nothing can violate because it rests on limitless unselfish love. The wife in "Eros Turannos" has chosen to deceive herself but has reached a point at which the extent of the deception and its origins are about to reveal themselves — with destruction inevitable. In "Veteran Sirens" the women who "cry out for time to end his levity" have discovered that the joke is on them and not on anyone else; the wife of "The Mill" needs only to know what she knows and to have heard her husband say "There are no millers any more." After that, what else can happen than does?

In creating his effects of fate and of "levity," Robinson relies heavily on a hard surface of objective statement, an intermittent current of humor — from gentle to sardonic — and a metric that seems frequently at odds with the subject matter, as though a pastoral elegy should be set to the tune of "Jingle Bells." The tripping, sometimes metronomic, measure alternates with sonorities, as the language alternates between the homely phrase and the "grand manner." In "Mr. Flood's Party" we see a similar technique in imagery: the juxtaposition of the grand and the ordinary, Eben Flood with his jug of hard cider to his lips "like Roland's ghost, winding a silent horn." The image and the language are at once evocative, original, and straight out of the tradition. And they are meant to be, for the "larger humor of the thing" as Robinson says in another place. The very objectivity with which Robinson views his destroyed and self-destroying characters allows him to forgo compassion and to present their plights with humor while he never shirks the rigor and the pity of the particular destiny. It is an appeal to us, as readers, to apply the same technique to our own capacities for self-deception, to see ourselves as "the clerks of time" or to watch "great oaks return / To acorns out of which they grew." The humor and levity arise from Robinson's refusal, when he is at his best, to consider human error as necessarily cosmically tragic. His Captain Craig, indomitable in defeat and death, is in fact a failure not only in the world's eyes, but in the eyes of the perceptive beholder and perhaps in his own too. And of course Robinson implies that all men are failures in this sense; "poets and kings are but the clerks of time." Hence "the larger humor," the levity, can be felt only by sensibilities realistic enough to understand their own plights and to relate those plights to the whole human condition.

Of course, there are occasions and poems when this sort of humor will not do, will not answer the call of a spirit too appalled at the workings of fate to achieve the right tone. In much of Robinson's work there is another face to the god of reality and under-

standing. Some facts are too horrible to face and too gratuitously
violent for understanding. Poems like "For a Dead Lady" and
"The Mill" belong to this category. In the former there is no at-
tempt whatever at mitigating the horror or at achieving acceptance
or understanding. Such things are simply *there*. To understand
would be to play God; to accept would be demonic. On the whole,
this side of the Robinsonian subject is less common than the for-
mer; it is not, for example, commonly to be seen at all in the longer
poems, where frequently violent acts, often perverted acts, create
denouement or tragic conflict almost as though violence has for
Robinson taken the place of what might be termed the irrational
principle in life. In *Lancelot* and *Amaranth*, to cite two of Robin-
son's best long narratives, understanding, acceptance, and the
promise of a new life form the very basis of the subject and the
theme, but it must be confessed that some of Robinson's finest
work moves in the direction of stating or implying that at the cen-
ter of our existence is something implacable, irrational, and not to
be propitiated. The old cliché often used of Robinson that he cele-
brated the success of failure and the failure of success has only a
limited application, notable in such a poem as "Old Trails"; actu-
ally, he found little reward in failure as such, nor do his failures
like Captain Craig and Eben Flood in any sense "triumph"; they
are as deluded as the man who congratulates himself on his success.
Men fall short of essential humanity and it is here that Robinson's
irony usually comes into play, in poems which treat of people in
particular situations which show them as inadequate to the human
demands made upon them. These poems have plot, action, place,
and time; they nearly always involve a man or a woman who is
confronted with a situation, involving others, which demands a
radical reappraisal of the self and one's conduct. The character is
called upon to discard a cherished image of himself, and nearly
always, in refusing or failing to do so, the character suffers disaster.

In order to see how Robinson works out the fates of such people
in such poems, it might be well to look closely at two or three of
the best examples and try to see what goes on. The best poems of
the sort described have a dense, deceptive surface, organized in a

seemingly careful, orderly way and proceeding quietly, baldly almost, while the narrator subtly assumes the point of view of the reader and imperceptibly helps him to assess and understand, finally leaving with him the realization that the ending is both inevitable and wholly human. The following analyses, then, attempt to show how certain of Robinson's best poems, each representative of a different aspect of the Robinsonian subject, achieve the desired effect.

"Eros Turannos" unfolds as narrative, compressed and suggestive yet without the trickery that occasionally irritates us, as in the case of "The Whip" or "How Annandale Went Out." Most noticeably, the language is general, the tone expository, the purpose of the poem communication rather than expression. Adumbrated in the first stanza, certain images, whose latent power and meanings are reserved until the final lines, have the function of motifs, repeated constantly and expanded as the poem opens out into suggestion. There are three such images or symbols: waves, tree, stairs leading down. Throughout, these symbols control and provide a center for the meanings possible to the poem, and from the mention of "downward years" and "foamless weirs" in the first stanza to the triple vision of the last four lines these elements recur, the same but altered. As is the case with so many Robinson poems, the reader must supply, from the general materials provided, his own construction, yet the poet has seen to it that there can be only one possible final product. The poem contains two complementary parts: the abstract, generalized statement and the symbolic counterpart of that statement, each constituting a kind of gloss upon the other; each moves through the poem parallel to the other, until at the end they become fused in the concrete images. In addition to the three symbols mentioned, we find also that of blindness and dimness, summed up in the single word "veil" yet continually present in the words "mask," "blurred," "dimmed," "fades," "illusion." All this culminates in the sweeping final image: "Or like a stairway to the sea/ Where down the blind are driven." Yet such inner order, such tight articulation as these examples may indicate, derives no more from the concrete than from the generalized; con-

trary to Marianne Moore's professed belief, not all imaginary gar-
dens need have actual toads in them, nor, conversely, do we have
to bother with the toad at all if our garden is imagined truly
enough. What we must have is room — for toads or non-toads, but
room anyhow, and Robinson seems to say that there will be more
room if we don't clutter the garden with too many particular sorts
of fauna and flora. For in "Eros Turannos" we are not told the
where or the wherefore; only, and it is everything, the how and the
just so. In the hinted-at complexity of the woman's emotion, in the
suggested vagueness of the man's worthlessness, lies the whole his-
tory of human trust and self-deception: none shall see this incident
for what it really is, and the woman who hides her trouble has as
much of the truth as "we" who guess and guess yet, the poem im-
plies, without coming nearer to the truth than men usually do.

"Eros Turannos" is the Robinsonian archetype, for in it we can
find the basic elements, the structural pattern, that he was to use
frequently and with large success. The most cursory reading af-
fords a glimpse into the potential power as well as the dangers of
such a form; Robinson's use of it provides examples of both. In
the poem in question he reaches an ultimate kind of equipoise of
statement and suggestion, generalization and concretion. The first
three words of the poem set the tone, provide the key to a "plot"
which the rest will set before us. "She fears him": simple statement;
what follows will explore the statement, and we shall try to observe
the method and evaluate its effect.

> She fears him, and will always ask
>   What fated her to choose him;
> She meets in his engaging mask
>   All reasons to refuse him;
> But what she meets and what she fears
> Are less than are the downward years,
> Drawn slowly to the foamless weirs
>   Of age, were she to lose him.

The epigrammatic tone of the verse strikes one immediately; we
are aware that here is a kind of expository writing, capable in its
generality of evoking a good deal more than the words state. Im-
portant though unobtrusive imagery not only reinforces and en-

riches the exposition but by calculated ambiguity as well sets a
tone of suspense and fatality. The man wears a mask: he conceals
something that at once repels and attracts her; notice the play on
"engaging" and the implications that involves. The motif is an
important one for the poem, as is that contained in the metaphor
of "weirs," since these two suggestions of deception, distrust, en-
trapment, blindness, and decline will be continually alluded to
throughout the poem, to find an ultimate range of meaning in the
final lines.

The second stanza will in such expressions as "blurred" and "to
sound" keep us in mind of the motifs mentioned, without actually
requiring new imagistic material or forcing us to re-imagine the
earlier metaphors. The intent here is not to be vague but to retain
in the reader's consciousness what has gone before as that con-
sciousness acquires new impressions. Hence, in stanza three, Robin-
son can now introduce a suggestive sketch of the man's nature
while he reminds of the woman's and continues to explore it:

> A sense of ocean and old trees
>   Envelops and allures him;
> Tradition, touching all he sees,
>   Beguiles and reassures him; .

That engaging mask of his becomes apparent to us here in this
man who finds a solace and security in the love of his wife and in
her solid place in the community, and yet the sinister note first
sounded in the image of "weirs" is lightly alluded to in the phrase
"a sense of ocean." Moreover, that he too is "beguiled" presents a
possibility of irony beyond what has yet been exploited.

> And all her doubts of what he says
>   Are dimmed with what she knows of days —
> Till even prejudice delays
>   And fades, and she secures him.

The possibilities are many. We grasp readily enough the pathos
of her situation: a woman with a worthless husband, proud and
sensitive to what the town is whispering yet ready to submit to any
indignity, to close her eyes and ears, rather than live alone. Surely a
common enough theme in American writing and one that allows

the poet to suggest rather than dramatize. Again, in "dimmed" we catch an echo of what has gone before, and in the last two lines the abstract noun "prejudice" with its deliberately general verbs "delays" and "fades" presents no image but rather provokes the imagination to a vision of domestic unhappiness familiar to us all, either in fiction or empirically. And of course the finality of "secures," ironic neither in itself nor in its position in the stanza, takes on irony when we see what such security must be: the woman finds peace only by blinding herself and by seeing the man as she wishes to see him.

Stanza four once again recapitulates and explores. Statement alternates with image, the inner suffering with the world's vision of it:

> And home, where passion lived and died,
> Becomes a place where she can hide,
>   While all the town and harbor side
>   Vibrate with her seclusion.

If this stanza forms the climax of the plot, so to speak, the next comes to a kind of stasis, the complication of events and motives and themes we see so often in Henry James. The outside world of critical townspeople, hinted at before, now comes to the foreground, and we get a complication of attitudes and views — the world's, the woman's, the man's, our own — and the poet's is ours too. Yet even in a passage as seemingly prosaic and bare as this Robinson keeps us mindful of what has gone before. In stanza four such words as "falling," "wave," "illusion," "hide," and "harbor" have served to keep us in mind of the various themes as well as to advance the plot, and in the fifth stanza Robinson presents us with a series of possible views of the matter, tells us twice that this is a "story," reiterates that deception and hiding are the main themes, as in the metaphorical expression "veil" and in the simple statement "As if the story of a house/ Were told, or ever could be." And at last, in the final lines, thematic, narrative, and symbolic materials merge in the three images that accumulate power as they move from the simple to the complex, from the active to the passive, from the less to the more terrible:

> Though like waves breaking it may be,
> Or like a changed familiar tree,
> Or like a stairway to the sea
> Where down the blind are driven.

For the attentive reader the narrative cannot fail; Robinson has given us the suggestive outline we need and told us how, in general, to think about this story. He has kept us constantly aware of place, time, actors, and action even though such awareness is only lightly provoked and not insisted on. In the last stanza the curious downward flow of the poem, the flow of the speculation, reaches an ultimate debouchment — "where down the blind are driven." Apart from the metrical power, the movement of the poem is significant; Robinson has packed it with words that suggest descent, depth, and removal from sight, so that the terrible acceptance of the notion that we must "take what the god has given" becomes more terrible, more final as it issues out in the logic of statement and imagery and in the logic of the plot.

If much of the poem's power depends upon the interaction of statement and suggestion, still another source of energy is the metric. Robinson here uses a favorite device of his, feminine rhymes, in alternating tetrameter and trimeter lines, and gives to soft-sounding, polysyllabic words important metrical functions; as a result, when he does invert a foot or wrench the rhythm or use a monosyllable, the effect is striking out of all proportion to its apparent surface value. Surely the plucking, sounding quality of the word "vibrate" in the last line of the fourth stanza is proof of this, though equally effective is the position of "down" and "blind" in the final line of the poem.

Contemporary verse has experimented with meters, rhyme, and rhythm to such an extent that one has to attune the ear to Robinson's verse; at first it sounds jingly and mechanical, perhaps inept, but after we make a trial of them, the skill, the calculation, have their way and the occasional deviations from the set pattern take on the greater power because they are deviations:

> Pity, I learned, was not the least
> Of time's offending benefits

> That had now for so long impugned
> The conservation of his wits:
> Rather it was that I should yield,
> Alone, the fealty that presents
> The tribute of a tempered ear
> To an untempered eloquence.

This stanza from "The Wandering Jew" shows the style. This is mastery of prosody — old-fashioned command of the medium. The reversing of feet, use of alternately polysyllabic and monosyllabic words, of syncopation ("To an untempered eloquence") are devices subtly and sparingly used. The last stanza of the same poem gives another instance, and here the running on of the sense through three and a half lines adds to the effect:

> Whether he still defies or not
> The failure of an angry task
> That relegates him out of time
> To chaos, I can only ask.
> But as I knew him, so he was;
> And somewhere among men to-day
> Those old, unyielding eyes may flash,
> And flinch — and look the other way.

Deviation implies a basic pattern, and although in many cases, particularly in the blank-verse narratives, syllable counting mars the prosody, nonetheless the best poems subtly attune themselves to the "tempered ear," syncopate on occasion, and jingle to good effect.

This analysis is technical and only partial; it seems to presuppose that we must lapse into Cleanth Brooks's "heresy of paraphrase." Granted. Yet this but begs a question, inasmuch as all of Robinson's poetry assumes that one will want to find the paraphrasable element the poet has carefully provided. These are poems *about* something, and what the something is we must discover. That is why we should consider Robinson as a poet with a prose in view; to read "Eros Turannos" or "For a Dead Lady" or "The Gift of God" is to feel that the scope of a long naturalistic novel has emerged from a few stanzas. Yet Allen Tate, in a brief essay, says that Robinson's lyrics are "dramatic" and that T. S.

Eliot observes this to be a characteristic of the best modern verse. One is really at a loss to know what the word "dramatic" means in this regard; Robinson's poetry is not dramatic in any sense of the word commonly accepted, unless it be that Robinson, like Henry James, frequently unfolds a scene. To look for anything like drama in the poems is idle, in that the excitement they convey is of a muted sort, akin to that which James himself generates. This poet wears no masks; he is simply at a distance from his poem, unfolding the "plot," letting us see and letting us make what applications we will. This directness, this prose element, in Robinson's verse is easy enough to find, less so to define or characterize. One can say this, however: just as Pope was at his best in a poetry that had morality and man in society as its subject matter and its criterion, so Robinson is happiest as a poet when he starts with a specific human situation or relationship, with a "story." "Eros Turannos" is *about* the marriage of untrue minds, but specifically it is not about just untrueness and minds; it is about untrue man A and suffering, self-deluding woman B, as well as about those worldly wisemen who conjecture and have all the "dope." Usually unsuccessful in speculative verse, Robinson excels in just this naturalistic case history, this story of a Maine Emma Bovary. If the theme is still failure, Robinson rings a peculiar change upon it, since at last the poem forces us to accept the implication that there *is* and must be a "kindly veil between/ Her visions and those we have seen"; that all of us must "take what the god has given," for failure is, in Robinson's world, the condition of man and human life. We do the best we can. In "Old Trails," the best one can is not often good, and what is indeed success in the world's eyes has a very shoddy look to those who recognize the success as merely "a safer way/ Than growing old alone among the ghosts." It is the success of Chad in James's *The Ambassadors*, who will go home to the prosperous mills and Mamie and Mom, not that of Strether, who could have had the money and the ease but took the way of "growing old among the ghosts."

A briefer, more compact poem than "Old Trails," one that deals with another aspect of the theme, is the sonnet "The Clerks,"

which for all its seeming spareness is a very rich, very deft perform-
ance. The octave opens colloquially, gives us a general location and
an unspecified number of clerks; the speaker is the poet, as poet
and as man. Robinson draws an evocative, generalized sketch of the
clerks' past, of their prime as well as of the slow attrition of time
and labor, and affirms that despite the wear they have sustained
these men are still good and human. It is in the sestet that the poem
moves out into suggestion, that it implies a conceit by which we can
see how all men are clerks, time-servers, who are subject to fears
and visions, who are high and low, and who as they tier up also cut
down and trim away. To call the poem a conceit is no mere exer-
cise of wit, for Robinson has clearly punned on many unobtrusive
words in the sonnet. What is the clerks' "ancient air"? Does it mean
simply that the men are old and tired? or that their manner is one
of recalling grand old times of companionship that never really
existed? or that one must take "air" literally to mean their musty
smell of the store? These possibilities are rendered the more com-
plex by the phrase "shopworn brotherhood" immediately follow-
ing, for then the visual element is reinforced, the atmosphere of
shoddiness and shabbiness, of Rotary club good-fellowship, and
the simple language has invested itself with imagistic material that
is both olfactory and visual. And of course, one may well suspect
sarcasm in the assertion that "the men were just as good,/ And
just as human as they ever were." How good were they? Yet lest
anyone feel this is too cynical, Robinson carefully equates the
clerks with "poets and kings."

As is the case with "Eros Turannos," this poem proceeds from
the general to the specific and back to the general again, a gener-
ality now enlarged to include comment on and a kind of definition
of the human condition. Throughout there have been ironic over-
tones, ironic according to the irony we have seen as peculiarly
Robinsonian in that it forms one quadrant of the total view. It
has to do here with the discrepancy between the vision men have
of their lives and the actuality they have lived. The poet here im-
plies that such discrepancy, such imperfection of vision is immuta-
bly "human" and perhaps therefore, and ironically, "good." That

the clerks (and we are all clerks) see themselves as at once changed and the same, "fair" yet only called so, serves as the kind of lie men exist by, a lie that becomes an "ache" on the one hand and the very nutriment that supports life on the other. You, all you who secretly cherish some irrational hope or comfort, merely "feed yourselves with your descent," your ancestry, your career, your abject position miscalled a progress. For all of us there can be only the wastage, the building up to the point of dissatisfaction, the clipping away to the point of despair.

Despite the almost insupportable rigor of Robinson's attitude, we can hardly accuse him of cynicism or of hopelessness. In every instance his view of people is warm and understanding, not as the patronizing seer but as the fellow-sufferer. Such feeling informs the poems we have discussed and fills "The Gift of God" with humanity no cynic could imagine, no despair encompass. For in this poem the theme of failure turns once more, this time in an unexpected way so that we see Robinson affirming self-deception of this specific kind as more human, more the gauge of true love than all the snide fact-finding the rest of the world would recommend. The poem is about a mother's stubborn, blind love for a worthless (or perhaps merely ordinary) son, and this in the teeth of all the evidence her neighbors would be delighted to retail. Again, the poem is a compact narrative; again the irony exists outside the poem, not in its expression. As in so many of the best poems, Robinson says in effect: here is the reality, here is the illusion. *You* compare them and say which is which and if possible which is the correct moral choice.

The metaphorical material we can roughly classify as made up of imagery relating to royalty, apotheosis, sacrifice, and love. From the first few lines we are aware of a quality which, by allusion to the Annunciation and the anointing of kings, establishes the mother's cherished illusion and thereby makes acceptance of the emergent irony inescapably the reader's duty; he must compare the fact and the fiction for and by himself; Robinson will not say anything in such a way as to make the responsibility for choice his own rather than the reader's. He will simply render the situation and leave us to judge it, for all of Robinson's poems presuppose an outside world of critics and judges, of ourselves, people who see and observe more or less clearly. His irony is external; it lies in the always hinted-at conflict between the public life and the private, between the thing seen from the inside and from the outside, with the poet, the speaker, presenting a third vision, not one that reconciles or cancels the other two, but one which simply adds a dimension and shows us that "everything is true in a different sense."

If the dominant motifs in "The Gift of God" are as indicated above, the progression of the poem follows undeviatingly the pattern suggested. In the first stanza Annunciation; the second, Nativity; the third, vision; the fourth, a stasis in which the mother seems to accept her son's unusual merit and her own vision of him as real; the fifth, a further extension of vision beyond anything actual; the sixth, the culmination of this calculated vision in the apotheosis. More than a schematized structure, the poem depends not only on the articulation of motifs and a plot, but equally on symbolic material that interacts with the stated or implied events in the "plot." Thus, from the outset the poet has juxtaposed the illusory vision and the "firmness" of the mother's faith in it; the language has a flavor of vague association with kingship, biblical story, and legend, notably conveyed by such words as "shining," "degree," "anointed," "sacrilege," "transmutes," and "crowns." Yet in the careful arrangement of his poem Robinson has not oversimplified the mother's attitude. She maintains her "innocence unwrung" (and the irony of the allusion is not insisted on) despite the common knowledge of people who know, of course, better, and Robinson more than implies the innocence of her love in the elevated yet unmetaphorical diction he uses. Not until the final stanza does he open the poem out, and suddenly show the apotheosis in the image of "roses thrown on marble stairs," subtly compressing into the last three lines the total pathos of the poem, for the son ascending in the mother's dream is "clouded" by a "fall": the greatness his mother envisions is belied by what we see. And who is in the right? For in the final turn of the "plot," is it not the mother who gives the roses of love and the marble of enduring faith? Is the dream not as solid and as real as human love can make it? If we doubt this notion, we need only observe the value Robinson places on the verb "transmutes" in stanza five: "*Transmutes* him with her faith and praise." She has, by an absolute miracle of alchemy, transmuted base material into precious; by an act of faith, however misplaced, found the philosopher's stone, which is love wholly purged of self.

What we have come to realize is that in these poems we have been considering we are concerned with narrative — narrative of a peculiar kind in which the story is not just about the events, people, and relationships but about the very poetic devices which are the vehicle of the narration and its insights. In "The Gift of God" symbol and theme have a narrative function; they must do in brief and without obtrusiveness what long passages of dialogue, exposition, and description would effect in a novel. As a result, the reader is compelled to take the entire poem in at once; he either "understands" it or he does not. Naturally there are subtleties which emerge only after many readings; yet because these poems are narratives, Robinson must concentrate upon communication, upon giving us a surface that is at once dense yet readily available to the understanding.

> As one apart, immune, alone,
> Or featured for the shining ones,
> And like to none that she has known
> Of other women's other sons, —
> The firm fruition of her need,
> He shines anointed; and he blurs
> Her vision, till it seems indeed
> A sacrilege to call him hers.

This is on one hand simple telling of plot: the mother sees her son as unique and feels unworthy to be his mother. Simple enough. But the story is more than this, more than a cold telling of the facts about the mother's vision of her son. We see on the other hand that it is her need of the son, and of the vision of him, which complicates the story, while the suggestion of kingship, ritual, and sacrifice in the diction, with the implication of self-immolation and deception, further extends the possibilities of meaning.

All this we grasp more readily than we may realize, for Robinson prepares for his effects very early and while he extends meaning is careful to recapitulate, to restate and reemphasize the while he varies and complicates:

> She sees him rather at the goal,
> Still shining; and her dream foretells
> The proper shining of a soul
> Where nothing ordinary dwells.

In these lines Robinson affirms the mother's illusion — it is a "dream" that "foretells" — and recapitulates the theme of kingship, of near-divinity, in the repetition of "shining." The stanza that follows gives the poem its turn, states specifically that the son is merely ordinary, that the mother deludes herself, that her motive in so doing is "innocent," and in stanza five the poem, as we have seen, turns once more, pivots on the verb "transmute," turns away from the simple ironical comparison we have been experiencing and reveals a transmuted relationship: son to mother, vision to fact, and an ultimate apotheosis of the mother under the guise of a mistaken view of the son. The poem is about all these things and is equally about the means of their accomplishment within the poem. This is a poetry of surfaces, dense and deceptive surfaces to be sure but still a poetry that insists on the communication of a whole meaning, totally and at once:

> She crowns him with her gratefulness,
> And says again that life is good;
> And should the gift of God be less
> In him than in her motherhood,
> His fame, though vague, will not be small,
> As upward through her dream he fares,
> Half clouded with a crimson fall
> Of roses thrown on marble stairs.

The recapitulation, the tying together, of the symbolic and thematic materials serves in this, the last stanza, a narrative as well as an expressive purpose. The tone is epigrammatic rather than prosaic and must shift delicately, come to the edge of banality, then turn off and finally achieve a muted sublimity that runs every risk of sentimentality and rhetoric yet never falters. The verse requires of us what it requires of itself: a toughness that can encompass the trite and mawkish without on the one hand turning sentimental itself or on the other resorting to an easy irony. The technique is the opposite of dramatic in that Robinson leaves as much to the reader as he possibly can; he uses no persona; the conflict-in-action before our eyes, as it unfolds itself at once, passes through complications, and returns to the starting point, the same yet altered and, to some degree, understood. To this extent Robinson is ratiocinative rather than dramatic; what we and the characters themselves think about the "plot" is as important as the plot, becomes indeed the full meaning of the plot.

Here, again, Robinson is likely to seem behind the times to certain readers. The narrative mode is unpopular in contemporary verse, and even poems about people who are not legendary or at least historical seem to be out of fashion. But the form is an old and honorable one with practitioners as variously gifted as Crabbe, Chaucer, Skelton, Prior, Tennyson, Browning, Kipling, certain Pre-Raphaelites and Decadents, a not inconsiderable company. And Wordsworth made a form of his own of it. Nearly always, the temptation is to move to the long narrative, the viability of which in recent decades is a vexed question. Nonetheless, however strongly dramatic monologue persists in our own era, the narrative lyric has largely disappeared, largely because of the tendency of most modern poetry to be, on the one hand, abstract, philosophical, didactic, or, on the other, rhapsodic, quasi-mystical, symbolist. Certain of the best practitioners in each mode transcend boundaries and mingle the two; one thinks of Stevens and Yeats here. But a Hart Crane, a Dylan Thomas, a Pound: these poets have a particular country from which they rarely stray with success. Robinson had, of course, a historical and local advantage: the nineteenth century was still available to him as an influence and a source, and his upbringing served to keep him isolated, during his formative years, from a too-doctrinaire rejection of his heritage. There is a disadvantage in rebellion and experiment, as there is in indiscriminate acceptance. Robinson took over much Roman-

tic feeling and practice because it suited him. What did not suit
him in it was its diction, its remoteness from real experience, and
its mere rhetoric. For him, the narrative lyric represented an eclec-
tic form combining many sorts of Romantic poetry, but with the
superaddition of a new vocabulary, a sense of real life in a particu-
lar time and place, and a zeal for solid truth. Hence his deliberate
omission from *Tristram* of the love potion. That was too much to
swallow!

For all that has been said of the shorter poems, we are still left
with the vexed question of the blank-verse narratives, the longer
and the shorter. Clearly, any attentive reader will single out for
first place among the latter such poems as "Isaac and Archibald,"
"Aunt Imogen," "Rembrandt to Rembrandt," and "The Three
Taverns." All are notable for the absence of that garrulity which
grew on Robinson, particularly in the last decade of his life, as
well as for their structure and genuine intellectual content: in
them Robinson thinks as a poet doing a job of work should think.
The first is a New England pastoral, muted yet rich in tone, gently
ironic yet lyrical, and marked by the poet's characteristic humor-
ous self-deprecation as well as his insight into both youth and
age. The second poem, less ambitious perhaps, is a marvel of es-
cape from a trap that seems to promise certain capture in senti-
mentality; it is the story of an old maid who finds her annual emo-
tional release in a month's stay with her sister and her children.
What saves the poem is its utter honesty of feeling and language;
the poem is not about pathos — pathos simply leaks out of the plain
account the poet gives. But "Rembrandt to Rembrandt," a more
ambitious piece, addresses itself to the problem of the solitary ar-
tist and in so doing is even more intimately autobiographical in
feeling than the others. Again, the poem never makes the mistake
of being about its own emotions; Robinson here concentrates on
the artist's agonized yet sardonic assessment of his own plight.
There is no solution, no dedication to the higher aims; only the
realization that he moves among demons of self-doubt, self-delu-
sion, and self-pity. Something of the same kind appears in "The
Three Taverns" in which St. Paul seems to be analyzing for us the

relative importance of faith and the Law. And here Robinson, abandoning a heritage of Calvinism and a more recent tradition of Puritan fideism, comes out strongly, in the persona of Paul, for a faith at once personal and from authority, ruled finally by wisdom slowly and painstakingly acquired. There are to be few sudden visions and visitations and those only for the elect.

If the foregoing remarks indicate, as they should, that in these shorter narratives Robinson is doing the poet's work with economy, high intelligence, and skill, what is to follow must of necessity show the other side of the coin. One must say candidly that with the exception of parts of the Arthurian cycle and of *Amaranth*, all the later long narratives are arid, badly thought out, and, as it were, tired. The reasons for this decay appear earlier and there is no need to rehearse them. Briefly, however, here are some of the qualities which these long poems show.

Merlin (1917), *Lancelot* (1920), and *Tristram* (1927) make up the Arthurian cycle and for all their failings surely treat the epic Arthurian theme with greater meaning and importance than do any other works of modern times, T. H. White's possibly excepted. The poems are of course allegorical in conception, at least in the case of the first two, and *Lancelot* really comes close to maintaining a successful interplay of the actual and the symbolic on an extended scale. Yet we have to admit that Robinson's besetting sins, the overelaboration of the obvious and whimsical garrulity, always potential in his work, here begin to exert their fatal influence. Everything Robinson wrote in blank verse in the last fifteen or twenty years of his life is too long, too diffuse, too manneristic. One feels that, like James, Robinson began to enjoy his own work too much, the sound of his own voice tended to intoxicate him. But enough — there are superb passages in *Merlin* and the characters of Vivian and Merlin are real and believable; Lancelot, Arthur, and Guinevere are also powerfully imagined, particularly Lancelot in the poem of that name. If Gawain is hopelessly tedious with the tedious whimsy that grew on Robinson, the figure of Lancelot emerges as heroic, human yet larger than life, a great soldier and a man of noble nature.

Fundamentally, the weakness of the whole cycle derives from Robinson's uneasy poetic and structural compromise: here is myth, symbol, allegory, yet here equally are men and women of the twentieth century. Reconciliation of these disparate parts is, if not impossible, at least an immensely formidable task. Robinson comes close to success in *Lancelot* only because myth, symbol, and allegory disappear when the poem is at its best and we have the powerfully conveyed triangular affair of Arthur, Guinevere, and Lancelot. In *Tristram* — Robinson's great popular success — there is much lyric beauty but the poem is fatally flawed by a love affair at once sticky and verbose and by characters more reminiscent of routine historical novels than of men and women out of myth and legend. And the later narratives, though perhaps less embarrassing in their portrayals of love and lovers, do fatally remind one of *Redbook*, if only in the names of heroines: Laramie, Gabrielle, Natalie, Karen. Only *Amaranth*, in returning to the old subject of failure and self-delusion in artists, touches reality and by fits and starts finds life and meaning. Robinson's last poem, *King Jasper* (1935), is another raid on the abstract by way of allegory and shows the poet's exhaustion — he was on his deathbed when it was completed — as do perhaps to some extent all these late narratives. "A series of conversations terminated by an accident." This dismissal of Ibsen's *A Doll's House* quoted by Yeats might serve to characterize the general effect of these poems on the modern reader, and if it seems sweeping and harsh, any qualifications can serve only to mitigate the judgment, not revoke it.

Yet Robinson stands alone among American poets in his devotion to the long poem. *Captain Craig* remains unique in our annals, rivaled in England by one or two of John Masefield's. In the narrative poem of moderate length, like "Isaac and Archibald," there is no one to touch him; Wordsworth's "Michael" and Keats's "Lamia" would seem the sole competitors in the genre throughout modern times. Robinson of course precedes Frost, in both time and originality, as a writer of short narratives. Frost's "The Death of the Hired Man," for example, lacks both the verbal complexity and the metrical subtlety of Robinson; when Frost turns to such a poem as "Out, Out," however, he is on firm ground indeed where none can outdo him. Both poets clearly find the compressed, elliptically told story their "supreme fiction." It is entirely possible that certain readers can never bring themselves to enjoy verse of this sort — muted, ironic, understated. For some, Robinson is less exciting than, say, Wallace Stevens, born only ten years after Robinson, just as Coleridge seems to many readers more exciting than Wordsworth, Hopkins more daring and absorbing than Tennyson. One might put it this way: Robinson in his best work has no specific religious or philosophical position to recommend, as neither Keats nor Wordsworth has; Hopkins, Stevens, Pound — these are poets who want to sell us something, a theory, a set of ideas or principles. If we like the principles we will love the poetry. For some, Robinson has a defect which goes far, in their view, to cancel out most if not all of his great merit; there is a certain dryness and mechanicalness of tone and feeling which for certain readers will always be an insuperable obstacle, as the "egotistical-sublime" of Wordsworth will always limit his audience. The reader who likes "Michael" will probably like "Isaac and Archibald." Robinson writes about himself in a guise some of us can recognize and enjoy; he does not pose, he does not try to give opinions. Personality in a poet is of the essence. We must like him as he speaks to us or we had better not read him.

That his poetic personality included a strong lyrical element cannot be denied, though it is frequently overlooked, largely because the poet rarely indulged it. We have seen that it was at least once overindulged in *Tristram* and we know that Robinson often kept it in reserve that its appearance might have the greater effect. The language, the imagery, of this lyricism derive largely from nineteenth-century sources, as in the opening lines of "The Man against the Sky" in which poem, as in "The Dark Hills," a deliberate use of highly colored rhetoric is central to the purpose. Unlike many poets of recent years, Robinson was not afraid of lyricism, nor, unlike still others, did he try to overwhelm the reader with "original" and striking imagery. The image of Eben Flood like "Roland's ghost winding a silent horn" is a typical example of one kind of Robinsonian lyricism in that it is euphonious, nostalgic, traditional — and wittily ironic.

But not all Robinson's lyrical flights are of these two sorts, the rhetorical or the ironic. Many occur as climaxes to poems which have begun in a muted, somber tone, rise gradually, and reach a peak of grandeur and eloquence in the final lines. We can observe the technique in such poems as "The White Lights," "On the Night of a Friend's Wedding," "The Sheaves," and of course, "The Gift of God." But there are still those poems which are primarily, almost purely, lyrical, and though few critics think of Robinson as a lyricist, or even as a poet of great versatility, a thorough reading of his work discloses a number of fine poems of quiet but powerful lyric intensity. "Luke Havergal" is one, a poem of almost macabre symbolism. Others, like "Pasa Thalassa Thalassa" and "The Wilderness," with their overtones of Kipling and Swinburne, seem Pre-Raphaelite in quality, as does the "Villanelle of Change." There remains nonetheless the conviction that Robinson's greatest triumphs and happiest effects derive from the "mixed" lyric, the poem rooted in situation which combines narrative, lyrical and ironic, often humorous, qualities with the intent of creating a more complex emotional state in the reader than that effected by the "pure" lyric. "The House on the Hill," "Veteran Sirens," "John Evereldown," and "New England," all display in their differing accents and rhythms the possibilities of this "mixed" form. Wit, pathos, lyrical power, and understatement combine in varied ways to produce complex states of feeling. It is one of the truly Robinsonian characteristics which can be called both modern and highly personal, characteristic of the man and the manner.

Finally, it must be avowed that any writer with a marked manner — and Robinson's manner is strongly marked — offends certain sensibilities, and those often the most acute. The defects and virtues of a poet are so closely allied that frequently they go hand in hand and it takes many bad poems to generate one good one. Robinson's fault was of course to mistake the attempt for the achieved thing. Can anyone say Robinson is alone in such misapprehension? We have seen the damaging effects on Robinson of exile from the kind of give-and-take the knowledge of the better contemporary minds can provide. He had protected his one talent so long and under such stress that we cannot wonder that he took little advice and criticism when it came to him. He was not a Browning; his latter days were divided between the MacDowell Colony in the summers, New York, and visits to friends and to "Tilbury Town," whither he now came as her most famous son — and can we imagine what that must have done to his long-battered pride? But he was not spoiled. He did not surround himself with doting women, or go to tea-fights and give readings — he shrank from these with horror, and a touch of cynicism. He kept on writing, as we have seen, and writing increasingly to satisfy, perhaps to justify, a conception of himself as poet and as man. The great fault of the nineteenth-century men of letters was to publish everything, and Robinson was of his time in this as in so much else. But his successes are many and large — in the narrative poem, the sonnet, the reflective lyric, the narrative lyric, and the dramatic monologue. Limited by environment, tradition, and circumstance, he yet managed to write the finest poems written in America between 1900 and 1920. In England and Ireland were Hardy, Yeats, and Wilfrid Owen and there were Pound and Eliot to be heard. Yet if we consider calmly, apart from notions of "influence" and contemporaneity, we will be forced to admit that the latter two men's work had not by this time achieved the self-contained excellence here under discussion. For all the obvious repetitiousness and aridity of Robinson's later work, twenty years of productiveness, and productiveness of excellence, is an unusually long period for an American writer. Robinson is not Great as Dante and Shakespeare and Milton and Sophocles are Great, but he is in the very front rank of American writers.

Marianne Moore

W E KNOW this poet by her voice, by her "astonishing invention in a single mode," by her delicate, taxing technique; we know her for the "relentless accuracy" of her eye.

This is Marianne Moore, ironist, moralist, fantasist.

She was born in 1887 in St. Louis, Missouri, and has written of herself that she is a Presbyterian and was brought up in the home of her grandfather, the Reverend John R. Warner, who was for twenty-seven years the pastor of Kirkwood Presbyterian Church in St. Louis, that her brother was a chaplain in the navy for forty and more years, and that the books to which she has had access have been, on the whole, serious.

Of her father, John Milton Moore, she has told us little. It is known that he left his family when his daughter was an infant. To her mother, Mary Warner Moore, she paid significant tribute in a postscript to the *Selected Poems*: "In my immediate family there is one 'who thinks in a particular way;' and I should like to add that where there is an effect of thought or pith in these pages, the thinking and often the actual phrases are hers."

In 1894 the family moved to Carlisle, Pennsylvania. It was at Metzger Institute in that town that she was educated and at Bryn Mawr, from which she graduated in 1909. The next year she studied at the Carlisle Commercial College and from 1911 to 1915 was in charge of the commercial department of the United States Indian School at Carlisle. If it remains a curiosity that she taught such subjects as typing and bookkeeping to young Indians it is less surprising, in view of her late pronounced interest in baseball and her early flair for tennis playing, that she coached the boys in field sports. In 1911 she spent a summer in England and France where, in Paris, she went to every museum but two. In 1918 she moved to New York, living on St. Luke's Place, teaching first at a private school. From 1921 to 1925 she was an assistant at the Hudson Park branch of the New York Public Library. Some critics have made something of this (part-time) library work, suggesting that her years of easy accessibility to so many card catalogues and pamphlets gave her the clue to her unique method of happening on a poem. But from Miss Moore's account she was more engaged in reviewing "silent-movie fiction" than in working behind the stacks with well-wormed collections of odd learning, and it would seem that her bent for collecting rare data and, taking "a wing here" and "a leg there," fitting something of them into poems was sufficiently native to her without the experience at the neighborhood library.

Her verse first appeared in *The Egoist*, an English periodical, in *Poetry*, and in Alfred Kreymborg's *Others* in 1915, and later she began to attend those small gatherings held at Kreymborg's apartment in Greenwich Village for such young experimenting poets as Wallace Stevens and William Carlos Williams. Although H. D. had been her classmate at Bryn Mawr, neither knew of the other's "interest in writing"; but in 1921 it was H. D. and Bryher (Winifred Ellerman, then Mrs. Robert McAlmon) who published through the Egoist Press, without the author's knowledge, *Poems*, a collection of twenty-four that had appeared in English and American magazines.

Ezra Pound had already spoken of her work and Mina Loy's as a kind of "dance of the intelligence" (*logopoeia*) and possessed of an "arid clarity" (*Little Review*, 1918) and in 1923 when a pamphlet of her poems, *Marriage*, was published in the United States and in England, T. S. Eliot wrote: "I can only think of five contemporary poets — English, Irish, French and German — whose works excite me as much or more than Miss Moore's."

By 1920 she was beginning to publish in the *Dial*, and in 1925 she received its award for "distinguished service to American letters" for *Observations*, her first book to be published in this country. In the same year she became acting editor of the *Dial* and remained with it until 1929 when it expired. *Selected Poems* appeared in 1935 with an Introduction by Eliot, famous for its pronunciamento: "My conviction, for what it is worth, has remained unchanged for the last fourteen years: that Miss Moore's poems form part of the small body of durable poetry written in our time."

Miss Moore has been brilliantly served from the beginning by the most astute of critics and the most perceptive of poets. If Pound and Eliot took up her cause, a poet-critic like Yvor Winters furthered it, and it remains for R. P. Blackmur and Morton Dauwen Zabel to have compounded penetrating estimates of her work. Of a later generation, Randall Jarrell, Lloyd Frankenberg, and Vivienne Koch have been brilliant and dedicated. She has not suffered from neglect or misunderstanding, and though her work went against the main current and tradition of (English) poetry, she was not scouted for it. Can we say that she was fortunate in being with the *Zeitgeist* rather than against it, or out of it? She has been compared with Emily Dickinson more than once and is it a proof of "progress" or was it a mere lucky accident that she was not penalized for her magnificent originality as Emily was?

In the fifties Miss Moore received from officialdom the recognition that poets, critics, and readers had given her for many years, her *Collected Poems* (1951) receiving the Bollingen and Pulitzer prizes and the National Book Award. In 1954 that long labor, her translation of the *Fables* of La Fontaine, appeared and in 1955 *Predilections*, a collection of her reviews and essays. She became a member of the National Institute of Arts and Letters in 1947 and of the American Academy in 1955.

"But we prove, we do not explain our birth," she wrote in "The Monkey Puzzle," and if this does not apply as sharply to life itself nevertheless let the poems lead the way.

Like William Carlos Williams she wanted, when young, to be a painter. But then she also thought of studying medicine and found the biology courses exhilarating. "Precision, economy of statement, logic employed to ends that are disinterested, drawing and identifying, liberate — at least have some bearing on — the imagination, it seems to me," she has said in an interview with Donald Hall in the *Paris Review*. We think we can see the bearing it has had. Might we not attribute to her what she did to Henry James: "a rapture of observation"? For who has held up to inspection more "skeined stained veined variety"? But this fascination with every shade and tone of the "minute particulars" was only one element of many in *Observations*.

Of *Observations* (1924) one might say: it is first and last a voice. The voice of sparkling talk and sometimes very lofty talk, glittering with authority. It has dismissed poetic diction, indeed is rigorous in its exclusion of the traditional or the romantic sensuous word, phrase, and implication. It works in a new area of language and meanings because it has new insights to bring to subjects not before then quite approximated by poetry. It is experimental and/or revolutionary because it is excluding the magical, the lyrical, the incantatory, and the musical; nature and the seasons, the moon, old Floridas of the imagination, the street scene and the fire sale. Bringing a new diction to another kind of "subject matter," it employed the cadences of prose in a rhythm based on speech. But whose speech? If at moments one might think of Congreve, at others of Henry James, it is essentially her uniquely mother-English own, running with a rapid, finely nerved energy. Held tautly to the line articulation, when so finely intermeshed, is meant, like a dance, to last just so long and not a second longer.

There are highly visual poems such as "The Fish," "A Grave"; there are epigrammatic poems out to discriminate, not describe; there is "Roses Only," a model of ambiguity, where a virtue is made of writing on two subjects as if they were one and of saying one thing while meaning another. But this is true of many poems.

The contours of these poems are sharp and fine-edged — Blake's "hard and wiry lines of rectitude" — like many of the objects de-

scribed: "the pierced iron shadows of the cedars," "sculptured scim-
itars." Her liking for the "strict proportions" of the hard and
definite equals her care for symmetries of pattern and such mathe-
matical niceties as in "The Fish" where the number of syllables
per line in each stanza is 1/3/8/1/6/9 and where the portioning
out of syllables works for a fine pointing up by sound, sight, and
meaning. That is, the word weights are so balanced and nicely
adjusted that (typographically aiding, too, the deaf) the force has
to fall where it does, on the telling when not the killing word —
i.e., the word that drives all the point of the poem home to the
heart. We hear it in

                              the chasm side is
                    dead.

Sound also tends to the crisp and quick, energetic consonants rather
than lolling alliterations: "Bundles of lances all alike, partly hid
by emeralds from Persia," or "Greece with its goat and its gourds."

With a concern to narrow limits, to reduce the means of expres-
sion to what is indispensable, she understands, like certain painters,
the necessity of not going beyond the line. Thus the firmness of
the contours, the self-containment of the poem, which often goes
by a crooked mile to its usually ringing, often epigrammatic close.

If many of the essential characteristics of her style meet the little
laws laid down by the Imagists — the absence of introspective
self, the concentration upon the object-subject, conciseness, a
rhythm "which corresponds exactly to the emotion or shade of emo-
tion" — can we say that Imagism was her distant parent? There
are the early brief "To a Chameleon," "An Egyptian Pulled Glass
Bottle in the Shape of a Fish," "A Talisman." Like most Imagist
poems they are static, concentrated on rendering the one instant of
the object as clearly and firmly as possible. But "A Talisman"
(1912), selected by Eliot as being the only poem to suggest a slight
influence of H. D., rhymes and is formally developed, unlike most
Imagist poems, and is conventional beside "To a Chameleon"
which is already more free and idiosyncratic and already (1916) tak-
ing the syllable as the measure rather than the foot, indicating
that if she had learned from the Imagists how to approach the ob-

ject with an intense scrutiny she had learned almost as soon how to take over a method for strictly her own purposes.

And if *precision* had become the watchword of the Imagists — T. E. Hulme, first Imagist and "father" of them all, is said to have introduced the word to modern literary criticism in his essay "Romanticism and Classicism" and it is known that Pound as early as 1912 was calling for poetry to be as precise as prose — these poems had it, and not only of the "minute discriminations" (Blake) but of the very articulation of movement.

Precision in this case also goes with wit and certain moral and intellectual convictions. Hers is no poetry of emotional conflict or discord or disillusionment. If in "Bowls" we have an implicit-explicit criticism of the blind worship of the present and in other poems satiric rejections of popular prejudices ("The vestibule to experience is not to/be exalted into epic grandeur"), there is little notice, head-on, of the disorders of the present. The open social scene was not her province. We do not have the flavors of the age in terms of rancid butter or oyster shells. (Her objectified world is in this sense interior.) Two lines in "New York" might sound a theme: "one must stand outside and laugh/since to go in is to be lost." If these lines suggest that laughter can be a weapon of self-preservation, do they not also suggest a recognition of differences about which nothing can be done? It is essential not to go in and be lost.

But in the decade of *The Waste Land* she partakes of no cynical or despairing view. From the first her highly defined world seems based on a clear-cut recognition of ethical values she considers still extant though many would have it proved that such values have been vitally assailed if not destroyed. It might be said that this poet, devoted to the paradox, strikes one as a figure of paradox too: with her clear moral and intellectual convictions not just exactly of the times, but with her forged weapons of technique the pure exemplar of the modernist. But what is a satirist (when she is) who doesn't have strong moral convictions? One is tempted to add that in her case morality seems a facet of sensibility.

One could remark also of her philosophic calm, that strong sense of being in touch with the *adagia*, with a resolute sense of wisdom about life, that it is what has been remarked of the Chinese, "a necessary armor to protect the excessive susceptibility to emotion."

Thus *Observations* brought to verse a new subject matter and to the line a new rhythm, the rhythm of prose in all its succinctness, by this latter completing the circle Flaubert had begun in 1855 when he wrote (in a letter) that he wished to bring the rhythms of poetry to prose. If this book has been equaled by her later books it has never been surpassed and exists a twentieth-century monument like *Harmonium, A Draft of XXX Cantos,* and *The Waste Land.*

Like Williams and Cummings she suspected the comma (Apollinaire was the first to do so) and thought it "wholesome" not to capitalize the beginning of lines, disliked the connective (but so did Emily Dickinson) in the interests of intensity. "Titles are chaff," she said in an early poem and circumvented the plague of having to title poems by making the first line serve as title. To such an instance of inventiveness can be added others: notes — listed at the back of each book — and, in the case of *Observations,* even an index appended!

If the notes can't be considered as what's left over of what couldn't be put into the poem, neither can they be considered as necessary for the deeper understanding of the poem. They frequently give us delightful information on, say, the price of unicorn horns, but primarily they serve as a reading list, giving us the authors of those phrases that as specimens of wit have been rescued for us. In this way Miss Moore is a kind of curator of verities and "briefs, abstracts and chronicles" of past literatures. "Acknowledgments seem only honest," said Miss Moore.

This inlaying of quotations with the black hooks that so nicely help to set a brilliance apart has been compared with the collage technique of Braque, Picasso, and Kurt Schwitters. Miss Moore first introduced it in 1915. And her innovation has since become a part of literary tradition.

Her approach to rhyme was also radical. In about half of the poems in *Observations* she avoids it altogether. In "The Fish," "Black Earth," "To Statecraft Embalmed," to name a few, the pattern is formal and the rhyme scheme elaborate. It is rarely insistent, however. Most of the time the rhyme endings are all but submarine in effect because the meaning of the line runs on to the next line and no pause is wanted by the reader, or are so light in sound and echoed so faintly — "Ming" and "something" — that they're almost not heard. (It might be noted that Hopkins wanted his verses to be recited as running on without pause, the rhymes occurring in their midst like a phonetic accident — which is what Miss Moore wanted and got.)

Also wanting a distribution of emphasis more light and even, as in French, she took the syllable as the measure rather than the foot, working always for the effect of unstressed or only faint and lightly stressed rhythms. This was, more or less, an extension of the prose effect. (In three poems puns are suggested on "feet" and we know that in 1918 Miss Moore wrote an article on the unaccented syllable in *The Egoist*. She also wrote in *The Oxford Anthology of American Literature*, Volume II: "Regarding the stanza as a unit, rather than the line, I sometimes divide a word at the end of a line, relying on a general straightforwardness of treatment to counteract the mannered effect.")

Almost from the beginning she proceeds by an express method of her own dialectic. The absurd will rest side by side with the exotic, the commonplace by the exquisite. "There is no progress without contrairies," said Blake and many of her poems seem to have their source in this dictum. They seem to move by the pull of contrasts and by that tension set up. The incongruities and the discrepancies, the contradictions and oppositions — these are what she harnesses and keeps either in tandem or under one yoke.

Juxtaposition of incongruities is of the essence. But not in the ways of other modernists. She is not working with a sensuous language for violently mysterious effects, or juxtaposing words for the sake of shocks of collision. Rather, her language is strictly tempered and clear, almost classical in its moderation and lack of rhetorical splurge. Verb is firmly connected to noun, there is no straining of language within the sentence unit for a tremor of associations setting up strange trains of disrelations. But she did put these clear lines together in such a way that the firm orderly

thought or epigramlike description is set next to another in a
manner not to have been foreseen. The surprise, the shock, exists
in between the spaces that have been leaped over by a swift imagi-
nation. Transitions thus seem more like transpositions, a strange
flowering of truth upon fact.

If the drama of many a poem lies in the strife of its particulars,
we have the same acting against and reacting in the pull of the
learned or scientific word against the idiomatic or concrete word:
"the elephants with their fog-colored skin/and strictly practical
appendages," for example, where "fog-colored" works against the
mockery of the abstract words applied to the simple trunk. And
words like "occipital" and "phenomena" or such phrases as "cy-
cloid inclusiveness," "fractional magnificence," "hairy carnivora,"
and "staple ingredients" frequently serve ironic purposes. Then
there is the august decorum of "he superintended the demolition
of his image in the water by the wind," and "the pulse of its once
vivid sovereignty," whose magnificence of phrasing has something
of the strange beauty of that poet of the sentence, Sir Thomas
Browne. This Latinate-laconic imperious elegance is to be found
less in later books. But formal balances and syntactical parallel-
isms persist. "He is swifter than a horse; he has a foot hard/as a
hoof; the leopard/is not more suspicious" (reminding us of Habak-
kuk) or "the/king gave his name to them and he was named/for
them."

In "Injudicious Gardening" (the title itself a small joke) it's as
if this poet mocks herself, turning against the musical inflections
of the first stanza with the slightly freezing abstractness of the sec-
ond:

> If yellow betokens infidelity,
>   I am an infidel,
>   I could not bear a yellow rose ill will
>   Because books said that yellow boded ill,
>   White promised well;
>
> However, your particular possession —
>   The sense of privacy
>   In what you did — deflects from your estate

> Offending eyes, and will not tolerate
> Effrontery.

The colder movement of the Latinate words drawn up to their full height and marched out to rebuke is felt in "Roses Only." Its effect of hectoring hauteur is dependent in part on the formal propriety of its diction and an elaborate sentence structure in which clause succeeds clause with all but martial progress to achieve the permanent brilliance of

> Guarding the
> infinitesimal pieces of your mind, compelling
> audience to
> the remark that it is better to be forgotten than to
> be remembered too violently,
> your thorns are the best part of you.

Both early and late Miss Moore has been a curator of that sacred cow, the statistic. In "Virginia Britannia" the hedge-sparrow "wakes up seven minutes sooner than the lark"; Lapland reindeer in "Rigorists" "run eleven miles in fifty minutes." But it is only in "New York" that the use of a business barbarism—"estimated in raw meat and berries, we could feed the universe" — crisply points up the grand uselessness of such an estimate. In this mimicking of the language of business and other clichés she escapes being flat by being so succinctly sharp. To say it another way, she was one of the first of the poets to take rather intractable antipoetic material, the business phrase, the statistic, the cliché, and by her arrangement of it in relation to other phrases, bend it to her own purposes — i.e., the poetry of the unpoetic. An example is her use of the banking phrase in "Roses Only": "You do not seem to realize that beauty is a liability rather than/an asset." The competency of that has entered the tone of many a poet.

"Marriage," that exercise in paradox, that divertimento of speculation on the "interesting impossibility," is a particularly striking example of the swift transition and the alternating between contraries. William Carlos Williams called it "an anthology of transits." One could also call it a tour de force of digressions, a masterpiece of sudden departures. Plying between homage paid to and

mockery made of "This institution,/perhaps one should say enter-
prise," we see that if it is the public nature of it that arouses deft
skepticism it is its private significance that is given such tribute as
"This fire-gilt steel/alive with goldenness." But since marriage is
both eminently private and public, she can be but in the position
of taking away with one hand what she gives with the other. To
the subject of love itself — not specifically amorous love but "'the
illusion of a fire/effectual to extinguish fire'" which makes mar-
riage seem "'a very trivial object indeed'" — she brings nothing
less than splendor in two passages, in one of which she puts Adam
and Eve into an Eden that has all the quaintness of a primitive
woodcut. "Plagued by the nightingale . . . dazzled by the ap-
ple." But nothing in this poem stands still. It is premised on the
necessity of swiftness and we are no sooner in Eden than out of it,
in some drawing room with the "shed snakeskin of politeness,"
just as we are never far from such sharp turnings of the tables as
"'For love/that will gaze an eagle blind . . . from forty-five to
seventy/is the best age.'" Its method of progression is not only
fleet but abrupt, connectives being dropped or leaped over. Darts
are released at women's prejudices against men and men's against
women; there are submerged hints of feminist argument at work
but these too are tossed off. Guarded, covering up its tracks almost
as soon as it makes them, it is a kind of masked dance on the ex-
cruciating point of how to be free though in bondage, and at the
close we learn that "liberty and union" are perhaps possible only
for those with a "simplicity of temper" — if the summary is more
important than the *aperçus* dropped along the way.

Does it seem to go by fits and starts? But how many overlappings
there are along the way. What matters is the sequence of airy no-
tions, what matters is that the wit not be grounded by the heavi-
ness that usually goes with too much expansion. What matters is
the impact which the successive words make on us. "Marriage"
is a rapidly moving train that once you are on it carries you from
glittering landing stage to stage, none of which you are really al-
lowed to get off at, or stay solemnly with. In grasping for analogies,
one thinks of Chinese painting which stretches out the viewpoint

along the entire panorama so that mountains and waterfalls all
appear to be moving toward us, although if such paintings avoid
leading the eye into a single depth, this scarcely applies to the
poem's action. Word playing on brilliant surfaces, it alludes as
much to depths behind depths. One is tempted to quote Henry
James: "To be explicit was to betray divinations."

In "The Past Is the Present" she has not only fallen upon her
form early, she is defining for us, although she is speaking about
Hebrew poetry, what it is that she is doing and going to be doing.
Or so, at least, we can interpret it in view of all the poems that
followed. Moreover she announces early (the poem was first
printed in *Others* in 1915) one of her touchstones. And this is no
less than the Bible. (We see by the notes in *Observations* how
many phrases from George Adam Smith's *The Expositor's Bible*,
Richard Baxter's *The Saints' Everlasting Rest*, A. R. Gordon's
The Poets of the Old Testament, how many phrases too from
ministers' sermons, are inlaid into poems. Is it incidental or not
that in a Foreword to the *Marianne Moore Reader*, 1961, she
should write: "My favorite poem? asked not too aggressively —
perhaps recalling that Henry James could not name his 'favorite
letter of the alphabet or wave of the sea.' The Book of Job, I have
sometimes thought . . .") If we remember that early pc. 'od when
the Imagists had already set verse free and damned rhyme, we can
think of this poem as being the last word in an intense argument
held in some book-lined room:

> If eternal action is effete
>   and rhyme is outmoded,
>   I shall revert to you
>   Habakkuk, as on a recent occasion I was goaded
>   into doing by XY, who was speaking of unrhymed
>   verse.
> This man said — I think that I repeat
>   his identical words:
>   'Hebrew poetry is
>   prose with a sort of heightened consciousness.' Ecstasy
>   affords
>   the occasion and expediency determines the form.

If external action (plot — in literature? resolution — in life) is effete and *if* rhyme is outmoded (assumptions of the unseen argufier made to seem both absurd and pretentious), if the new broom of the present wants to sweep half the past away, she will revert to Habakkuk. Nothing later than that minor prophet of the Bible, and nothing more fashionable. Is the goading XY the same "this man" who delivers the energizing definition of Hebrew poetry that can and will be applied to her own work? "Prose with a sort of heightened consciousness"? The Reverend Edwin H. Kellogg is credited in the notes with "Hebrew poetry is prose" but to this has been added the very important "with a sort of heightened consciousness." The heightening of consciousness is all and an answer in the argument. There is verse and verse. Bad free verse is simply prose without that heightening. Moreover she herself is using rhyme in this poem, unlike old Habakkuk. And in the last line she kicks away from the contradictions inherent in the situation to hand us with abrupt decisiveness the keys to the secret of the creative instant. "Ecstasy affords the occasion and expediency determines the form." "Expediency" is the shock word here following so close on "ecstasy." You might say that it disinfects a word so much distrusted in this century. (Much later, in "The Hero," we have: "looking/upon a fellow creature's error with the feelings of a mother — a/woman or a cat" where "cat" takes the curse off "mother," let alone "woman.") Nevertheless, ecstasy it is. One does what one can with the lightening flash. How to seize it except by the most expedient method at hand? Form, it would seem, is determined by the raptus. "Spirit creates form" ("Roses Only"). Is form to be equated with the shell that the mollusk makes, his being's expediency too, the artist's form as organic to himself as the shell is to the snail? Miss Moore has defined it for us: "I feel that the form is the outward equivalent of a determining inner conviction, and that the rhythm is the person."

The force and fire of biblical language is also a subject of "Novices" but before we arrive at it an artillery of wit is brought to bear on a kind of overrefined and underfed modern literary mind

"confusing the issue," "blind to the right word, deaf to satire."
The poem glitters with so much summed-up intensity that its en-
ergy feels like — is it Irish? fury? A fury of byplay, at least. "Ac-
quiring at thirty what at sixty they will be trying to forget . . .
they write the sort of thing that would in their judgment interest
a lady; / curious to know if we do not adore each letter of the alpha-
bet that goes to make a word of it." The raillery continues:
"according to the Act of Congress, the sworn statement of the
treasurer and all the rest of it," which is surely calculated to reduce
the opponent to a recognition of his own asininity. Other sidewise
allusions, metaphorical extensions such as in the lines beginning
"Dracontine cockatrices" and those on the "lucid movements of
the royal yacht," contribute to the argument more elaborately, the
latter lines preparing for the tremendous onslaught of the power-
ful and dazzling conclusion. And certainly the finical quibblings,
the "willowy wit" of those, one suspects, all-too-precious novices,
who are bored incidentally by "the stuffy remarks of the Hebrews,"
get what they deserve as the "unforced passion of the Hebrew lan-
guage" is hurled at them. What begins in witty ire ends in a gran-
deur not far from the Miltonic sublime as two authorities meet —
the sea and biblical language:

> Obscured by 'fathomless suggestions of colour',
> by incessantly panting lines of green, white with concussion,
> in this drama of water against rocks — this 'ocean of hurrying
>   consonants'
> with its 'great livid stains like long slabs of green marble',
> its 'flashing lances of perpendicular lightning' and 'molten fires
>   swallowed up',
> 'with foam on its barriers',
> 'crashing itself out in one long hiss of spray'.

The action of language is developed in terms of the action of the
waters, and all in a blaze of glory and claps upon claps of energy.
The method is to rush you into splendor and leave you with
dazzle. "People's Surroundings" ends with such a triumphant
progress, "The Monkeys" in a burst almost as breathtaking:

> — strict with tension, malignant
> in its power over us and deeper

than the sea when it proffers flattery in exchange for
    hemp,
rye, flax, horses, platinum, timber, and fur.

This roll call of nouns in the last line is a choice example of
Moorish sound at its finest and it is an effort to remember that
they are but shipper's items transmuted into splendor. The un-
expected contiguity of flax with horses and timber, so hard a sub-
stance, with rich fur — thus this poem that begins with the
drolleries of the zoo moves into high comedy when a cat makes a
speech worthy of any autocrat defending the art of the few against
the Dunciad many. His astringent remarks on those protesting
that they can't understand the new and difficult in art (Brancusi,
Picasso? — this poem was first published in 1917) has a further
refinement of irony, for the cat scorns these objects of his wit for
suspecting art to be just what it really is: "strict with tension,
malignant in its power over us and deeper than the sea . . ."

"The Labours of Hercules" undergoes a similar mutation, com-
mencing with the absurd and by a series of progressions closing
on the note of a moral rhetoric which is to have an echo later in
"In Distrust of Merits" and " 'Keeping Their World Large.' "
Formally it is a series of propositions couched in the infinitive,
"To popularize the mule," etc., and with the same kind of sym-
metrical nicety closes with another kind of grammatical repetition:

> 'that the Negro is not brutal,
> that the Jew is not greedy,
> that the Oriental is not immoral,
> that the German is not a Hun.'

Shifting after its humorous opening to the literary-critical note,
"to teach the bard with too elastic a selectiveness/that one detects
creative power by its capacity to conquer one's detachment," it
arrives after two extensions or witty divagations at

> to prove to the high priests of caste
> that snobbishness is a stupidity,
> the best side out, of age-old toadyism,
> kissing the feet of the man above,
> kicking the face of the man below

which in its directness of putting the quality of bootlicking under
the most searching light has an effect of almost shockingly savage
insight. Beginning with humor, ending with the moral impera-
tive, this poem has, like "The Monkeys" and "Novices," its pattern
of progress until, the reversal achieved, we are in another field
of thought.

"Those Various Scalpels" not so much progresses as changes
key, if one may revert to the musical analogy, and in the phrase
"rustling in the storm/of conventional opinion" drives with ruth-
less swiftness to the heart of the matter: all this wrought artfulness
of appearance, this Renaissance-jewel-encrusted and farthingaled
semblance of the utmost of aristocratic vanity — for what? Nothing
more than *conventional opinion*? We are prepared and not pre-
pared for this swift reversal by the ringing insistence of the repeti-
tions "your hair," "your eyes," "your raised hand" which, for all
the tribute that so much intent attention implies, warn us by their
pain-suggesting images of "eyes, flowers of ice/and/snow sown by
tearing winds on the cordage of disabled ships" and "your cheeks,
those rosettes/of blood on the stone floors of French châteaux"
with its hint of shadowy plots and sudden assassinations. That
this epitome of sterile cruelty whose arrows are lances (nicely hid
by jewels), whose weapons are surgical instruments, that this idol
of a frigid self-involvement whose beauty can give nothing but
pain, is rebuked with a brilliance surpassing the brilliances that
described her is a spectacular achievement:

                                        But
why dissect destiny with instruments which
    are more highly specialized than the tissues of destiny itself?

Otherwise one sees in this poem how the visual is tempered by
the abstract, how repetition of phrasal structure is employed for
an imposing rhetorical effect, how the symmetrical stanzas (two of
nine lines and three of eight lines) have in each stanza a one-
syllable first line, a last line of four, three, or two syllables, a third
line usually of twelve or fourteen syllables, and how the whole
effect of shape, of repetition, emphasizes the formal splendor of
the phrasing. The effect makes for a sense of volume, of receding

planes and sudden perspectives as in architecture, or in baroque music.

Miss Moore created a new form (to fit her manner) primarily by means of a new rhythm, a new way of organizing details and the insights that spring from them. But there is no critical terminology for this new form and one has to fall back on old ways of classifying. Call "A Grave" a soliloquy if you like, and "New York" too. Or call "Roses Only," that lecture to a flower who is also, it would seem, a woman, a kind of version of the moral essay. Call "People's Surroundings," that study of the kind of places people make for themselves, and "Sea Unicorns and Land Unicorns," that fanciful treatise on the power of the mind to make immoderate legends and to reason almost anything into existence — call them both descriptive essays. But the terms "moral essay" and "descriptive essay" are grab-bag terms and don't really apply. The culmination, in any case, of this kind of free-ranging discursive structure for which there is no term is to be found in "An Octopus," that stupendous aggregate of minerals, animals, weathers, while "Sea Unicorns and Land Unicorns" anticipates the more circuitous organization of Miss Moore's later work. In the latter, her manner with the marvel, the fantastical, is to be methodical, as if giving us information in part. This treatment of the fabulous as if it were quite as probable as the so-called fact wonderfully emphasizes its rare lusters. The poem rises and falls, alternating between passages like " 'cobwebs, and knotts, and mulberries' " and "Britannia's sea unicorn with its rebellious child." In a differing fashion for purposes of humor and for the subtle sake of contrast there will be amidst the rare knowledges and textures the opposing note of " 'in politics, in trade, law, sport, religion' " — a broad sober worldly tone which counteracts the elegant quaintness and faery richness of " 'myrtle rods, and shafts of bay.' " And this dynamics of some high pitch of verbal excitement frequently succeeded by a calm or ironic or dryly prosaic passage is to be found in many poems.

(This poem is also an instance of the way she makes a new unity out of parts of old learnings and culled phrases. In later work, from "The Jerboa" to "Elephants," one sees even more complex examples of this drawing upon all kinds of sources to create a new imaginative reality. In "The Plumet Basilisk" Miss Moore weds the legendary, the naturalistic, and history with a scarcely restrained sumptuousness to present to us the half-miraculous attributes of a very real creature. Chinese legends relate him to the great dragons of the East; myths of "the chieftain with gold body" and the jade, the amethysts, and the pearls of half an Incan empire are gathered in to gild his little gorgeousness. A love of the marvelous is combined with factual notations (obtained from the *Illustrated London News* and other sources) to re-create a beast whose very being seems to be one more proof of Nature's pure fantasy. Has zoology truly such instances? Yes. And in "Nine Nectarines" there is the haunting bit of knowledge on the "red-cheeked peach" that according to ancient Chinese thought "cannot aid the dead,/but eaten in time prevents death." Declared in passing, that knowledge is there to give us the tang, the taste of incredible theory.)

"People's Surroundings" is notably a shuttling between the opposites, a play on that favorite eighteenth-century device, the antithesis, as it tacks here and there, creating rich effects that it contradicts a few lines later, pitting splendors against absurdities, the utilitarian against the artful, movement being one of its powers. Stylistically the poem alternates between the crisp speech rhythms setting forth the plain or efficient and two grand flights, the one beginning with Bluebeard's tower and the closing section which is a very Whitman catalogue, if you will (one line beautifully echoes him: "in magnificent places, clean and decent"), a very cavalry charge, a pure poetry of namings:

> captains of armies, cooks, carpenters,
> cutlers, gamesters, surgeons and armourers,
> lapidaries, silkmen, glovers, fiddlers and ballad-singers

The rich appreciation of the ridiculous in this poem, from the "vast indestructible necropolis" of office furniture to "the municipal bat-roost of mosquito warfare," crops up again in "England" in the greatly gay originality of "plain American which cats and dogs can read!"

And when there is not the satirical that crisps the line, there is its easier twin, humor. If the irony preserves (like amber), the humor sweetens. In later work humor becomes allied with fantasy. In *Observations* it frequently seems a kind of irrepressible out-burst — from the fir trees, "austere specimens of our American royal families," to "the spiked hand/that has an affection for one/and proves it to the bone" (though the first is a joke and the latter a pun).

At one or not with this sense of humor is the apt harnessing of the likely with the unlikely, even the "antipoetic." Thus the "in-dustrious" waterfall, the not lulling but plaguing nightingale, young bird voices compared to the intermittent "squeak/of broken carriage-springs," this latter a refreshing accuracy that produces in the reader that nervous response which to some extent resembles what is provoked by the experience itself. Not only has an un-hackneyed equivalent been found, but a new association has widened the field of reference, modified it too. For it is the squeak of *carriage-springs*, the something slightly antiquated.

And isn't humor that relishes the incongruity and notices the irrelevancy a facet of candor and honesty, and a part of a desire to see the whole and not to exclude the just incidentally thorny or what cannot be classified, the contradictory? Surely in league with it seems the appreciation for "naturalness" whether it is that of the hippopotamus or Peter the cat or the "mere childish attempt . . . to make a pup/eat his meat from the plate."

This taste for the spontaneous, the "beautiful element of un-reason," "a tireless wolf," "a wild horse taking a roll," might be contrasted to the connoisseur's zest for "the hair-seal Persian sheen," old Waterford glass, or for what, when it is rare, could not be more rare, when it is jeweled, the most jeweled, when it is blue, a dragonfly blue. The larger, looser, bolder touch — "The tug . . . dipping and pushing, the bell striking as it comes," and "when the wind is from the east,/the smell is of apples, of hay" —

is about as strong an element in her work as these curio-collector notations are.

In nine poems Miss Moore is both poet and critic, writing incidentally about literature in general or poetry in particular. Was she also telling her readers just what it was that she herself had set out to do? Jean-Paul Sartre has said that there is no new technique without a metaphysic. And because her approach to the poem was so radically different, did she have her interests in setting forth as plainly as a subtle mind might her own intentions? One might make a case for this in looking at the celebrated "Poetry" with its shocker of a first line: "I, too, dislike it: there are things that are important beyond all this fiddle." It is an early poem (1919). It is also a difficult poem. Seemingly straightforward, it is oblique when you look into it and complex in terms of what's left out as well as what's put in. And with its iconoclastic and reformist frankness it is upsetting a good many applecarts.

The tone of the opening is cutting. "Reading it, however, with a perfect contempt for it." Why should poetry have to be read with a perfect contempt? And whose poetry? All poetry? Then it turns out that it is not all poetry that is being talked about, that it is possibly just the poetry of her contemporaries — or even not all her contemporaries. It is the poetry of "half poets" and when she dislikes their "fiddle" it is when it is "so derivative as to become unintelligible." What, then, is being argued for? The opposite of the derivative — the original, the honest, the "genuine." A new touchstone is being set up. This touchstone is not the old and famous *beautiful and true*. It is the *genuine*. There is more to be said about the *genuine*. "Hands that can grasp, eyes/that can dilate, hair that can rise,/if it must, these things" — signs of the emotional animal — "are important not because a/high-sounding interpretation can be put upon them but because they are/useful." The *genuine* is, then, the *useful*, the functional. But since there are a great many uses of the word "useful" and we are most acquainted with it in its dreariest, most utilitarian sense, the word has a double edge. *Useful*. Isn't the poet just possibly taunting the aesthetes by choosing a word with such hateful, factual, hard edges? A word that can also be called an epitome of understatement — as if to say the sky is *useful*, or rain, the sun, or for that matter poetry. There is another challenging section. We learn of what is more important than "all this fiddle." It is "the bat/holding on upside down . . . elephants pushing, a wild horse taking a roll . . . the base/ball fan, the statistician . . . and 'business documents and/school-books.' "

A prodigious activity somehow gets set up between these assorted items and by their selection Miss Moore tells us as exactly as analogy can do "what is important." Not only the star, the rose, the sea, but matters and subjects not already made acceptable by literary tradition. "One must make a distinction/however: when dragged into prominence by half poets, the result is not poetry."

A fresh subject matter is not enough. In order to make it seem true poets must be "literalists of the imagination." A poet must imagine so exactly and astutely that, in the words of Morton Dauwen Zabel, he can "see the visible at the focus of intelligence where sight and concept coincide and where it becomes transformed into the pure and total realism of ideas."

Furthermore, without the "imaginary gardens (with real toads in them)" which is a symbol for the aesthetic order, the arrangement of these "phenomena" in a modifying structure and texture, the wolf or the whatnot, will only seem "dragged in." It will not have been assimilated, it will acquire no new reality, and it will have lost its original own. There will be no poem, in short. Only a half poem.

(Miss Moore's heightening of the phrase of William Butler Yeats on Blake — "He was a too literal realist of the imagination" — is famous. By portmanteau effect she rendered a daring new meaning. Like many of her finest phrases it combines opposites as compactly as possible. Such paradoxes are her elixirs.)

When this poem appeared in the second edition (1925) of *Observations* it was quite another animal, for it was stripped from its original thirty lines (in *Poems*) to thirteen lines, stripped, too, of its complexities. The bat, et cetera, are still there, but they are "pleasing" rather than "important," and the main emphasis is upon clarity:

> but when they have been fashioned
> into that which is unknowable,
> we are not entertained.
> It may be said for all of us
> that we do not admire what we cannot understand;
> enigmas are not poetry.

In *Selected Poems* it returns to the original version save for the omission of three phrases, and has not been altered since.

If Miss Moore was making a strong stand for intelligibility and clarity in this version of "Poetry" she criticizes the "unknowable" in other poems. "In the Days of Prismatic Colour" there are the lines

> complexity is not a crime but carry
> it to the point of murki-
> ness and nothing is plain

and a variation in "Picking and Choosing":

> Words are constructive
> when they are true; the opaque allusion — the simulated
> flight
> upward — accomplishes nothing.

"When I Buy Pictures" concludes:

> It comes to this: of whatever sort it is,
> it must be 'lit with piercing glances into the life of things';
> it must acknowledge the spiritual forces which have made it.

In other poems there are other critica dicta as triumphantly perceptive.

In his Introduction to the *Selected Poems* T. S. Eliot classified the poetry of Marianne Moore as descriptive rather than lyrical or dramatic. But to what new uses description is put! And is such a poem as "New York" simply descriptive? Is it not a turning and unfurling upon a given point: the commercial statistic that New York (in 1921) was the center of the wholesale fur trade? A bizarre enough "fact" in view of all else that the city was the center of — from which the poem leaps straight off into "starred with tepees of ermine and peopled with foxes,/the long guard-hairs waving two inches beyond the body of the pelt." This latter line of a strange half-humorous beauty, a detail (of furrier's knowledge) within a detail, is complemented by an even more rarefied detail on deerskins and these two by the aside, later on, that quotes the follied vanity of a Gonzaga duchess: " 'if the fur is not finer than such as one sees others wear,/one would rather be without it.' "

If these extensions of texture (in more ways than one) act as brief rests or pauses, the poem otherwise moves swiftly in a continuousness of visual action which allows for no intrusion of what would thin out its density. Thus by no other transition than the phrase "It is a far cry" we are with " 'the queen full of jewels' " and "the beau with the muff" and the contrasting of two pasts with some only implied hint that English palefaces bought furs from redskins at that fur-trading center, the conjunction of the Monongahela and the Allegheny. For this is not the vital point: the vital point is that "scholastic philosophy of the wilderness/to combat which one must stand outside and laugh/since to go in is to be lost." If the subjective depth of this sets up many questioning echoes, we have at least one answer. "It is not the dime-novel exterior,/Niagara Falls, the calico horses and the war-canoe." It is not even "the plunder." It is, in Henry James's phrase, " 'accessibility to experience.' " *Accessibility to experience* – a prescription for the artist! The poem juggles with the past, the present, Europe, America, outlandish and wonderful Indian names until the grand light of James's phrase gives one answer, too, to staying outside. *Accessibility* suggests that one may go inside, even be lost, agreeably.

Of these specificities which are not cloyed by generalizations, one remembers that "to explain is to deform." In this poem of as much wit as description, passage must be rapid. Another poet might have lingered with the beauties of deerskins and wilting eagle's-down in which case the point of the wit might have been dulled. And if we are with the furs one moment and the " 'queen full of jewels' " the next, it is up to us to consider the impact of the contrast between two pasts, both of which are our heritage.

Of the maintenance of such tension Miss Moore has this to say in an essay called "Feeling and Precision," first published in the *Sewanee Review* in 1944: ". . . expanded explanation tends to spoil the lion's leap — an awkwardness which is surely brought home to one in conversation . . . Yet the lion's leap would be mitigated almost to harmlessness if the lion were clawless, so precision is both *impact* and exactitude, as with surgery; and also in music, the conductor's signal . . . which 'begins far back of the beat, so that you don't see when the down beat comes. To have started such a long distance ahead makes it possible to be exact. Whereas you can't be exact by being restrained.'"

One is exact just because one is so aware of so many shades of meaning or of "ivory white, snow white, oyster white and six others." And in the same way that the conductor's beat must begin far back of the downbeat, the poem acquires its power by virtue of the distance it has to travel before the poet's perceptions can encompass the range of his feeling.

Again, "The Monkey Puzzle" encloses its theme so thickly in arresting particulars that it is tempting to be adrift with them, charmed by the strange freshness, simply content with the outraying allusions to the Foo dog and Flaubert's Carthage. Its subject is, however, a rare pine tree, "a complicated starkness," a "this [that] is beauty" growing in a fastness and like Gray's desert flower, unseen, unknown, "in which society's not knowing is colossal,/the lion's ferocious chrysanthemum head seeming kind by comparison." The force of this astounding comparison (and the oxymoron that makes the lion a little less fearful but far more beautiful) serves only to intensify the plight of this rare tree that "knows" (trees have prescience, cats talk like artists, elephants philosophize, and jaybirds don't know Greek) "'it is better to be lonely than unhappy.'" Its isolation as profound as any early American genius's, what can it do but endure its own singularity in its own irreparable solitude? This is to bring perhaps too much to the surface what is implied and embodied in a visual intricacy not unlike the tree's own thicket.

This concreteness can sometimes make a poem seem almost unpossessable on first reading because the meanings are so realized in the specificities themselves. These lines from "The Jerboa" might serve to illustrate: "Those who tended flower/beds and stables were like the king's cane in the/form of a hand." It is for the sake of compression and the desire not to obstruct the movement of the poem that the king's attitude toward the poor is personified. But the sting of the observation may not come at once: that the king depends on the poor as he would on a cane, that they are simply commodities to him, to be useful, as a cane is. The visual strangeness of a cane "in the form of a hand" may so divert the reader that he forgets to consider its significance. Sometimes, too, the argument of a poem may be submerged, only to emerge openly, at certain moments. The poem moves in its maze of associations, the disconnected connections magnetized in a manner we cannot see on first acquaintance. And always Miss Moore states but doesn't "explain." Or lines may be of such an epigrammatic rigor that the very parts seem like wholes, or poems within poems. This alone (from "Snakes, Mongooses"), "one is compelled to look at it as at the shadows of the alps/imprisoning in their folds like flies in amber, the rhythms of the skating rink," is but one example of those perceptions compact as definitions, brimming with the energy of having pinned it down and gotten it right. Charles Lamb has spoken of the obscurity of too much meaning. Intense clarity can also blind, like the sun at noon.

But as to all this and as to those poems where the clarity of the image and the density of allusion make for that fascinating combination of what is both lucid and ambiguous at the same time, Miss Moore has, as usual, the last word: "A few unexplained difficult things — they seem to be the life-blood of variety."

As for that magnitude of particularities "An Octopus," though it does not necessarily divert "one from what was originally one's object" (to quote from "England"), it does delay one along the way as description becomes a kind of plot and its own drama. All is in action, from the old glacier itself that "hovers forward 'spider fashion/on its arms'" to its fir trees with "their dark energy of life," its animals, seen in some characteristic behavior and on the move, even its stationary flowers active in their complications of colors and designs.

In its serial construction there is a regular recurrence of outriding phrases that allow for sidelights, tangential glances sometimes pert in tone such as the line on the icy glacier itself, "made of glass that will bend — a much needed invention," or lines that permit us to consider the sheer deadness of Park Portfolio language when it is legal or such purely "poetic" extensions (of the ponies with glass eyes) as "brought up on frosty grass and flowers/ and rapid draughts of ice-water." Not to forget the mountain guide in his "two pairs of trousers" reminding us of Thoreau's Irishman who wore three. The aside, the brief digression, the Jamesian parenthesis might be called a part of the Moore method and are to be found in many poems. They serve, as they do in "An Octopus," to make for a kind of brio of the irrelevantly relevant and for the effect that R. P. Blackmur phrased so acutely: "husky with unexhausted detail . . . containing inexhaustibly the inexplicable."

In the last section, about the Greeks, which also gives another character to the glacier,

> Relentless accuracy is the nature of this octopus
> with its capacity for fact

(as if it were a terribilita of an artist), one sees how the tempo at which one must read is dictated. The passage begins slightly after "The Greeks liked smoothness"

> ascribing what we clumsily call happiness,
> to 'an accident or a quality,
> a spiritual substance, or the soul itself,
> an act, a disposition, or a habit,
> or a habit infused, to which the soul has been persuaded,
> or something distinct from a habit, a power —'
> such power as Adam had and we are still devoid of.

As if Experience were correcting Theory, this kind of Schoolman's ethereal speculation in finely defining phrase upon phrase, one qualifying the other and all kept in musical suspension, is given this forceful, brusque stop, a stop even to our hopes.

In "Camellia Sabina" there is the same kind of rapid moving out onto a single hard flashing line after the airy humors and mercurial play of the "upland country mouse," that "Prince of Tails," dashing around the *"concours hippique"* of the grape-arbor "in a flurry/of eels, scallops, serpents/and other shadows . . . The wine-cellar? No/It accomplishes nothing and makes the/soul heavy" — the abruptness of this and the swift change of rhythm severely preparing us for the renunciatory "The gleaning is more than the vintage."

From the *Selected Poems* (1935) on we see more "inscape," hear more music, meet more fantasy and far more animals. Stanzaic structure is more elaborate together with a new complexity of detail, the line is more musically nuanced, with more verbal interplay and more sub-patterns of internal rhymings and end rhymings. The ironist and the satirist has been succeeded by the fantasist-humorist, and the hard-driving electrical speed of the free-verse line (as exemplified by the ruthless, relentless progression of a poem like "A Grave") by more light and subtle rhythms. Seven of the eight new poems of *Selected Poems* are seven new departures. One is not like the other. In each a new version of a form is explored. In "The Frigate Pelican" one can fancy that form is in part imitative, so deftly are the rhythms of flight suggested by certain lines and by wordplays; there is a gliding from one stanza to another, like the feints of bird-winging. The thickly woven texture of "The Plumet Basilisk," that essay on dragonhood, is so closely qualified that it suggests the very density of tropical vegetation. Of later poems "Virginia Britannia" (*What Are Years*, 1941) takes description to a new height. As one of her many place poems, it is of flowers, birds, and history so interwoven that its long lines seem to move like feelers, reaching out and advancing on all sides at once, the theme of colonizing arrogance (as symbolized by the strangler figs) growing out of the very elements of the scene and at one with it. In these instances detail is given a new kind of day and with it, necessarily, a slowing of tempo, or delayings and detainings by Hopkinsesque word clusters. Such word clusters do what Hulme in 1915 or so asked the new poetry to do ("to make you continuously see a physical thing, to prevent you from gliding through an abstract process") and aid in compacting multiple parts swiftly for the sake of impact.

The high interest in design and pattern, first seen in "The Fish" (1918), is carried on in "Nine Nectarines" in which precision of sight — even a subdividing of it — is heard in the intricately echoing fineness of sound. And "The Jerboa" with its neatness and firmness achieves an especial kind of visual and aural beauty by virtue of its flexibly confining pattern, the six-line stanza with a rhyme scheme that exerts the nicest control over the faint chimings. Working with highly selected clarities of dapple dog-cats and small eagles, it evolves (in the first section) into a kind of tale-telling, a rigorously simplified recounting of the habits and tastes of a people forgotten save by historians and encyclopods. They are "violently remembered" in this poem:

> Lords and ladies put goose-grease
> paint in round bone boxes with pivoting
> lid incised with the duck-wing

> or reverted duck-
> head

The acuteness of the visual achievement might be exemplified with the power of

> the wild ostrich herd
> with hard feet and bird
>   necks rearing back in the
>   dust like a serpent preparing to strike,

and delicacy of sound by "They looked on as theirs/impallas and onigers."

The concern to strike for the resonances of color that we see in the "coachwheel yellow" of "Critics and Connoisseurs" — which gives us at least two sensations at once, the pleasure of the coachwheel and the shade of its color — is to be found in "duck-egg greens, and egg-plant blues" (note the nice balancing of consonants) or "calla or petunia/white." Instead of a metaphor we are given a further qualification. Such precisions both intensify the experience and keep it under close control as the measurements

and temperatures of what's seen are exactly taken. Her "pride,
like the enchanter's,/is in care, not madness." With the lines

> in the stiff-leafed tree's blue-
> pink dregs-of-wine pyramids
> of mathematic
> circularity

she circumvents the near-impossibility of translating so exotically
natural an impression by pinning down, first of all, the mixture
of hue and likening it to something definite but unexpected —
yes, and not wine but dregs-of-wine — and next by comparing its
form to the at first concrete *pyramids* and then abstract *circularity.*
But the eye that can see "boats/at sea progress white and rigid as
if in a groove" has long since found the secret way of getting at the
truth of the pure first shock of visual impression. Is it a "science of
the eye" or the free daring of imagination that brings opposites
together that had never met before?

Held up to inspection with the same bold fidelity are her ani-
mals who, if they are frequently parts of a web of allusions that
ally them to more philosophies than they could dream of, are
always known first and last to us by their beautiful *thisness* of
claws, dapples, quills, delineated with the vital accuracy of a Bew-
ick, the English engraver who cared just as much for the origi-
nality of the particulars. We see them not only in their fine suits of
fur and feather, we see them also in the fitness and niceness of
those "skills" by which they earn their livings, defend themselves,
and keep up their populations. We see them as craftsmen and we
see them as artists, too. The frigate pelican hides (as "impassioned
Handel") "in the height and in the majestic/display of his art,"
the jerboa's leaps "should be set/to the flageolet," the "wasp-nest
flaws" on the paper nautilus are compared to "the lines in the
mane of a Parthenon horse." And sometimes they are compared
to works of art or artists. The pangolin, "Leonardo's indubitable
son" (in the *What Are Years* version), is "compact like the furled/
fringed frill/on the hat brim of Gargallo's hollow iron head of
a/matador."

Gide in *Travels in the Congo* wrote of his rare tamed antelope:

"I must study Dindiki's ethics and aesthetics, his peculiar manner
of moving and defending and protecting himself. Every animal
has succeeded in finding out his own particular manner, outside
of which there seems to be no salvation for him." It is the beast's
particular manner that Marianne Moore has found. The style of
the poet — style, "that specialisation of sensibility" — has met the
"style" of the animal. Her celebrated objectivity exemplifies that
detachment that the West Wind symbolizes in "Half Deity." If
it is his delighted disinterest that spurs the butterfly into really
becoming a half deity, that same detachment in the artist permits
the object, the beast, to be seen for itself, brought into existence
or a second existence. Cézanne said: "The landscape is reflected
in me and I am its consciousness." When the plumet basilisk is in
danger and all his forces leap into play, when he is that "nervous
naked sword on little feet," when he has the black eyes of a "mo-
lested bird" "with look of whetted fierceness/in what is merely/
breathing and recoiling from the hand," we can only feel that the
poet has entered into the blood and breath of the beast, transmit-
ting its very reality into our hands, and that observation has be-
come a passion.

Thus her "studies" are always dramas. Each animal poem be-
gins at the point of an action. It's night and the pangolin is setting
forth or the frigate pelican has just robbed another bird of its fish,
all in midair. We have no stuffed animals. She does not, as Audu-
bon did, paint her birds when they're dead. But she is no "ex-
ternalist." "The power of the visible/is the invisible." Thus the
jerboa of the "Chippendale" claws, described as if some Supreme
Cabinetmaker had thought him up, is no "conqueror"; he is "free-
born," "has happiness" in the abundance of all that he needs which
is almost nothing, not even water, and becomes the occasion for a
secret discussion on the powers of a being to live in an energy of
delight, in spontaneous accord with his portion of the universe.
And in "The Pangolin" three refrains of Shakespearean munifi-
cence and hymnlike sobriety work against the descriptive weave.
As in "The Frigate Pelican" there is the sudden outbreak of the
personal voice — "*Festina lente.* Be gay/civilly? How so?" — in the

midst of this impersonal improvisation on a bird's flight, so this personal-impersonal refrain is set against the pangolin's "exhausting trips" until at the close, our cousinship with this " 'Fearful yet to be feared' " animal so insinuatingly established (as it was in "Peter" who is "one of those who do not regard/the published fact as a surrender"), we see ourselves and him in a universal context:

> The prey of fear, he, always
> curtailed, extinguished, thwarted by the dusk,
>   work partly done,
> says to the alternating blaze,
>   'Again the sun!
>   anew each day; and new and new and new,
>   that comes into and steadies my soul.'

Danger is three-fourths of an animal's life and its every element; these poems don't let us forget it. For the plumet basilisk it is only nightfall that protects him from men who can kill him. The ostrich has circumvented extinction by his solicitude for his young; the butterfly is pursued by a child, the young birds by a cat; the devilfish must zealously guard her eggs. What thorns of a rose are "proof" against "the predatory hand"? "All are/naked, none is safe." And if "Hercules, bitten/by a crab loyal to the hydra,/was hindered to succeed," there are those who "have lived and lived on every kind of shortage," not unlike the jerboa.

We come into the themes of armor and unarmedness and self-protectiveness, to humility "His shield," to the pangolin again, the "frictionless creep of a thing/made graceful by adversities, con/versities," to the not aggressive, tentative snail whose "contractility" of horns "is a virtue as modesty is a virtue." In "The Fish" the "defiant edifice" with "marks of abuse" upon it "has proved that it can live/on what can not revive/its youth. The sea grows old in it." And one can add "resistance with bent head, like foxtail/millet's" and "tough-grained animals as have . . . earned that fruit of their ability to endure blows," or "that which it is impossible to force, it is impossible to hinder" (as true of poetry as of this vital vegetable, the carrot, of "Radical") and see how many times difficulty, deprivation, "society's not knowing," struggle (even for a strawberry) are themes implied in the early work, more openly stated in the later. In "The Monkey Puzzle" the solitude of singularity is accepted, to be endured, but in "Sojourn in a Whale" it is suggested that the impossible, the constricting condition can be circumvented by the power of the being to "rise on itself" as water does "when obstacles happened to bar/the path" (which is one answer to the complacency of the proverb "Water seeks its own level").

As the themes of the scarred but defiant and enduring interact with the theme of the wild animal's precarious existence, so the themes of bondage and freedom interact with these. "What Are Years?" — that exultant psalm — is built upon the paradox that only in the acceptance of limitations can one be released from them (as the caged bird, "grown taller as he sings, steels/his form straight up" and in "his mighty singing/says, satisfaction is a lowly/thing, how pure a thing is joy"). This Christian paradox is not abandoned. In "His Shield" freedom is defined as "the power of relinquishing/what one would keep"; in "Spenser's Ireland" a reversal: "you're not free/until you've been made captive by/ supreme belief." The devilfish's "intensively/watched eggs coming from/the shell free it when they are freed" suggests not only the gestation of a work but much else. The poem frees the poet when he has expressed it and delivered it. The devilfish who possesses her eggs is as much possessed by them; so is the jailor by the jailed. The freedom of the one is the freedom of the other. In "The Jerboa" the people "who liked little things" but had slaves, kept "power over the poor," and even put baboons to work for them are in bondage compared with the jerboa, both indubitably himself, a happy animal, and emblem of the spirit; they are in bondage to their materialities, their petty customs, rituals, superstitions. The jerboa with nothing but immaterial abundance is free.

So is the elephant of "Melancthon" (formerly "Black Earth"), that earliest of heroes (1918), who has richly accepted the rough conditions of existence, who has survived earthquakes and lightning. He does what he does which pleases no one but himself, his spiritual poise is not in pride (though he is too confident to be humble) but in that kind of seeing and hearing which the senses only have when the soul is master. He trumpets: "My ears are sensitized to more than the sound of/the wind." He is the hardy master of the ("patina of") circumstance like any Chinese sage. Lesser heroes are the cat of "Silence" and "Peter" himself, both eminently self-reliant and honorably what they are, with no apologies.

Other heroes are the student of "The Student" who can "hold by himself" and the hero of "The Hero" who is a kind of hero-in-reverse, without the heroics. Of touchy nerves he doesn't like "suffering and not/saying so." He can also be vexing or, like "Pilgrim having to go slow/to find his roll; tired but hopeful." He is certainly the opposite of the tragic hero or the standard nerveless hero. But, jumpy like the pangolin, he is not empty: he knows "the rock crystal thing to see — the startling El Greco/brimming with inner light — that covets nothing that it has let go."

A facet of the hero is the "decorous frock-coated Negro" "with a/sense of human dignity/and reverence for mystery, standing like the shadow/of the willow." The willow, most pliant of trees and fragile of bough. Heroism, like any good thing, is precariously maintained. (It is also "exhausting.") The seemingly random course of this poem rather beautifully fits the exposition of a hero full of inner hesitations and if it could be said that this poem is a poem about a person who has found his spiritual rock to abide by, it could also be said of "The Steeple-Jack" that it presents us with a vision of the place where this rock might be. Certainly this poem remains one of Miss Moore's most charmed ones. That "Dürer would have seen a reason for living/in a town like this, with eight stranded whales/to look at; with the sweet sea air coming into your house/on a fine day" is already more than enough to establish the tone from which nothing thereafter, not one accent, departs, the tone of a state of what seems to amount to purest felicity. As well, it expresses so fine an appreciation for the irregular, the not self-conscious, the moderate, modest, and free, the slightly crooked, the not-correct but vital, that it remains a triumph of the unex-

pected, of things caught in their essential dress, their *quidditas*.
Nowhere does Miss Moore's zest for the idiosyncratic and genius
for selecting the exactly right and irresistible detail shine forth
more warmly, from "the whirlwind fife-and-drum of the storm" to
the action that keeps danger and hope in tension when the steeple-
jack lets down his rope "as a spider spins a thread." There is in
this local setting endeared the gusto of a very idiomatic, very
home-grown paradise, the only paradise that some of us can be-
lieve in, the one that's found, when it is found, on earth, when
"there is nothing that ambition can buy or take away."

And in another mode "A Carriage from Sweden" creates out of
the view of a "museum-piece . . . country cart/that inner happi-
ness made art" some platonic ideal of "stalwartness, skill" and fey
grace. The musical "Spenser's Ireland" creates all the wayward
elusiveness of an enchanter's place. Remarkable for its "flax for
damask" passage, its "guillemot/so neat and the hen/of the
heath," it is the presence of the unsaid far underneath the said
that produces at least a half of this delicate combination of magic
and ruefulness.

Returning to the subject of the hero, are there not-heroes? Very
few. Even her animals are "good," as Randall Jarrell has pointed
out. But in "The Hero" there is a "sightseeing hobo," a fool of
shameless questions. Very little time is spent on her, no more than
is spent on that group of people in "The Icosasphere" who are
"avid for someone's fortune." "Through lack of integration" —
could understatement be more excessive? — "three were slain and
ten committed perjury,/six died, two killed themselves, and" —
studied anticlimax — "two paid fines for risks they'd run." For
why flay a dead horse? "Heroes need not write an ordinall of attri-
butes to enumer/ate/what they hate." If presidents punish "sin-
driven senators by not thinking about them," Miss Moore, it might
be inferred, prefers too to ignore certain obvious forms of tawdry
or berserk behavior. However that may be, this Websterian plot
of misconduct (lacking only incest) is mentioned only in passing
and is simply one element in a poem that sets up very dryly rela-
tionships between the "rare efficiency" of birds' nests made in "par-

abolic concentric curves" and the icosasphere that an engineer,
lacking the instinct of the birds, had to take infinite pains to learn
how to make, and the still living enigma of how the Egyptians
ever got their obelisks up. That the birds' nests put mortal "lack
of integration" to shame, and the obelisks Mr. J. O. Jackson's ico-
sasphere, it is left up to the reader to "make out."

Interacting veins between early work and later work are evident
not only in themes but in certain imagery. The elephant, for ex-
ample, has two whole poems to himself but his trunk turns up in
at least four other poems. The sea appears both early and late,
and so does water imagery. In "The Fish" there is the vividness
of all that scuttling under water life of volatile flux and flow (and
the mysterious correspondence of the "crow-blue" mussel shell
"opening and shutting itself like/an/injured fan" with the
hatchet-scarred cliff). There is "A Grave," that masterpiece that
calls the sea "a collector, quick to return a rapacious look"
haunted by the beauty of the metaphor that wins life from
death:

> men lower nets, unconscious of the fact that they are
>   desecrating a grave,
> and row quickly away — the blades of the oars
> moving together like the feet of water-spiders as if
>   there were no such thing as death.

In "An Egyptian Pulled Glass Bottle in the Shape of a Fish"
there is "a wave held up for us to see/In its essential perpendicu-
larity" while water in "The Steeple-Jack" is "etched with waves
as formal as the scales/on a fish." In "Dock Rats" there is the
"steam yacht, lying/like a new made arrow on the/stream" and
the sea's "horse strength." Not to forget the concluding lines on
the grandeur of the waters in "Novices."

In "Marriage" the image of " 'the heart rising/in its estate of
peace/as a boat rises/with the rising of the water' " suggests not
only the image of water in "Sojourn in a Whale" but the central
image in "What Are Years?" of the one who "in his imprisonment
rises/upon himself as/the sea in a chasm, struggling to be/free."

The birds of "A Grave" that "swim through the air at top

speed" remind one of the seagulls in "The Steeple-Jack" "flying back and forth over the town clock" and the beautiful merry-go-round study of the frigate pelican's flight. In "In the Days of Prismatic Colour" we might associate the cliff of "The Fish" with what survives, what is organic to existence, the very bedrock of things as it is celebrated in the lines

> Truth is no Apollo
> Belvedere, no formal thing. The wave may go over it if
> it likes.
> Know that it will be there when it says,
> 'I shall be there when the wave has gone by.'

But though certain themes and imagery appear and reappear, there is a continuous unfolding, a deepening and widening of range, a constant experimenting with new modes or new aspects of a form. "Half Deity," notable for its symmetrical beauty, is a little model of dramatic development, the West Wind acting as a *deus ex machina* to allow for the butterfly's full emergence, full achievement of his transfiguration. ("Bird-Witted" is another, less formally elaborated.) "In Distrust of Merits," written during World War II, achieves, with its powerful rhythmic impulsion, its refrain, "They're fighting, fighting, fighting," majestic scope and harrowing depth. But it is particularly by the veracity of the poet's own directly subjective voice questioning, self-questioning, holding dialogue with itself, that the poem achieves its moral power. "They're fighting that I/may yet recover from the disease, My/Self; some have it lightly; some will die. 'Man/wolf to man' and we devour/ourselves." It is in such ways that Miss Moore's "morals" become a way of seeing the eternal. Again the theme of heroic acceptance that is also withstanding, that may become transcendence, is exemplified in the lines " 'When a man is prey to anger,/he is moved by outside things; when he holds/his ground in patience patience/patience, that is action or/beauty.' " (And "Beauty is everlasting/and dust is for a time" the poem concludes.) We see again her democratic hero's aristocratic self-sufficiency based upon his endeavor at self-knowledge, the aesthetic of his ethics. Indeed, Miss Moore's awareness of the incessant conflict

that the "firebrand that is life" is grounded in gives her poetry that
gusto of what she has called "helpless" sincerity.

It is an aside to point out that at least two of her animals, the
impalla and the tuatera, will soon become extinct unless they are
put on a list of animals-to-be-preserved-in-zoos, though it is an
aside pertinent to other rareties always in danger of becoming
extinct. Against such general pervasive threat her various later
poems, "Efforts of Affection," "Voracities and Verities," "By Dis-
position of Angels," yield us searching insights to "steady the
soul," ending on "Bach-cheerful" tonic chords of affirmation. One
all but hears the lofty resoluteness of Lutheran hymns.

But how awkward it is to paraphrase. It goes against the tight
grain of these poems to expatiate upon their themes, for they are
never as openly stated as this kind of generalizing might lead
some innocent reader to suppose. Rather, insights always seem
pulled from out the very heart of the particulars:

>   What is there
>   like fortitude! What sap
>   went through that little thread
>   to make the cherry red!

This comes in "Nevertheless" as if it had been a secret wrenched
forth just at that moment when happening upon the trials of a
plant she discovered how in its élan vital it had persisted. And
thus her moral insights seem "proved on the pulse" to use Keats's
phrase; they taste of the savor of conflict, they are the secret
truths fought for and not the hawked wise-saws, the maxims of
the copybooks.

Marianne Moore is, as she said of William Carlos Williams,
"indomitably American," whether she is with sweet reasonable-
ness correcting its critics (in "England") or joking upon "the
original American menagerie of styles" (in "An Octopus"), al-
though the earlier debate between past and present, Europe and
America, is far less noticeable in her later work. Like Emily Dick-
inson she is irresistibly original. With Thoreau she dislikes the
showy ("I don't like diamonds"), which includes gardenia scent

and the overemphatic, all of which is at one with her capacity to make us feel the finest shadings.

By the patience and passion of her "eye" she has proved that the stripes of the tulip *can be counted*; her greater glasses, one might say, have revealed to us how much had not been seen until she saw. By her excitable "detecting" (a numinous word for her) she has given us a new world of marvelous specifics or a new-old world of what had been seen before but seen without feeling. This is to say it had not been seen at all.

A few words may be in order regarding the *Complete Poems* which appeared in 1967 on Miss Moore's eightieth birthday. As a kind of preface the terse warning "Omissions are not accidents" prepared the reader for the reduction of "Poetry" to three lines from twenty-nine (the original version is printed in the Notes) and for small but never insignificant excisions in twelve of the poems that first appeared in *Observations*. Poems are also excluded, notably "Melancthon," that had survived up until this volume. "Roses Only," long ago rejected, and three other poems from *Observations* remain outside the pale. Likewise rejected from the canon are "Walking-Sticks and Paper-Weights and Water Marks," "Half Deity," and "See in the Midst of Fair Leaves" from *What Are Years*. But if some poems are retired, others are returned. "The Student," from *What Are Years*, left out of the *Collected Poems* is now back in the *Complete Poems*. An early poem, "To a Chameleon," which appeared in *Poems* under another title, and "A Jellyfish" from *Observations* were included in *O to Be a Dragon* and both are in the *Complete Poems*. "Sun" from *Observations* appeared in *Tell Me, Tell Me* and is also in the *Complete Poems*. "To a Prize Bird" from *Observations* reappears again in the *Complete Poems* after having been absent from the *Selected* and *Collected Poems*. "I Máy, I Might, I Must," an early poem that did not even appear in *Poems*, appears both in *O to Be a Dragon* and the *Complete Poems*. All the later poems from the volumes after the *Collected Poems* are included without omissions, plus four poems hitherto uncollected and nine selections from *The Fables of La Fontaine*.

There are other revisings to be noted: the restructuring of "Nine Nectarines" and "Camellia Sabina" for the sake of turning an internal rhyme into an end rhyme and the removal of stanzas from "The Frigate Pelican" and "The Buffalo" (although periods kindly tell us of their absence) and of phrases from "The Plumet Basilisk." However, "The Steeple-Jack," which was severely cut when it appeared in the *Collected Poems*, is now restored, save for a few alterations, to its original state as we knew it in the *Selected Poems*.

It might also be noted that the later poems undergo a change. For all of their "gaiety in finished form," their elaborate lightness and quickness, they tend on the whole to work more on the surfaces, to be open at the loss of that previously intricate relationship between the surface and the depths. Some are rather public, like the two poems about baseball that are a tour de force of specificities for the initiated but less than that for the uninitiated; "Rescue with Yul Brynner" and "Carnegie Hall: Rescued," also public, are more mannered than vital. Do Mr. Eisenhower's tiringly earnest phrases in "Blessed Is the Man" serve the good that the antipoetic has done in other poems? Or "the drip-dry fruit/of research second to none" in "Saint Nicholas"? But there is the rich and humorous robustness of "Tom Fool at Jamaica" with its

> Sensational. He
>   does not
>   bet on his animated
>
>   valentines

and the tact with which nostalgia is avoided in the evocation of that childish charm of "An Old Amusement Park," implication being all, for where it was is now LaGuardia Airport. "No Better Than a 'Withered Daffodil'" and "The Sycamore" work in a new measure of music, the latter with its small blunt shock:

> We don't like flowers that do
>   not wilt; they must die, and nine
>   she-camel hairs aid memory

and its last lines:

retiringly formal
    as if to say: "And there was I
    like a field-mouse at Versailles."

And if Miss Moore does not explore new veins, or mine the former ones as deeply, her major poems to which many of these later ones are minor will remain as a part of our heritage and the achievement of the language. "Freckled integrity," Tom Fool's "left white hand foot — an unconformity; though judging by results, a kind of cottontail to give him confidence," independence, resolution: these are some of the qualities that forge the armor of what becomes no longer armor but "patience/protecting the soul as clothing the body/from cold, so that 'great wrongs/were powerless to vex.'" In our sort of age Miss Moore's "mirror-of-steel uninsistence," her faculty for digesting the "hard yron" of appearance, as Wallace Stevens said, triumphantly speaks for man forever caught on the horns of his own dilemma but man resisting by grace of his understanding, by grace through his works of the vision of the underlying order of the universe.

Conrad Aiken

Eʀʟʏ in his work Conrad Aiken wrote:

> There are houses hanging above the stars
> And stars hung under a sea.

These suave, unsettling lines from *Senlin: A Biography* (1918) suggest in miniature much of what was to follow. The world of these verses is no other than the round world on which we live. Man's visual logic, if he tries to extend it very far, is turned upside down by the gravitational logic of the globe. "Can the same be true of all of man's mental life?" Aiken seems to be asking. In that event our thoughts and feelings are subject to fields of force in which fall is flight and flight is fall and high and low are interchangeable. Aiken's work in both verse and prose is concerned with just such circularities and reversibilities and his success with them is the success of all his best writing.

In the late 1940s the American critic Lionel Trilling, in a troubled appraisal of his favored "liberal imagination," remarked that "the sense of largeness, of cogency, of the transcendence which largeness and cogency can give, the sense of being reached in our secret and primitive minds — this we virtually never get from the writers of the liberal democratic tradition at the present time." There are, however, grounds for considering the best of Aiken's work as having provided some of what Trilling said he could not usually find. That work has now extended over more than half a century and has encompassed haunting poetry, prophetic criticism, varied fiction, and journalism. He has been justly called, by Allen Tate, "one of the few genuine men of letters left."

Conrad Aiken was the first (1889) of three sons born to New England-bred William and Anna Aiken. His surname points to the Scotch blood he shares with his thematic and stylistic ancestor Poe. His birthplace, Savannah, Georgia, was the city in which his Harvard-trained father practiced medicine, and the family lived on one of those pleasant squares whose back alleys provided a playground for boys of the neighborhood, both black and white. When Aiken went to Harvard in the fall of 1907 he joined without being at first aware of it one of the most influential groups of writers and intellectuals in the twentieth century. The classes of 1910–15 matriculated, among others later famous, T. S. Eliot, John Reed, Walter Lippmann, E. E. Cummings, and Robert Benchley.

Since his graduation Aiken has pursued one of the most distinguished careers in his literary generation, capturing and holding from the time of his earliest publications to the present an audience in both England and the United States. Along with this there has been a broad and genial exchange with many of his most luminous contemporaries. Outspoken and often unfashionable in his public statements on literary affairs and reputations and sometimes waspishly bantering in his conversation on such matters, Aiken has nevertheless been blessed with a gift for friendship with his artistic peers. The public record of this is characterized by cooperation without hint of coterie machinations and controversy unmarked by tones of rancor. The mutual regard of Allen Tate and Conrad Aiken, for example, is some sort of monument to the transcendence by affection of deep differences in temperament and virtually diametrical perceptions of art and politics. Working to please himself, sometimes in New York, sometimes in Sussex or on Cape Cod, more recently in Georgia as well, Aiken has earned most of his living solely by writing and has memorialized his experiences in a remarkable autobiographical work of human and artistic self-analysis, *Ushant: An Essay* (1952).

Ushant, of which more must be said later, touches upon major aspects of Aiken's life and art: the unstinting dedication to poetry; the interest in psychoanalytic doctrine and "musical" form; the self-reversing attachments to the United States and England; the conscious continuance of a family tradition of liberalism and humanism; and the overcoming of tragedy in his early life. The third-person protagonist of *Ushant*, "D.," a reference to the character Demarest in the novel *Blue Voyage*, is a persona of Aiken himself and if there is such a thing as an interior-monologue autobiography of a literary man, perhaps *Ushant* is it. Indirectly candid in factual reference, it provides a Proustian regress toward the tragedy of Aiken's eleventh year (when both his parents died by the hand of the father, and he, "finding them dead, found himself possessed of them forever"). A high point is the scene in which the New England grandmother who has taken an interest in the orphaned D. gradually and tactfully brings his suicide father into the conversation, thus restoring the father to a place of conscious respect — and turns over the writings of the tragic man to the child so that the child can reach for identification with what was best in the father's life and work. Since it is these more profoundly personal aspects of *Ushant* that will monopolize our attention later on in this essay, it is necessary to notice here that the work has an important public interest as a chapter in modern literary history. Providing an informal commentary on literary men Aiken has known, it presents them in half disguises: Ezra Pound, for example, is "Rabbi Ben Ezra"; Eliot, the "Tsetse."

The global generality of the fragment quoted above from one of Aiken's earliest reputation-making poems might hint even to a reader who has not yet read *Senlin* that he gives himself freely to rhapsodizing forms. The play with incongruities, especially in

the complex concreteness with which the poet evokes a relativ-
ized viewpoint, seems to be a prevision of lines by Dylan Thomas:

> And I am dumb to tell a weather's wind
> How time has ticked a heaven around the stars . . .

Consider the masterly larger unit of verse containing the lines
quoted at the head of this essay:

> It is morning, Senlin says, and in the morning
> When the light drips through the shutters like the dew,
> I arise, I face the sunrise,
> And do the things my fathers learned to do.
> Stars in the purple dusk above the rooftops
> Pale in a saffron mist and seem to die,
> And I myself on a swiftly tilting planet
> Stand before a glass and tie my tie.
>
> Vine leaves tap my window,
> Dew-drops sing to the garden stones,
> The robin chirps in the chinaberry tree
> Repeating three clear tones.
>
> It is morning. I stand by the mirror
> And tie my tie once more.
> While waves far off in a pale rose twilight
> Crash on a coral shore.
> I stand by a mirror and comb my hair:
> How small and white my face! —
> The green earth tilts through a sphere of air
> And bathes in a flame of space.
>
> There are houses hanging above the stars
> And stars hung under a sea.
> And a sun far off in a shell of silence
> Dapples my walls for me.

(It should be noted that Aiken has sometimes made changes
in his poems before reprinting them in selected or collected
editions. The quotations included here are taken from the latest
editions, for the most part from *Collected Poems* of 1953.)

Surely the young Aiken richly let himself go in *Senlin* and the
other pieces — *The Charnel Rose* (1918), *The House of Dust*
(1920), *The Jig of Forslin* (1921), *The Pilgrimage of Festus*
(1923) — that make up *The Divine Pilgrim*, the long sequence of

"symphonies" written in the years 1914 to 1920, when he was in his late twenties. The literary influences are unconcealed. Swinburne's tone had already been present in *Nocturne of Remembered Spring* (1917): "After long days of dust we lie and listen / To the silverly woven harmonies of rain . . ." *The Divine Pilgrim* shows Aiken as the rapt reader of others who had preceded him. Poe: "For seven days my quill I dipt / To wreathe my filigrees of script . . ." Browning: "Here's my knife — between my fingers I press it, / And into the panic heart . . . / Do you still hear the music? Do you still see me?" Wilde: "Death, among violins and paper roses . . ." As R. P. Blackmur says, Aiken's readiness to continue to call upon the conventional poetic vocabulary that he relied upon in this early work has remained with him all his life. At the same time the inventive advances he achieved in these pieces constitute some of his strongest claims to attention. *Forslin*, says Allen Tate, is the first poem in the English language in which a symphonic texture is employed to develop a philosophical theme. In this blend of the lyric and the narrative the lyric predominates and is centered on the feeling and thought of a single character.

These poems, besides showing how closely Aiken along with other *littérateurs* of his generation at Harvard studied Arthur Symons' *The Symbolist Movement in Literature* (1899), tell us much about what kind of an artist Aiken wished to be. A first clue is his interest in drawing upon music for suggestions about the forms of poems, an interest centered upon the capacity of music for presenting simultaneously several different levels of sound and meaning. This perhaps Wagnerian preoccupation with a thematic plurality of voices is directly connected, in turn, with Aiken's leading intuition of human character and circumstance. Influenced by the early psychoanalytic movement, Aiken sees man as a creature existing in both awareness and unawareness. The voices from the unawareness deserve to be rendered. But how? Aiken's solution is one that has now become conventional but was not always so. He makes these voices carry a symbolic content in which traditional and psychoanalytic motifs are blended. The manner is also what the composer might call "chromatic" and "impressionistic." It is worth noticing that although Aiken himself has made not a few references to the French Symbolists, he attached himself to them far less programmatically than some other American poets of his generation and his own style is that of impressionism — impressionism strongly tinged with that still older school that the French called Parnassian. Such predilections led him to produce poems whose strength lies in their brilliant and fulsome rendering of typical human temperaments. Let us consider his own analysis of his method.

In *Poetry Magazine*, in 1919, Aiken remarked that the arrangement of the four parts of *The Jig of Forslin* was such that part IV gains, in its position, a certain effect it could gain at no other position in the sequence. Each emotional tone in the poem is employed like a musical tonality. "Not content to present emotions or things or sensations for their own sakes . . . this method takes only the most delicately evocative aspects of them, makes of them a keyboard, and plays upon them a music of which the chief characteristic is its elusiveness, its fleetingness, and its richness in the shimmering overtones of hint and suggestion." This idea of impressionistic musicality in poetry follows suggestions popularized by, among others, a writer who was a noticeable influence upon Aiken and his generation, Walter Pater. In his essay on "The School of Giorgione" Pater lent his elegant pen to the notion that any art (painting, for example) could learn from another art (music, for example, or literature) employing another sensuous medium and (somewhat contradictorily) that "all art constantly aspires to the condition of music."

Aiken himself sometimes used the word "chorus" in connection with his method. A character in the early poems is conceived as generating a wide-range band of voices from various levels and temporal sectors of the psyche; and the themes carried by these voices are elaborated in a sequence of variations somewhat in the way the composer undertakes the expansion and development of themes in a symphony or, perhaps more properly, a tone poem. While it is certainly true that Aiken's poems do have parts in which the mingled voices of many selves of the principal character seem to vocalize together in the same lines at the same time, the word "chorus" is not entirely satisfactory. The reason is that the various aspects of a character also are frequently rendered in a manner quite different from that of the chorus: it is a regular occurrence for them to appear in separate successive solos. The method is operatic or oratoric rather than choral, and might as well be called so.

Although Aiken referred to a "chorus" in the sense of its use as a musical rather than a dramaturgical device, there is a sense in which he could just as properly have emphasized the latter meaning. A trait of the chorus in an early Greek play was that it took a standpoint distinct from that of both the protagonist and the audience, serving as a narrative and meditative "we" disjoined from both. One of the expository advantages of this was that the chorus could be made to share information and feelings with the audience that were not made available to the protagonists, thereby generating one type of dramatic irony. There is a sense in which the voices emanating from the unawareness of the agent in a poem by Aiken serve similar purposes. The principal resemblance lies in the fact that these voices make available to the reader a certain knowledge of the agent not possessed by the agent himself. This involves the use of the now-familiar literary device best known as "interior monologue." Aiken early employed it in his poems to obtain a contrast between a character's conscious and unconscious motivations, thus effecting what we might term "psychoanalytic irony." It is not clear that Aiken himself was entirely aware of what he had hold of here. His comments on his own work do not fully identify the originality of a form he had discovered partly as a result of his interest in psychology.

Senlin is crucial to our analysis so far. A dreamlike poem, like a dream, represents the same relatively simple thing over and over again, whatever the disguises and semi-disclosures.

What does *Senlin* represent and render? A poem influenced by Eliot's "The Love Song of J. Alfred Prufrock," it is concerned with a raw young man forced by his age and his character into a state of intense self-consciousness. On one level he is expressing and struggling with self-pity and a sense of isolation. On another he is expressing and struggling with solipsism. On both levels he is confronted with the problem of the relativity of perceptions and judgments. One of the results and signs of Senlin's crisis is the confusion between the stages of his life. While still not aged, he acts old, thus missing his youth. This habit of acting while young and raw as if he were older and more jaded is both the cause and the effect of his incomplete identity. A particular form taken by this crisis is the fear that he may be hurt by women or that this expectation will itself eventuate in his hurting them. When all sections of the poem are taken into account the basic statement of *Senlin* is this:

A young man keeps walking and climbing, with a feeling that he has been abandoned by the goal that is at the end of the road and the powers that are at the top of the stairs. He is returned incessantly to a situation in which he digs up a young woman.

This can be condensed:

A young man digs up a young woman.

This sentence states the whole dramatic meaning of *Senlin*: the ascent to the transcending other of a fatherly greater maleness, greater age, and wisdom is unsuccessful or at least difficult. Attempts to ascend to this are always accompanied or followed by rediscoveries of the dead traces of the non-male in the self. Senlin is too much like a woman to be a woman's lover. Yet the non-male in Senlin is not alive and active; it is, in every sense except recollection of it, dead.

When Aiken, in the early and middle 1920s, directed much of his attention toward fiction he marked, one might say, not only the beginning of a new kind of productivity but the end of a stage of the old. If Aiken had never collected more of his poems than those represented in the dozen or so that culminated in *Senlin*, he would have been assured of a place in twentieth-century American writing. In the period from the early twenties to 1940, however, Aiken completed not only new poems in new forms but also all of his novels, most of his short stories, and a fair share of his prose and criticism. The move into fiction had its adventurous elements as we shall see when we examine the work itself, but it may also have had its elements of necessity. Aiken was the father of three children by his first marriage (1912) and he remarried twice after that, once in 1930 and again in 1937. His own small patrimony was probably not adequate for these financial responsibilities and what he could earn by his pen was therefore crucial to him. Although Aiken never became a big seller in fiction his success in the field was not, to his gratification, solely an artistic one. Its artistic merits, however, along with its developmental place in his lifework, invite our attention now.

Few fictional works by a modern poet are as well known as Aiken's "Silent Snow, Secret Snow." A tapping into the stream of consciousness of a boy who appears to be relapsing into isolation and death wish, it is one of the best of the short stories in which Aiken has demonstrated his skill. Admiring Chekhov, James, and Andreyev, Aiken has worked mostly in the twentieth-century form of psychological fiction that we associate with Édouard Dujardin, Joyce, Dorothy Richardson, and Virginia Woolf. We should take special notice of Aiken's ability to repossess from the writers of fiction some of the tools they borrowed so readily from poets. The question of the relation between the poetry and the prose of Aiken might seem to be satisfied by referring to the blend of the symbolic and the psychological that we find in both. This reminiscence of the ambidextrous Poe is reinforced not by any interest of Aiken's in shrewd plotting but by his general attraction to the macabre and by the pleasure he sometimes takes in poetic texture as a resource of prose. Yet while most of Aiken's short stories offer complexity of character rather than plot they are not eventless. They ground themselves in those slowly gathering expectations that create suspense, provide the basis for dramatic reversal in the condition of the characters, and qualify the pieces as stories rather than portraits. The same is true of his novels.

Blue Voyage, earliest of his five novels, appeared in 1927. Returning to his ship's bunk each night, William Demarest recreates not only the events of the day and his expectations of the day to follow but also his deeper past. Does he possess a true identity — or rather, will the interactions of the voyage reveal one to him? This question is seen as pivoting on his chase of Cynthia, the girl of his past who has turned up as a passenger of the very ship on which he has sought to reach her in Europe. Aiken establishes a nice contrast between the sophistication ascribed to Demarest by his co-passengers and the abdominal Jello that is Demarest's other self, though he is probably dilatory in exploiting the comic possibilities in his portrait of a shipboard prig. As Demarest (which could be read as the Latin-like *de mare est,* "from the sea he is") comes toward the end of his voyage, having lost Cynthia even before the voyage began, we have been treated to episodes vitalized by an action whose course has described a circle.

Great Circle (1933) employs a massive flashback to explore two events separated in time by a generation. The later event is the protagonist's stealthy discovery of his wife's infidelity; the earlier is his parallel loss of childhood innocence when he is the witness of a tragic affair between his mother and his uncle. A sort of Harvard Square *Hamlet, Great Circle* is not so much a novel as a morality play in print, vexed by problems of viewpoint, tone, and central action. The binary pattern, in which each of the crises, past and present, is at once more important and less important than the other, is true enough to the temporal relativism of the twentieth century. But Aiken's symbolic loadings, such as the hero's loss of one eye — emblem perhaps of his Oedipal situation — seem arbitrary and distracting. The best section of the book is one in which the hero's Harvard classmate, who has alcoholically graduated into the status of a completely self-understanding and clairvoyant bum, provides an amateur psychoanalysis of the hero in exchange for an evening of drinks.

King Coffin (1935) is a descendant of Hogg, Poe, Stevenson, and Dostoevski and a predecessor of Camus' *The Stranger*. Jasper Ammen, the hero, has become obsessed with his observations of a stranger, Mr. Jones. Jones is unaware that Ammen has not only voyeuristically selected him for study but also elected him as the future victim of a gratuitous homicide. Told in roughly chronological sequence from a viewpoint somewhere "just back of" third-person protagonist Ammen, it shows us how Ammen's plan to commit the Raskolnikofian murder of the stranger, Jones, is reversed by the mournful birth of a stillborn baby to Mrs. Jones and its seemingly perfunctory burial. The death of the baby, by linking Jones with the banality of human life in general, disqualifies Jones as the pure and single stranger-victim of the crime. After the infant's burial, Ammen's desire to kill Jones evaporates, leaving Ammen himself as the only possible victim for the supreme jape in "Nietzschean" aggression that he has been cryptically telling his friends about.

In view of this construction, it might be thought that Aiken would foreshadow without revealing the unexpected appearance in Jones's life of a baby; but both the reader and Jasper Ammen become too early aware that a baby is to be born to the Joneses and this works against the force of the denouement. The convergence apparently intended between the simpler plot (Ammen's exposure of his vague plans to his confidants; his challenge to them to reveal those plans; and their alerting of his father) and the more complex plot (the transformation of Jones into a family- and life-connected person who cannot be defined as a pure ritual victim) does not fully work. Yet there are passages of remarkable success in the book. The experiments of Ammen with the air paths of the smoke of his cigarette signal to us, perhaps before Ammen himself knows it, that he is verging toward suicide by self-asphyxiation. Equally moving are the sections in which Aiken renders the succession of psychosomatic calms and storms through which Ammen passes on his way to final self-isolation and self-destruction.

These productions, along with *A Heart for the Gods of Mexico* (1939), with its quest motif, and the Cape Cod comedy *Conversation* (1940), with its portraiture of children, show that Aiken is the many-gifted literary man who turns with fascination, confidence, and professional energy toward current forms of fiction, and they demonstrate that he can work with them quite as well as many practitioners and better than most. (His one attempt to write a play, *Mr. Arcularis*, by turning a short story into a script, was not, however, a success.) He offers us no large-scale "Conrad Aiken World" of narrative prose but rather a winding "Post Road" through eastern American urban and suburban social scenes, passing through self-conscious counties connected with those of C. Brockden Brown in the past, Robert Coates among his contemporaries, and John Updike in the present. It is quite understandable that Aiken was one of the very first (in 1927, in a review in the *New York Post*) to recognize and raise significant questions about the genius of Faulkner.

Discussion of Aiken's fiction leads us naturally in the direction of his other major experiment in prose narrative, *Ushant*. Readers of this work meet in it the two principal masks of the artist-hero D. created by Aiken. The first is seeking the gratification he thinks he will be content with. The second is a gloomier bemoaning the loss of the gratification or its excessive price. The title itself indicates not only this polarity but others as well. Ushant is a dragon-shaped rock on the French side of the English Channel's opening into the Atlantic. Its associations include both departure and landfall, the idea of a westward limit to inquiry but also the notion of a taking-off place from Europe. This title was plainly offered in the expectation that it would be received as a Joycean transliteration of "You shan't" and as a metaphor both for the Ten Commandments and the superego. The work strives to render, by the expansion of a single state of the consciousness of D. (a moment in a steamer bunk, late in his life), the totality of D.'s struggle with the world and himself. The forward movement in time is left to be reconstructed by the reader from nonchronological recollections concerning three conscious goals of the writer's life: literary excellence, women's favors, and self-understanding.

This anthology of formative scenes in D.'s life is rendered with less clinical self-analysis than one might have tolerated and this has the advantage of leaving it up to the reader to complete the connections where he himself thinks they make sense. There is a chilling moment when D.'s mother comes to tuck him in as a child of seven or eight and asks him if, when he grows up, he will "protect her." This scene may point forward to D.'s family tragedy — and more than that; it may even foreshadow the episodes in the life of D. when his pursuit of women can be interpreted as a response to exorbitant demands made upon him as a child. A burden of comic complaint running through the book is that the searcher for art and love cannot attain both.

How are the disclosures of *Ushant* to be taken? If psychology is wrong or irrelevant about such lives as Aiken's or if Aiken is wrong or irrelevant about how it applies to them, the retrospection of *Ushant* produces not an autobiography but, as Jay Martin suggests, an art work half revealing and half veiling the life of an author — D. — *Ushant*'s author. On the other hand, if psychology is right and relevant about such lives as Aiken's and if Aiken is right and relevant about how it applies to them, the work has a kind of biographical weight over and beyond the artfulness of its portraiture. It seems appropriate here to assume that Aiken himself understood that *Ushant*'s readers would be pulled in the direction of both interpretations. Therefore, even if the reader inclines toward enjoying *Ushant* more as a literary artifact than as a biographical record he is compelled to have considered the latter dimension as a built-in aspect of the former. *Ushant*, it is clear, obliges us to take a much closer look at Aiken's relation to psychological teachings.

Aiken's first acquaintance with psychoanalytic thought was

made while he was still an undergraduate at Harvard, around 1909, just about the time when Freud delivered to Americans his now-famous lectures at Clark University. From almost the beginning Aiken was regarded as an accomplished hanger-on of the movement, especially in the conversational games of "Latent Motive" and "Dream Analysis" as they were then practiced by devotees upon each other. As a consequence of Freud's admiration for Aiken's novel *Great Circle*, there was an opportunity for Aiken to be himself analyzed by Freud in Europe, with a friend offering the necessary financial aid. Aiken decided not to undertake the experiment. Years later, in *Ushant*, he wondered whether this might not have been a mistake. More or less characteristically, he could not make up his mind about the forgone opportunity. There is no doubt, however, that the fifth *Divine Pilgrim* "symphony," *The Pilgrimage of Festus*, has qualities that permit us to view Aiken as philosophical expositor as well as artistic exploiter of psychoanalytic views.

Aiken describes *Festus* as a study in "epistemology" and so it is. According to Freud, the cognitions of man are reshaped and distorted, as in a warped lens, by wishes that are the father to the thought. Festus, the hero, who is a kind of Faustus as well as a *Festung* (or fortress) and *festive*, is seen constructing a world out of his own "projections." Extending this theme to its limit, Aiken portrays Festus as a "paranoid" giving free rein in his fantasy and his actions to a sadistic vein. The whole poem is an exploration of the idea that knowledge is obtained when a Subject fully imposes itself upon an Object — the perception that Freud expressed by arguing that a surgeon's therapeutic violation of the body can be considered as the sublimation of an impulse originally cruel. Knowledge begins in hurting as well as wishing and willing and searching; and we had better recognize that systems of knowledge, being systematic, are also sadistic. As a remapping of the Faust legend, *Festus* implies the recognition of and recoil from the fact that scientific experiment sometimes is driven to contaminate its own object of research even to the point where, as in biology, it kills its specimens and thus denatures the nature it aims to study. Moreover Festus himself is, in effect, his own victim.

On the basis of what has been said so far, what can be suggested about the role of psychological theories in Aiken's life and in Aiken's work? To begin, some generalizations on the biography whose tragedy and triumph were sketched above:

First, Aiken's life story is quite unlike that of many of his artistic contemporaries who were also interested in Freud. The aberrations that in their families may have lain under the surface were in Aiken's family the conditions for a tragedy that was acted out to its end. Aiken, we can imagine, was drawn toward a general psychiatric interest in his own past more forcefully than most of his artistic contemporaries.

Second, his general psychiatric interest in his own past was stimulated by his knowledge of certain factors in his background, namely hereditary and organic ones, which happen to be, by definition, precisely the sort from which Freud withdrew his interest in the course of developing his nonsomatic theory of mental disorder. We are told in *Ushant*, for example, that Aiken's mother and father were cousins, and there are remarks in the work suggesting that Aiken was aware that he may have inherited a strain of petit mal, the milder form of epileptic seizure.

Third, Aiken's active response to the threatening disorders of the period of his latency had probably already brought him to a certain state of mental health before he ever heard of Freud.

Fourth, the "Oedipal conflict" in Aiken's life was presumably left uncompleted in Freud's terms because of his father's self-removal from the family scene while Aiken was between eleven and twelve. The same act that deprived the child of the conflict also deprived him of his mother, the conflict's prize.

It is Aiken himself, in *Ushant*, who provides the data of these four speculations. In this situation it would be irresponsible for us to follow certain valuable self-denying ordinances of modern criticism. What is required is precisely what these ordinances forbid: the pursuit of clinical themes in the work and the linkage of these themes with the makeup of the writer.

Given the four biographical conditions of Aiken's relationship to psychological doctrines, it can be suggested that one would not expect to find in Aiken's work a fully developed concern with Freud's Oedipus theme. Nor do we. It also follows that a generally psychiatric, as opposed to specifically psychoanalytic, concern for his own past would be at work in Aiken. The psychoanalytic interest would arise only when he had to consider the consequences for his own identity of having been deprived of the Oedipal conflict. This is noticeable also. Although there are hints of the Oedipal theme in *Senlin* (II, 8), it is broached more overtly in *Blue Voyage*, when Aiken's hero relocates his girl Cynthia only to learn that she is already engaged to be married. Read "mother" for "Cynthia" and the Oedipal rivalry theme is complete. It also turns up in *Mr. Arcularis*, in which an uncle is substituted for a father as the mother's lover. It appears in somewhat the same form in *Great Circle*. In all these references, the weight of the Oedipal theme is not heavy and the emphasis is almost entirely on the jealous search for possession of the mother, hardly at all on the direct struggle with the father. Although *King Coffin* portrays an open enmity between father and son, it is offered chiefly as one of the explanatory conditions of subsequent events and is not much dwelt upon in itself. The poems, the prose, and *Ushant* all suggest that this weighting reflects Aiken's own life and preoccupations. Even D.'s discovery later in his life that he had been taking his rebelling grandfather as a model can be interpreted as a conventional and mild critique of D.'s father.

This does not exhaust, however, the relationships joining Aiken's biography, his psychologizing, and his work. In a section of *Ushant*, D. recalls a picture drawn of him in early infancy by his father. Retrospection tells him that in this portrait his father showed an infant possessing godlike self-assurance. The passage implies that the picture dramatizes the father's recoil before the potential power of his first child, a male. After such infantile omnipotence, what innocence? D.'s comment is simple, brilliant, and touched by Mark Twain: "That child's father and mother were already as good as dead" — a boldly ironic apology for being born. Here Aiken seems to acknowledge both as doctrine and as indirect biography the idea that the son of a father who has killed himself may sometimes feel the event as the materialization of his own wish. It is not odd therefore that the themes and situations developed by Aiken in his early work involve fantasies of horrid actions, nightmares capable of serving to rationalize a guilt already felt. One fantasy after another is tested in order to see which one fits best a preestablished mood of guilt. *The Charnel Rose* explores survivals of the "infantile polymorphous perverse"; *Forslin*, the autistic stages of mentality; *Senlin*, the homosexual identification of self; *Festus*, "paranoid" sadism. Later, in *Punch* (1921), Aiken explored another face of sadism.

Since our major interest here is directed not toward Aiken's life but toward his writing, the foregoing speculations can be useful to us chiefly because they suggest how Aiken's psychologizing influenced his self-definition as an artist. The identification of five characteristics seems in order here. First of all, his intellectual appeal to psychological doctrine as a clue to the meaning in life. Second, his concern with substitutes or "surrogates" in human experience — Aiken early wrote of himself as having an interest in "the process of vicarious experience by which civilized man enriches his life and maintains emotional balance." Third, his employment of a "musical" method in verse composition, a method which emphasizes the associative stream of imagery both in the minds of the characters represented and in the compositional habits of the writer. Fourth, his exploration of themes of ego, identity, and the "defense mechanisms." Fifth, his use of phallic symbolism in a manner suggesting that the reader can be expected to possess a knowledge of that code. The doctrinal details of these concerns dominated Aiken less and less as he matured.

Despite these conjectures pressed upon our attention by the masquerade of *Ushant* it will occur to many readers of Aiken that even if his life experiences had been different, his art might have demonstrated the same concerns; and that, for readers who know nothing or who could not care less about his life, the poems present themselves not as fragmented history but as the make-believe of art. It follows that they make a claim to be concerned with the destiny of all men rather than one man alone and that this exploration of the general as opposed to the particular involves an examination of the evils that all men encounter and a search for sources of value that all men can share. In effect, this involves a research into the depths of universal guilt, conscience, and indeed the sense of human solidarity. Aiken's approach to these matters deserves greater clarification than it has as yet received.

Lest what needs to be said about this seem to make Aiken a rhetorician rather than a poet it would be well to look for a moment at how well Aiken defended the claims of art in his criticism as well as in his poetry. For the intellectual background of Aiken's beliefs about the relation between life and art presents itself quite clearly in his criticism, not because it is programmatic but because, despite its range, it is consistent and coherent in its drive. Aiken undertook considerable reviewing, much of it at the behest of Marianne Moore for the *Dial*, and his criticism has the vitality of taste-in-the-making. It is rather to its credit that his is not the sort of criticism that labors first of all to preestablish a position of defense for the writer's own poetry. Nor does it rework ground already covered by others. One could summarize its strength by noticing Aiken's early perception of grandiose confusions in Pound. To get an idea of Aiken's range and perception as a critic one has to turn only to *Scepticisms* (1919), in which he writes freely and incisively about himself as well as his contemporaries. Or one may take advantage of Rufus Blanshard's service to Aiken's reputation by examining his *A Reviewer's ABC*, a 1958 publication which reprints most of the pieces on which Aiken is willing to rest his critical reputation. As displayed in the *ABC*, the ranginess and independence of this work calls up Hazlitt and Baudelaire; and what may most distinguish it is the magnanimity by which it rises above the professional animus and often intrusive pedantry that burden much of the criticism in English that has appeared in the twentieth century. A most perceptive and helpful commentary on Aiken's development as a critic is provided by Jay Martin. According to Martin, Aiken's early attitude toward literature leaned toward that of Tolstoi in *What Is Art?* The stress was placed upon the moral effects of the artist upon his audience. Later, Martin tells us, Aiken gradually articulated quite a different position, one that gave rather more attention to the artist as autonomous explorer of reality. Perhaps it would be fair to say of this process that Aiken has given up Tolstoi in order to replace him with Croce. Yet even though Aiken's criticism leans closer and closer to a Crocean core as it proceeds, it does not forsake all sense of the instruction that is found in art, and may even, like his poetry, constitute more of a teaching than Aiken has been prepared to admit.

We should keep in mind these aspects of Aiken's attitude toward the poetic art as we try to come closer to an understanding of how Aiken involved himself in poetry as a channel of total feeling and thinking. In the "symphonies" Aiken undertook to study the engulfing vice or virtue of a human temperament from the point of view of new scientific doctrines about such matters. While the background of this can be seen extending from Aristotle and Theophrastus to Ben Jonson and La Bruyère, the particular intellectual source of Aiken's "symphonies" is the interest in characterology handed forward by such men as Wilhelm Dilthey from early nineteenth-century philosophies to Freud, Spranger, Scheler, Jung, Fromm, and Erikson. This line of thought is concerned quite as much with "identity" as with "personality" and it includes a consideration of ethical problems. Since Aiken is true to this tradition — the moral worth of a character such as that of Senlin is studied in the poem in the light of his perilous preoccupation with himself — it is hard to understand the habit of minimizing the moralist in Aiken. But it appears that there are two reasons for this judgment, one involving a development in philosophy and one involving Aiken's manner of constructing the moral orientation of his characters.

The first, or philosophical, consideration is that we have witnessed a narrowing of the province of ethics in Great Britain and the United States since the turn of the century. This is seen in the tendency of ethics to pursue "normative" as contrasted with "descriptive" inquiry. For philosophers following such men as Bradley and McTaggart and for critics such as Eliot and Winters, a system of ethics appears to be validated largely by showing that it is entailed by the nature of an ultimate reality. But this can only be an article of faith rather than philosophy, since no system of ethics can be validated merely by this warrant. Besides, there are those who hold that descriptive as well as deductive inquiry is required in ethics; and Aiken is one of these. The source of ethics that others seek in an intuition of duty to a metaphysical realm Aiken seeks in an intuition of human purposes in the realm of nature; and his poems constitute a teaching in this ancient tradition of moral judgments — a tradition which is as evident to us in Epicurus and Lucretius as it is in Freud. And if we pursue this line of investigation more fully we shall see why Aiken employs a particular and significant method for developing the moral orientation of his characters.

David Bakan, in one of the chapters of his work in progress on modern psychology, has called attention to the power of dynamic psychology as a system of metaphor. He suggests that thought is renewed from time to time by revolutions in its systems of metaphor and that not the least of Freud's contributions was of just this sort. This is one of the principal ways in which Aiken understood psychoanalysis and it is a way that is not yet grasped by many who claim to understand Freud. Along similar lines John Chynoweth Burnham, in one of the chapters in his forthcoming study of the intellectual climate in which modern psychiatry arose, notes that Edwin B. Holt of Harvard, in *The Freudian Wish and Its Place in Ethics*, as early as 1915 saw Freud as translator into modern terms of the idea that knowledge, including knowledge of self, is a virtue. Aiken read this book when it first appeared. Scattered throughout Aiken's work, including *Osiris Jones* (1931) and *Preludes for Memnon* (1931), appear systematic comments along this line. Aiken's Freudian belief in the determination of all mental life by all of its past did not make him a psychological determinist in the sense that Hardy was an environmental determinist and Dreiser a naturalistic determinist. Rather it encouraged him to develop the voluntarism and relativism of his minister grandfather's dissenting brand of the Unitarian view.

As a consequence Aiken moved from the very beginning toward views of human nature that stand in contrast to comparable concerns in many of his artistic contemporaries. For them the center of interest is the family as the source of an oppressive cultural superego and they seek a new compact with the guilt they believe has been forced upon them by their upbringing. Aiken on the other hand is concerned with the development of ego in situations in which the outside world must be substituted for the family. From the outset, therefore, he is led in the direction of an interest in character disorders rather than the neurotic or the psychotic. The questions he asks himself are more like those asked by a psychoanalyst such as Harry Stack Sullivan, with his sensitivity to social aspects of personality, than like those of earlier and more "classical" masters of the field. By accident and insight Aiken anticipated the interest in "identity" as contrasted with the interest in "personality" that appeared in fullest form in the American school of Freudian revisionists. Aiken's relationships to dynamic psychology are therefore about as different as they can be from the picture of them provided by some critics of Aiken's work such as Peterson, Martin, and Hoffman and even by some opaque remarks in Aiken himself. "The cosmic ironist" in Aiken pivots not so much upon a struggle of personality for a place in an impersonal cosmos as upon the struggle of the human being, over and beyond being possessed of a "personality," to arrive at an identity.

Consider the persistence of this theme in the eloquent late poem
"The Crystal":

> At seven, in the ancient farmhouse,
> cocktails sparkle on the tray, the careful answer
> succeeds the casual question, a reasoned dishevelment
> ruffling quietly the day's or the hour's issue.
> Our names, those we were born with,
> or those we were not born with, since all are born nameless,
> become the material, or the figment, if we wish,
> of which to weave, and then unweave, ourselves.
> Our lives, those we inherited, of which
> none can claim ownership in fee simple, but only
> a tenant's lease, of unpredictable duration,
> rented houses from which have already departed perhaps
> those others, our other selves, the children . . .

It is important to notice that whereas Frost's Social Darwinism
and Eliot's anthropology and Pound's culture-history have all
dated, Aiken's psychology anticipated a half century ago a major
viewpoint in psychology today. We do not dismiss writers for the
obsolescence of the intellectual fashions that once nourished
them any more than we praise them for their anticipation of
scientific world views. On the other hand we can praise them
for the coherence with which a unified view of man is drama-
tized in, and dramatizes, their work. On this score Aiken dis-
plays an intelligent consistency that makes some contemporaries
of his, for example Pound, sound incoherent and others, for ex-
ample Stevens, seem bloodless. Thus, in analyzing how Aiken's
view of man led him to undertake certain crucial experiments
in form we dare not fail to evaluate what he says about man and
for man — all the more so because Aiken has avoided the
role of guru accepted for themselves by some of his best known
contemporaries.

With this observation, however, we are brought close to a
crucial question not only for Aiken but for others in his gener-
ation. It is ordinarily expressed in the following terms: does
the twentieth-century poet inherit a set of beliefs that make the

triumphs and the failures of men significant? A set of beliefs that, because they are general beliefs about human action, assist the artist to portray human actions as possessing a sharp contour, against a clear-cut ground? The question develops some of its importance out of the observation that even poets such as Eliot or Claudel who have attached themselves to the authoritative belief system of traditional Catholicism have not been able to present in verse or in drama anything so artistically clear-cut as the doctrine itself claims to be in dogmatic terms. It develops further importance out of the observation that an artist who, like Brecht, has attached himself to the doctrinaire prophecies of Marx, has not been more convincing than the traditionalists as a dramatizer of man's good and evil. Aiken did not escape such difficulties by his attachment to a psychological liberalism that, if anything, supplies even less dramatizable contrast in human affairs. Even if it be true that classical Freudianism "rescues" for us some of what we still possess of the dramatic and the tragic, Aiken has not chosen that line of psychoanalytic thought. He has chosen rather an outlook that deemphasizes contrast between absolute good and absolute evil, and disqualifies traditional hard-line distinctions between passion and action. The more experienced, anguished, and pessimistic version of this viewpoint, with its simultaneous rejection of Greek beliefs in fate, Christian assurance of salvation, and revolutionary expectations of a new social order, is probably to be found in such a Continental writer as Camus. Aiken's version of it, like that of most Americans who espouse it, is not so pessimistic as the European and contains as a major element its radical rejection of two leading American intellectual traditions of the nineteenth century: the earlier Scottish realism, with its inadequate account of the human emotions, and the later Kantianism, with its glowing assurances that the universal law outside of man was reflected in, and reflected, the moral law within him.

Such a world view multiplies the difficulties of the literary artist in his attempt to objectify and dramatize the moral orientation of the characters he is representing. One reason, suggested and developed by the philosopher Maurice Mandelbaum in *The Phenomenology of Moral Experience,* is that in making judgments of the moral worth of fictional characters as well as real people we make a distinction between two situations. One occurs when we make a judgment of an agent's "actional" traits; in this situation we can pass a judgment upon the action without second thoughts about the motive. The other appears when, in passing a judgment upon his action, we dare not dismiss the agent as lacking this or that moral attribute without inquiring into his motives and thus into the history of his relationship to the action. Aiken, in the "symphonies" and in *Punch,* invites us to judge his characters almost entirely in the latter terms and hardly at all in the former. Each character, that is, is like a delinquent standing before a liberal-minded judge: nothing that he has thought or done is to be judged independently of the temperament or disposition he evinces and represents. Aiken, whose true interest is in character and identity rather than personality and ego, achieves by this approach a singular power in the rendering of certain character types. The price of the method is shown, however, by the difficulties Aiken experienced in going from the portrait-poem and lyric to the narrative poem.

Aiken's biggest experiments with the narrative poem came toward the beginning and after the end of his novel-writing years, in *John Deth* (1930) and *The Kid* (1947).

John Deth follows its subtitle, *A Metaphysical Legend,* in being too complex. Inspired in part by the names on an English tombstone and in part by Aiken's Jungian advertence to the idea of mankind's collective dreaming, it draws on medieval myth. Aiken's own commentary on the genesis and the aim of the poem multiplies the difficulties of the piece. Yet it can be read with great enjoyment, as Jay Martin reads it, as a derivation from the dance of death allegories, with a dreamlike persuasiveness and a certain narrative get-up-and-go.

The Kid is Aiken's contribution to the "lyric-epic" tradition that began in the United States with Whitman, was continued by

Crane and Williams, and is also represented in sequences of the later Stevens. In this poem William Blackstone (inexplicable man who was willing to be Boston's first settler) is seen transmogrified into a sequence of American heroes in search of an inner frontier that is related to but not identical with the physical and national frontier to the westward. The poem owes as much to Owen Wister and Theodore Roosevelt as it does to Hart Crane and William Carlos Williams. *The Kid* contains wonderfully sustained passages, concludes with less than the obsessive brilliance of Crane's *The Bridge* or the pawky mythography of Williams' *Paterson*. The truth is that few poems of Aiken's force us to construct their protagonists so fully that we see and hear them ever after. His poems are not intended in this way any more than Ovid's or Spenser's poems are. The most persistently narrative efforts in Aiken's poetic work are aimed at representing an adventurous and problematic pursuit as it is undertaken by an allegorized temperament.

Aiken's definitely mixed accomplishments with narration and dramatization in verse pivot, as has been said, upon the difficulties inherent in moving from a poetic form that achieves a lyrical rendering of a character type whose actions and whose thoughts constantly flow into each other to a poetic form in which a character — since he exists among other characters — must be objectified clearly as someone who actually exists in the viewpoint of those other characters. A better understanding of how this familiar challenge presented itself to Aiken is obtained by examining more closely than we have so far the methods of composition that he employed in the early groundbreaking "symphonies." It can be shown that these methods were largely as successful as they were ingenious — but that they also entrenched habits that exerted a limiting influence upon Aiken's later experiments in narrative.

In those important early long poems that Aiken called "symphonies" the unit next largest to the whole is a section headed by a subtitle (or in some cases by a Roman numeral) that deals pretty much with one emotional tone or one emotional episode. This unit is perhaps the "movement" of the "symphony." The next smaller unit of composition is a group of traditional stanzas separated from their surroundings by an Arabic numeral, or by a space, from similar units before and after it. This unit, in turn, is composed of subsections fairly tightly unified by rhythm and by coterminous grammatical units. These subsections, written generally in lines of end-stopped character, are frequently enough made up of lines in couple, triple, or quadruple formation; each succeeding line undertakes to develop by repetition or variation a theme stated in the opening line. Here are examples of the part-Imagist, part-biblical manner:

> Things mused upon are, in the mind, like music,
> They flow, they have a rhythm, they close and open,
> And sweetly return upon themselves in rhyme.
>> *The Jig of Forslin*, i, 7

> Rain slowly falls in the bitter garden;
> It rains: the streets grow dark.
> The leaves make a sorrowful sound in the hidden garden;
> It rains, and the streets grow cold.
>> *The Charnel Rose*, ii, 2

This crucial smaller unit of Aiken's prosodic and poetic organization which I have called the "subsection" seems to me to be the fundamental building block of most of Aiken's poetry. As it is seen in the early work, it possesses an expressive unity reinforced not only by anaphora and other types of repetition but also by its formation around a unified cluster of sensuous impressions. Within this basic unit Aiken increasingly learned to build up such variations upon imagery that certain other features of its construction pass unnoticed. Of all the figurative devices that Aiken employs, one of his favorites is the substitution of a sign associated with one sense for a sign associated with another sense: synesthesia. Made both famous and fashionable by Baudelaire's sonnet "Correspondences," this device has been exploited by Aiken in ways that are particularly his own. Emphasizing the mutual substitution of the auditory and the visual, he also likes to play the natural and the artificial off against each other. Thus, when he makes reference under the auditory component to a natural sound such as the sound of rain, he likes to make reference under the visual component to something artificial; when he makes reference under the auditory component to an artificial sound, such as the note of a trumpet, he likes to make reference under the visual component to something as natural as the shape of a flower. This is why, for example, the interchange of the visual and the auditory in the opening movement of the title poem from *And in the Hanging Gardens* (1933) speaks for him so typically:

> And in the hanging gardens there is rain
> From midnight until one, striking the leaves
> And bells of flowers, and stroking boles of planes,
> And drawing slow arpeggios over pools,
> And stretching strings of sound from eaves to ferns.

Now the more we read early Aiken the more we notice the single-cast construction of his subsections. But what do single-cast, coupled- and tripled-line structures have to do, even in freely unrhymed fashion, with poems of the kind that Aiken said he wished to write? Is the unconscious so tidy? Would not the movements of the psyche with which Aiken claims to deal render themselves more persuasively in line and sentence arrangements less sweetly formal than this? The dependence on end-stopped clusters of lines in the subsections of the "symphonies" introduces a prosodic formality that forfeits some of the gains made by abandoning formal stanza patterns. Such early critics of Aiken as Blackmur and Winters, it is to be guessed, felt not only an over-smooth, redundant, and even cloying tone in some of Aiken but also this related problem in the prosody of the "symphonies." We can safely say, in any event, that this method and texture is even less adaptable to the requirements of narrative verse than it is to those of the symphonic poem. The reason is that although it may facilitate the force of single-character portraiture by repetition, variation, and expansion, it does not contribute to narrative what narrative needs: the deft introduction to the reader of distinguishable characters and the rapid rendering of events linked to each other in time and in causality.

Clearly a question of language in general, as well as the question of the figurative and prosodic modalities in smaller basic parts of Aiken's poetry, presents itself to us here. It is probably fair to say that during the years of Aiken's greatest poetic productivity a general debate was proceeding on questions of poetic diction. To a large extent the issues were lexical rather than, as they tend to be today, structural. That is to say, the poetic practitioner or critic examining, say, a poem by Robert Frost paid somewhat more attention to the general choice of usage, idiom, and word than to the ways by which Frost deployed the underlying intonational patterns that reinforce the sense of English in order to place his emphasis precisely where he wanted it to be in the line or verse-paragraph. Most discussion of Aiken's "texture" focuses its attention therefore on such lexical questions as his unmodish pleasure in adjectives and his willing dependence upon verbal constructions which had first been made expressive and then stereotyped by the progress of Romantic literary experiment. The point is not an unreasonable one even though it probably has been overemployed as a critique of Aiken's style. Since such observations have been a staple of Aiken criticism for a long time, it is necessary here only to acknowledge them and to suggest that other dimensions of Aiken's language are equally worthy of study: his sentence, for example.

The sentence in which Aiken achieves his cadence is the familiar informal declarative run-on sentence of American speech, made rather more formal in most respects than speech itself — Aiken is as free with the artful and unvernacular flourish ("This is the shape of the leaf and this of the flower") as any poet of his time. Generally, it is his habit to use a fairly loose sentence, adding clause upon clause in an unperiodic structure that follows the pulse of association as waves follow each other to a shore. The grammatical antecedents sometimes grow vague, and a natural accompaniment of this sentence is a good deal of anaphora and echolalia, as if the propulsion of feeling could be renewed from point to point only by associative returns to climaxes previously passed:

> It is morning, Senlin says, and in the morning
> When the light drips through the shutters like the dew,
> I arise, I face the sunrise,
> And do the things my fathers learned to do.

Little in the sentence structure of Aiken achieves a tension between what is carried in a principal clause and what is carried in a subordinate clause. The compound-complex organization, with its emphasis upon the compound, simply takes the form of refined rumination as it reaches the level of speech, adapting itself readily to the compulsive repetition that Aiken emphasizes in his rendering of the movement of human feelings. Anticlimax in this mode of composition is related to the employment of underconnected independent clauses that prevails in Hemingway ("He swung the axe and the chicken was dead") and Eliot ("Six o'clock. / The burnt-out ends of smoky days").

The language Aiken worked out for himself is the result of imitation, intuition, and trial and error. Successful though it is, it is far from being the sophisticated product of a "structural-linguistic" talent such as we find in Cummings and Thomas, remaining by and large at the conventional and lexical level characteristic of American linguistic thinking before, say, Leonard Bloomfield. It is a mistake to take Aiken's own somewhat ponderous comments on the "problem of language" as evidence for a keen philosophical or technically informed sense of the matter. They add little to our understanding and critical attention to them adds even less. The main thing to notice is Aiken's William Jamesian determination to let the thought think itself — and to stand by the consequences of the experiment. In his more ventriloquistic constructions the reader does not always know who is speaking or from what situation or from what context. The separation of the author and the fictional agent and the separation of the situation from the agent's sense of it has little of the clarity with which these matters are represented, in, for example, Frost. Nor are they necessarily intended to. The purpose of Aiken's style as well as of his total construction is to evoke mood and character and not to dramatize. It pictures, and it expatiates upon what has been pictured; and it represents what a character dreamed or wished or hoped as being on somewhat the same level as what he did or had done to him.

It was a tincture of cosmic purple among other things that was responsible for some of the bad reviews Aiken received in the 1920s — and even later, when it had become more frequent to speak of him as being overdetached from social values. It appears that points were sometimes missed about the earlier poems. It will help us to understand this if we go back for a moment to the famous earlier "Discordants" (*Turns and Movies,* 1916):

> Music I heard with you was more than music,
> And bread I broke with you was more than bread;
> Now that I am without you, all is desolate;
> All that was once so beautiful is dead.

The effect of "Discordants" arises partly from a trochaic foot in which the sharpest stresses combined with the highest pitches are placed toward the end of each line, to be reinforced there by the terminal junctures. It also depends upon alliterations and consonances attached to these strong-stressed and high-pitched syllables; and upon the placement toward the line end of most of the consonantal collisions heard in the poem, almost all of them bringing together smoothly a voiced consonant (a consonant requiring the voice box to vibrate, such as "b" contrasted with "p") with another of the same kind. The smoothness of the piece suggested to some that this was about the best that Aiken could do with English prosody — and that perhaps he had "done" too much.

But surely this was grudging praise and Aiken after 1930 forced a gradual reversal of such judgments by the meditative poems of *Preludes for Memnon, Time in the Rock,* and *Brownstone Eclogues.* In these poems he pursued the verbal refinement of all that he had learned before — and much that was new.

This movement away from the quasi-dramatic or narrative is reinforced and enriched by Aiken's gradual discovery of freer variations and part of the excitement of the *Preludes* is our participation in Aiken's finding of new rhythms. The Wagnerian brass line of the earlier poems is transposed for woodwinds; and although the lines are still heavily end-stopped, the freedom and variation seem both effortless and endless as if from a self-renewing source:

> Watch long enough, and you will see the leaf
> Fall from the bough. Without a sound it falls:
> And soundless meets the grass . . . And so you have
> A bare bough, and a dead leaf in dead grass.
>
> *Preludes for Memnon*, XIX

Consider also this section:

> Two coffees in the Español, the last
> Bright drops of golden Barsac in a goblet,
> Fig paste and candied nuts . . . Hardy is dead,
> And James and Conrad dead, and Shakspere dead,
> And old Moore ripens for an obscene grave,
> And Yeats for an arid one; and I, and you —
> What winding sheet for us, what boards and bricks,
> What mummeries, candles, prayers, and pious frauds?
> You shall be lapped in Syrian scarlet, woman,
> And wear your pearls, and your bright bracelets, too,
> Your agate ring, and round your neck shall hang
> Your dark blue lapis with its specks of gold.
> And I, beside you — ah! but will that be?
> For there are dark streams in this dark world, lady,
> Gulf Streams and Arctic currents of the soul;
> And I may be, before our consummation
> Beds us together, cheek by jowl, in earth,
> Swept to another shore, where my white bones
> Will lie unhonored, or defiled by gulls.
>
> *Preludes for Memnon*, II

It should be evident by this point that Aiken speaks in terms of a creed, liberalism, which has been on the defensive among the most inquiring poetic minds of the past two generations. He has written, to be sure, in terms of not classical political economic liberalism but rather the social-psychological liberalism which since the 1880s has rejected that earlier laissez-faire liberalism almost as much as it rejects absolutism. The coherence of creed and art in Aiken is rather more noticeable than it is in many of his contemporaries. Yet Aiken's own vaguenesses as well as the development of psychological doctrine in his own lifetime are probably responsible for some of the oversimplified views of the Freudianism that was a formative element in his art, liberalism, and relativism. It has not yet been said clearly enough that the classical Oedipus complex plays a minor part in his work; that his early interest in the ego and identity as over against the theory of complexes distinguishes his work utterly from the Freudian rhetoric of Robinson Jeffers and Eugene O'Neill; that, despite his interest in characterology, his poems have rarely received the "Freudian reading" that they deserve; that for better or worse (some think better), his Freud approaches the Freud of the "revisionists"; and that despite his reputation as a poet of chaos his work embodies a total, consistent, and normative view of man.

The orientation is visible in the earliest accomplished work. Certain common tones in Pound's "Hugh Selwyn Mauberley" (1915), Aiken's *The Jig of Forslin* (1916), and Eliot's "The Love Song of J. Alfred Prufrock" (1917) remind us of what these writers shared with each other. The central figure of each is a self-involved man out of tune with his warring time and not getting any younger. He is sketched by a method that recalls Browning's dramatic soliloquy while at the same time it deliberately disarranges this form toward impressionistic vagueness and Symbolist mystery. *Forslin*, because it includes a version of the Salome story in its middle passages, invites special attention to that theme. Mallarmé's poem *Hérodiade*, followed by a short tale by Flaubert, a prose poem of Huysmans, a novel by Sudermann, an opera by Strauss, paintings by Moreau, and a verse play by Oscar Wilde, all show a preoccupation with the theme at the century's turn. Developing the vampire figure of Romantic writing, this motif became a flaming fashion during a time when the feminist move-

ment was acquiring respectability and effectiveness and it
touches on the discomfiture of the male in a period when he was
continuing to lose his traditional dominance. Appearing almost
simultaneously in "Prufrock" and *Forslin*, the theme helps us to
understand the differences in the effects of the two poems.

In both poems an analogy is suggested between the absence
of masculine initiative in love and the absence of the ability to
experience, feel, and create. In Eliot's version we see the male
dismissed or even victimized by the female and his own atti-
tude toward her; and the whole relationship is passionately em-
balmed from an ironic and comic point of view. In Aiken's
version we see the female told off by the male in a series of fan-
tasies in which the male counter-anticipates the power of the
female; and the whole relationship is rehearsed from a more or
less melodramatic and pathetic point of view. Just as there is
something like a European *tedium vitae* in the attitude taken
by Eliot toward the battle of the sexes, there is something "con-
trary" and American about Aiken's choice of the other attitude.
Not apart from these perspectives, the reader of today is likely
to feel that Eliot, by going in the direction of ironic and comic
treatment, attained somewhat greater control over his material
than Aiken but also that he played it more or less safe by
taking the myth at its inherited value.

Given these strategic choices that Aiken made when young,
the important thing is that the poetic gifts he brought to them
attained a richer and more controlled form when he was older.
Consider this poem, "Doctors' Row" (in the *Brownstone Ec-
logues* of 1942):

Snow falls on the cars in Doctors' Row and hoods the headlights;
snow piles on the brownstone steps, the basement deadlights;
fills up the letters and names and brass degrees
on the bright brass plates, and the bright brass holes for keys.

Snow hides, as if on purpose, the rows of bells
which open the doors to separate cells and hells:
to the waiting-rooms, where the famous prepare for headlines,
and humbler citizens for their humbler deadlines.

And in and out, and out and in, they go,
the lamentable devotees of Doctors' Row;
silent and circumspect — indeed, liturgical;
their cries and prayers prescribed, their penance surgical.

No one complains — no one presumes to shriek —
the walls are very thick, and the voices weak.
Or the cries are whisked away in noiseless cabs,
while nurse, in the alley, empties a pail of swabs.

Miserable street! — through which your sweetheart hurries,
lowers her chin, as the snow-cloud stings and flurries;
thinks of the flower-stall, by the church, where you
wait like a clock, for two, for half-past two;

thinks of the roses banked on the steps in snow,
of god in heaven, and the world above, below;
widens her vision beyond the storm, her sight
the infinite rings of an immense delight;

all to be lived and loved — O glorious All!
Eastward or westward, Plato's turning wall;
the sky's blue streets swept clean of silent birds
for an audience of gods, and superwords.

Explorations of Aiken led by Blackmur and Tate and later
by Schwartz, Blanshard, Martin, and Hoffman have laid the
foundations for a fuller view of his work. Aiken is the poetic,
less carapaced, side of the American mentality of his genera-
tion that represents itself on the more intellectualized and dis-
cursive side in the confident criticism of Edmund Wilson. As
artist and as man, he displays an affection for the very world
that he attacks for being too distinct a giver of pain, too un-
certain a giver of pleasure, and too monstrous to be grasped by
a divided consciousness. His perception of suffering is not
Christian, or Nietzschean, or tragic, or skeptical, or withdrawing.
It is liberal, ironic, humane, conscious of the discontents that
civilization itself imposes and therefore relativistic and partly
hopeful. It is probably inconsistent for those who emphasize in
Aiken a sympathy for the Freudian formula of the "pathology
of everyday life" to see him as a poet of clear-cut pessimism

about personality or culture. There is to be found in Aiken as well as in Freud the belief that "Where id was, there shall ego be" — enough of a commitment to a rationalistic hope to leave major aspects of Freud's thought and Aiken's poetry this side of tragedy. Of all the themes that Aiken inherits from Freud, he emphasizes the one that is "non-tragic" in the inherited sense of the word, but painful enough in its human meaning: the quietest life, devoid of tragic incident or suffering, is already the victim of the internalized aggression that, in the form of conscience, punishes gratuitously the psyche that it inhabits.

This almost Baudelairian theme of the "heroism of everyday life" was well realized in "Tetélestai," written in 1917, when Aiken was twenty-eight. The title, drawn from the last words of Jesus in John 19:30 ("When Jesus therefore had received the vinegar, he said, It is finished; and he bowed his head, and gave up the ghost"), has the meaning, in John, of fulfillment as well as conclusion. An elegy for the obscure heroes of everyday life, this poem of Aiken's calls up a line like that of Marlowe to decorate the theme that Gray's *Elegy* is remembered for and Whitman himself would have understood:

> How shall we praise the magnificence of the dead,
> The great man humbled, the haughty brought to dust?
> Is there a horn we should not blow as proudly
> For the meanest of us all, who creeps his days,
> Guarding his heart from blows, to die obscurely?
> I am no king, have laid no kingdoms waste,
> Taken no princes captive, led no triumphs
> Of weeping women through long walls of trumpets . . .

Close to forty years later the humanism and the relativism were still there, finding a sparer and pithier form in part IX of the title poem of *A Letter from Li Po* (1955):

> The winds of doctrine blow both ways at once.
> The wetted finger feels the wind each way,
> presaging plums from north, and snow from south.
> The dust-wind whistles from the eastern sea
> to dry the nectarine and parch the mouth.
> The west wind from the desert wreathes the rain

too late to fill our wells, but soon enough,
the four-day rain that bears the leaves away.
Song with the wind will change, but is still song
and pierces to the rightness in the wrong
or makes the wrong a rightness, a delight.
Where are the eager guests that yesterday
thronged at the gate? Like leaves, they could not stay,
the winds of doctrine blew their minds away,
and we shall have no loving-cup tonight.
No loving-cup: for not ourselves are here
to entertain us in that outer year,
where, so they say, we see the Greater Earth.
The winds of doctrine blow our minds away,
and we are absent till another birth.

There can be little doubt that Aiken's independence of the neoclassicism brought in by such men as Hulme and Eliot and his equal independence of the automatic Marxisms of the 1930s were costly to his vogue. Nor did the New Criticism find his work congenial to explication, an activity that could have made it more well known than it has been to university students of recent decades. One result, quite apart from the matter of his fame in general, is that much remains to be understood about the interaction of Aiken and his time. It is not merely that he has still to receive due credit for the concerned, cosmopolitan, and equable attitudes he displayed toward the nightmare issues and events of social politics in the last fifty years. It is also that his art, with its manifold sources in American rebellion and European sophistication, is worthy of even fuller exploration than it has received.

The anonymous writer of the lead article in the London *Times Literary Supplement* of April 19, 1963, credited Aiken with being original in advance of his time and the possessor of a cosmic sense that outsoars Eliot and Pound. The writer continued: "Increasingly poetry has become a way of writing, not a way of thinking. Yet not to like Aiken (or Shelley, of course) is a confession of not being capable of thinking in poetic terms; that is to say with the whole consciousness."

Aiken has created a fluent and colorful picturization of man learning to enjoy and realize himself. The process is conceived of as a response to a universal challenge, first in the sense that the ancestral gods are against enjoyment and ultimately in the sense that enjoyment leads to a need to transcend itself. The poetic art in which he embodies this view of life is Indian in its luxuriance, repetition, and decoration. It stands over against the sparer poetic line that has won much of the lip service as well as some of the practice of the more influential poets since Hulme and Pound made their voices felt half a century ago. The energetic profusion of Aiken has a masculine bouquet that allies him more closely with Yeats and Tate than with most of his contemporaries. Aiken, as they say, has written lines below his own best level and was thoughtful enough in his *Selected Poems* of 1961 to anthologize himself at his best. His lifelong performance in a luxuriant style is not only one of the strongest testaments to the power of his youthful insights but also the preserver of a tradition whose vitality, we should be glad to say, he has helped to pass on.

E. E. Cummings

O BEDIENT to the world spirit of change, in the early decades of the twentieth century a group of notable poets, by diverging from traditional practices, transformed American poetry. The most thorough "smasher of the logicalities" among them was a transcendentalist: one who views nature as a state of becoming rather than as a stasis and who believes that the imaginative faculty in man can perceive the natural world directly. He was also a troubadour who said: "enters give/ whose lost is his found/ leading love/ whose heart is her mind." He was not only poet but novelist, playwright, and painter. In following his vision he roused hostility in academic critics and readers, apparently repelled by his idiosyncratic typographical and stylistic devices, but he was from the beginning admired by his fellow innovators, William Carlos Williams, Marianne Moore, Ezra Pound, and T. S. Eliot — and eventually he won the esteem of his critics.

"I am someone," remarked E. E. Cummings late in his career, "who proudly and humbly affirms that love is the mystery-of-mysteries . . . that 'an artist, a man, a failure' is . . . a naturally and miraculously whole human being . . . whose only happiness is· to transcend himself, whose every agony is to grow." In a world oriented to dehumanized power, transcendentalism is a synonym for absurdity. Cummings recognized this early. In an address at his Harvard commencement in 1915, he had said, "we are concerned with the natural unfolding of sound tendencies. That the conclusion is, in a particular case, *absurdity*, does not in any way impair the value of the experiment, so long as we are dealing with sincere effort." The manifesto he issued then was that of one man to himself. He would experiment, and he would not fear being absurd; he would use the absurdity principle to the limit of its usefulness. As he worked at his trade of wordsmith, the implications of what he had said in 1915 were clarified in a remarkable stream of poems. From the start he used absurdity to leaven the commonplace, to startle readers into "listening" instead of merely hearing. In his later years he discovered a new significance in the concept: experimental living and the practice of his craft had redefined absurdity; it came to mean the truth of earthly living and a promise of eternity.

Edward Estlin Cummings, son of the Reverend Edward Cummings (lecturer at Harvard and Unitarian minister) and of Rebecca Haswell Clarke Cummings, was born at Cambridge, Massachusetts, on October 14, 1894. His parents had been brought together by their mutual friend William James. Dr. Cummings was a woodsman, a photographer, an actor, a carpenter, an artist — and talented in all that he undertook. Mrs. Cummings was a shy woman who overcame conventional influences to respond joyously and effectively to life. The son was educated in public schools and at Harvard University where he received an A.B., *magna cum laude*, and an M.A. for English and classical studies.

While Cummings was in graduate school he helped to found the Harvard Poetry Society. He and some of his friends in the society put together *Eight Harvard Poets* (published in 1917). In it, by a printer's error, according to one story, Cummings' name and the "I's" as well were set in lowercase letters. He seized upon this as a device congenial to him and later had "e. e. cummings" legalized as the signature to his poems.

After Harvard, Cummings went to New York. In this city he

held his first and only job, three months with P. F. Collier & Son, Inc., mail-order booksellers. He was twenty-one at the time. In mid-1917 he went to France to serve as a volunteer ambulance driver. There he was interned for a minor military offense — what happened was that he refused to say he hated Germans; instead, with typical Cummings care for precision, he repeated: "I like the French." From his experiences at La Ferté Macé (a detention camp) he accumulated material for his documentary "novel," *The Enormous Room* (1922), one of the best war books by an American.

Upon his release, he returned to the United States, but when the war ended he went back to Paris — this time to study art. He made the acquaintance of the poet Louis Aragon and of Picasso and their circle of poets and painters; he became friendly with many visiting writers such as Archibald MacLeish and Ezra Pound. On arriving back in New York in 1924 he found himself a celebrity — for his documentary novel and for *Tulips and Chimneys* (1923), his first book of poems. The next year he won the *Dial* Award for "distinguished service to American Letters." A roving assignment from *Vanity Fair* in 1926 permitted him to go abroad again, where he established a routine he was to follow most of his life: he painted in the afternoons and wrote at night.

From his experiences in the two cities he loved, New York and Paris, came the material for scintillating or extravagant essays on burlesque, the circus, modern art, and the foibles of the day, later collected into *A Miscellany* (1958) and *A Miscellany, Revised* (1965). He wrote forewords to books and brochures for art exhibits, and he sold sketches and paintings. Three volumes of poetry appeared in quick succession: *&* (*And*) and *XLI Poems* in 1925, *Is 5* in 1926. The play *Him*, a phantasmagoria in 21 scenes, which was a forerunner of what is now called the Theater of the Absurd, was published in 1927 and produced by the Provincetown Players in 1928 and was acclaimed by avant-garde critics. In 1931 he published a collection of drawings and paintings, *CIOPW*, which took its title from the initial letters of the materials used: charcoal, ink, oil, pencil, watercolor. In that same year came *W* (*ViVa*), a thick book of poems. A travel journal published in 1933, *Eimi* (I Am), recorded his revulsion against an even more "enormous room" than the military detention camp: the collectivized Soviet Union.

After 1930, although Cummings continued to travel abroad, he divided most of his time between a studio apartment in Greenwich Village, at 4 Patchin Place, and the family farm at Silver Lake, New Hampshire. This yearly contact with New England soil occasioned one of his finest poem-portraits: "rain or hail/sam done/ the best he kin/ till they digged his hole." A similar earthy wisdom is in a poem that may be a comment on himself: "my specialty is living said/ a man(who could not earn his bread/ because he would not sell his head)."

Because he had in common with T. S. Eliot not only a New England Unitarian background but also cosmopolitan traits, it is stimulating to observe the differences between them. Eliot became a British citizen. Cummings, responding to French art, always admiring the French civilization, nonetheless spent most of his life in the United States. He was a goldfinch needing a native tree to sing from. Through the years, from his perch, he continued to pour forth his songs: *No Thanks* (1935), *50 Poems* (1940), *1 x 1* (*One Times One*, 1944), *Xaipe* (1950). A *Collected Poems* appeared in 1938. The ballet *Tom* was published in 1935 and the plays *Anthropos* and *Santa Claus* were published in 1944 and 1946.

Honors and rewards came with frequency — now. In 1950, for "great achievement," he was given the Fellowship of the Academy of American Poets. In 1952 he was invited to give the Norton Lectures at Harvard (published as *I: Six Nonlectures* in 1953), an urbane but lively analysis of the Cummings quest to discover "Who as a writer am I?" These lectures could have been subtitled "And who as a person are you?" because — like Walt Whitman with his phrases addressed to future generations who would cross on Brooklyn Ferry — Cummings was always reaching out from the persona, the neutral "i," to the "you" out there. In 1955 he received a special citation from the National Book Awards for

Poems 1923–1954 (1954) and in 1957 he received both the Bollin-
gen Prize for Poetry and the Boston Arts Festival Poetry Award.
A year later the last of his poetry collections to appear during
his lifetime was published, *95 Poems*. Cummings the painter was
also honored: he had one-man shows in 1944 and 1949 at the
American-British Art Centre, and in 1945 and 1959 at the Ro-
chester Memorial Gallery. His wide-ranging interest in the visual
arts was reflected in *Adventures in Value* (1962) on which he
collaborated with his third wife, photographer Marion More-
house.

Cummings died on September 3, 1962, in New Hampshire. He
left a manuscript of poetry published the following year as *73
Poems*.

"The artist's country is inside him," said Cummings. This
was another way of saying that he would abide only by the laws
of his own mind. His formalities — the literary devices he devel-
oped — were intended to show how the outer appearance rein-
forces the inner vision. His disordered syntax and typographical
disarrangements were intended, not to bewilder, but to heighten
the understanding. He described what he was trying to do in the
1926 Foreword to *Is 5*: "my theory of technique, if I have one, is
very far from original; nor is it complicated. I can express it in
fifteen words, by quoting The Eternal Question And Immortal
Answer of burlesk, viz. 'Would you hit a woman with a child? —
No, I'd hit her with a brick.' Like the burlesk comedian, I am
abnormally fond of that precision which creates movement." One
of his methods to achieve this was tmesis (the separation of parts
of words by intervening words). It became almost like a signature
for him. As Karl Shapiro put it in his *Essay on Rime*, Cummings
was concerned with the "Integers of the word, the curve of
'e',/ Rhythm of 'm', astonishment of 'o'/ And their arranged
derangement." By the analysis of words into their parts, both
syllables and individual letters, and by considered use of space
and punctuation marks, as well as by "arranged derangement,"
Cummings hoped to extend meaning beyond traditional limits.

Cummings used space in his typographical rhetoric to indicate
tempo of reading: single words may have spaces within them to
force the reader to weigh each syllable, as in "can dy lu/ minous";
or words may be linked, as in "eddieandbill," to convey the act
of boys running. A comma may be used where a period is ex-
pected, within a poem or at the end of it, to produce a pause for
the reader to imagine what the next action might be. Or commas,
colons, and semicolons may be used within a word to arouse new
sensations and intuitions. In examining the poem beginning "as
if as" (*No Thanks*) the reader disentangles from the typography
the idea that it is a poem about sunrise. But it is not like other
accounts of sunrise, nor, probably, does it reflect the reader's own
experience. Toward the end of the poem the word "itself" is
fractured into "it:s;elf." The "s" suggests the sun as well as the
viewer. "Elf," relating to an earlier phrase, "moon's al-down," is
a hint, in this instance, of the supernatural impact of dawn. The
daily sun is no longer a habit but a miracle. In a later work
(Number 48 in *73 Poems*), the word "thrushes" is divided into
"t,h;r:u;s,h;e:s" so that the reader may perceive, with the poet,
the individual sleepy birds gripping a branch at moonrise and, by
implication, the transcendental relationship between all living
things. Of the exclamation point beginning the first poem in
50 Poems, "!blac," Cummings himself said that it might be called
an emphatic "very"; the unpronounceable "?" and ")" are often
similarly used. To focus the reader's attention a capital letter may
be thrust into the middle of a word. In the opening poem of
No Thanks capitals are used to imitate the roundness of the
moon and to imply the eternity of the circle:

> mOOn Over tOwns mOOn
> whisper
> less creature huge grO
> pingness

In "i will be" (*And*) the word "SpRiN,k,LiNg" is manipulated to
make a visual representation of sunlight filtering through wing
feathers. In this poem, too, a parenthesis is used in the middle of

the word "wheeling" to place simultaneously before the reader's mind the flutter of the pigeons and their effect on the sunlight:

> whee(:are,SpRiN,k,LiNg an in-stant with sunLight
> t h e n)l -
> ing . . .

Cummings made varied use of parentheses: for an interpolated comment or to split or combine words as a guide to his thought. Frequently they occur, in poem-parables, to clarify the relationship between two sentences that run simultaneously through the poem. In "go(perpe)go," published in *No Thanks*, we have a typical Cummings juxtaposition. The parenthetical sentence is a surrealist collection of "perpetual adventuring particles" describing the action of a disturbed ant heap and an anteater getting his dinner. The sentence outside the parenthesis, "go to the ant, thou anteater," is an allusion to Proverbs 6:6: "Go to the ant, thou sluggard." The poem is description and social comment, disguised as a joke. Critic Norman Friedman analyzed it succinctly: "Cummings is satirizing a certain kind of worldly and prudential wisdom. The ant's activity represents for Cummings merely busy work rather than a model of industry, and he who is advised to 'go to the ant' is the one creature who can possibly profit from such a visit — the anteater. In thus reducing the proverb to its simply 'realistic' aspects — by refusing to make the metaphorical transference intended — Cummings deflates the whole implied point of view."

Some of Cummings' poems utilize the "visual stanza" in which lines are arranged in reference, not to rhyme and meter, but to a shape reflecting the poet's thought. This kind of typographical design, with poems contrived in the form of roses, diamonds, and hourglass figures, was in fashion during the Elizabethan age and continued to be used in the seventeenth century. With changes in taste and technical practice in the last two centuries, this device fell into disuse, although it has been revived occasionally as when Lewis Carroll used it for his mouse's "long and sad tale." More recently it appeared in the *Calligrammes* of Guillaume

Apollinaire and in the "quaint" patterning of Dylan Thomas'
poem "Vision and Prayer." However, the visual appearance of
Cummings' poems can be largely accounted for by his interest
in contemporary art forms, rather than by influence from other
writers. From artists like Picasso who were bringing new vitality
to painting, he learned the effectiveness of distorting lines and
reshaping masses; and he juxtaposed words as they did the pig-
ments (in John Peale Bishop's apt phrasing) — to bring perception
of things into sharper focus. Cummings specifically disclaimed any
stylistic influence from Apollinaire's mimetic typography, and as
Gorham B. Munson observed very early, Cummings' typographi-
cal design, unlike that of the *Calligrammes*, reinforces the literary
content of his poems. Some of Cummings' poems are designed to
be read vertically; in others, stanzaic structures are balanced for
mass, as are certain colors in painting. Effective examples of Cum-
mings' use of the visual stanza are the poem "!blac" and the
ironic dedication to *No Thanks,* which lists in the shape of a
wineglass all the publishers who had rejected the manuscript. In
XLI Poems there is a poem, "little tree," that visually suggests a
Christmas tree, and another that on the page resembles smoke
puffing out of a locomotive:

>   the
>   sky
>   was
>   can dy lu
>   minous

Another important device by which Cummings intended to
enlarge the reader's comprehension was word coinage. He kept
already existing root words, joining to them new affixes. In such
compounded words the prefixes are familiar enough, but his use
of the suffixes *-ly, -ish, -est, -ful* and adverbs (such as *less*) in un-
expected combinations, a dimension natural to classical and
romance languages, produces in English an intensifying of per-
ception. Introduce one or two of these words — *riverly, nowly,
downwardishly, birdfully, whichful, girlest, skylessness, onlying,
laughtering,* etc. — into a verse of recognizable words and the

reader has to explore possibilities in a creative way. In reading creatively a phrase like "on stiffening greenly air" he will cross the threshold of transcendence. Articles and particles were rearranged by Cummings for the same purpose — "some or if where." One part of speech may be used for another as in the first line of a much-anthologized poem from *And*, "Spring is like a perhaps hand." The charm of this line is due in large part to the use of an adverb where an adjective is expected, to emphasize the tentative nature of springtime. This is reinforced by an image of the window dresser who moves things and changes things "without breaking anything," in contrast to the destructions of winter.

In all of these ways Cummings broke language from its conventionalized mold; it became a nourishing soil through which "faces called flowers float out of the ground" (*Xaipe*). Cummings' virtuosity was directed to capture in words what the painter gets on canvas and what children, violently alive in response to objects and seasons, display in their street games. His poems are alive on the page, as he told the printer when he instructed him not to interfere with the "arrangement." Any change would be an injury to living tissue. In discontinuous poems he tried to pin down the "illuminated moment," to ransom from oblivion the fleeting present, in words seasonal, contemporary, and timeless — like a writer of haiku. To get at the realities, Cummings smashed the logicalities, an idea in harmony with Oriental art and philosophy, with which he had acquaintance as shown by a quotation from the Tao that appears near the end of *Eimi*: "he who knoweth the eternal is comprehensive . . . therefore just; just, therefore a king; a king, therefore celestial; celestial, therefore in Tao; in Tao, therefore enduring." Cummings' perpetual concern with transcendental ideas led to the shining leaps on the page that make his work unique.

One needs to remember, however, that this innovating poet was practiced in conventional Western literary tradition. The young Cummings learned from Elizabethan song and eighteenth-century satire, as well as from the Pindaric ode. He was rooted in

the same soil as Thoreau, Emerson, and Emily Dickinson. Inter-
mittently he read Aeschylus, Homer, and the French trouba-
dours — as evidenced by his quotations in the *Six Nonlectures*. He
cut his literary teeth on the strict rules of villanelle, roundel, and
ballade royale. Nonetheless his genius led him to quite different
patterns: a poem in *ViVa*, for example, records phonetically not
only a conversation but a revelation of the hearts of lost men:
"oil tel duh woil doi sez/dooyah unnurs tanmih eesez pullih
nizmus tash,oi/dough un giv uh shid oi sez. Tom." The emphasis
is deliberate and made with care.

Cummings said that Josiah Royce (who appears in one of the
poem-portraits) directed his attention to Dante Gabriel Rossetti,
especially to Rossetti's sonnets, and that made him a sonneteer.
Certainly Cummings wrote some of the finest sonnets of our
century: celebrating love, savagely ridiculing human stupidity,
and recording his pilgrimage to the transcendental. From the
somewhat conventional, Cummings' sonnets developed, as Theo-
dore Spencer has said, to achieve "specific gravity." Yet the only
discernible influence of the Pre-Raphaelite school is in the early
lyrics and might as easily have been been picked up direct from
a reading of the sonnets of Dante. There is internal evidence that
Shakespeare was the dynamic influence in his sonnet-making:
sensory details, the absence of hypocrisy, even the rhythm of the
snap at the end, as in a couplet from "being to timelessness as
it's to time" in *95 Poems*: " — do lovers love?Why then to heaven
with hell./Whatever sages say and fools,all's well." In an inter-
view with Harvey Breit in 1950 Cummings said: "Today so-called
writers are completely unaware of the thing which makes art
what it is. You can call it nobility or spirituality, but I should
call it intensity. Sordid is the opposite. . . . Shakespeare is never
sordid . . . because his poetry was the most intense."

Cummings' experimentation was clearly within Western liter-
ary tradition, as was Eliot's, but, finally, whatever he did resulted
in poems that could not have been written by anyone else. He has
had no successful imitators. And because of its nature Cummings'

work cannot be held within the bounds of conventional literary analysis. The critic must stretch his own powers to find the significant new insights waiting to be revealed by this poet's language in action. What is required is "intelligence functioning at intuitional velocity" — Cummings used the phrase to characterize a work of the sculptor Lachaise but it admirably describes the approach a perceptive critic-reader must take to Cummings' writing.

For a study of Cummings' philosophy and of his devices to achieve art in motion and at a peak of excitement, the play *Him*, called by the critic Edmund Wilson "the outpouring of an intelligence, a sensibility, and an imagination of the very first dimension," is especially useful.

The action is divided between "exterior" and "interior" happenings that develop the love story of a man and the predicament of an artist. The satirical exterior scenes are presented before a garish curtain like that used in carnival shows. The deliberate lack of a third dimension is one of the poet's "absurdities"; it symbolizes the "unworld." The curtain and the parodies of circus and burlesque in the play's action reflect his interest in folk amusements. The interior scenes explore the psyche of the creative temperament. Connecting the two phases is the chorus: the three Fates, Atropos, Clotho, Lachesis. They are disguised as the Misses Weird and are nicknamed "Stop," "Look," and "Listen." They sit with their backs to the audience, rocking and knitting, as they swap a nonsensical version of backfence talk and advertising slogans. The stage directions integrate the themes and devices of the play.

In the complex design of *Him*, described by one commentator as "a play of lucid madness and adventurous gaiety," Cummings sets up a confrontation: man, a social being, versus the artist. In the *Six Nonlectures* he repeats: "Nobody else can be alive for you; nor can you be alive for anybody else. . . . There's the artist's responsibility . . ." Yeats knew this human instinct to fulfill strenuous conditions for the sake of an ideal: writing of the Irish playwright J. M. Synge, he said, ". . . to come out from under the shadow of other men's minds . . . to be utterly oneself: that is all the Muses care for." At first glance Yeats's statement seems callous but when it is illustrated in the creative life it leads to service for the community. In the poems beginning "i sing of Olaf glad and big" (*ViVa*) and "a man who had fallen among thieves" (*Is 5*), Cummings is urging awake the sleeping conscience of his fellows. And in *Him* Cummings develops a metaphor, found with varying emphasis in his poetry, that strikingly illustrates his view. The artist is likened to a circus performer who sits astride three chairs stacked one on top of the other and balanced on a high wire. He explains to his lover, "Me," that the three chairs are three facts: "I am an Artist, I am a Man, I am a Failure."

The label on the top chair, "Failure," is disconcerting but acceptable when the reader becomes familiar with the paradoxes of Cummings' vocabulary. To distinguish true accomplishment from the disappointing successes of the salesman-politician-warmongering world, he uses words that for him state the ultimate emptiness of the prizes the crowd pursues and often captures. Throughout Cummings' poems occur the words *failure, nothing, nobody, zero,* and the prefixes *non-* and *un-*. They are also scattered through the prose of *The Enormous Room* and *Eimi*. By these negatives he separated his ideals from the pleasures of a conformist world and showed his condemnation of "mobs" and "gangs" and his concern for the individual. The phrase "you and i" dominates his response to relationships: lovers, mother and child, a man and a city, a man and a tree.

The other two "chairs" of *Him* have a subordinate but vital function in the metaphor. The experiences of the man are limited to the senses until they are fused with the perceptions of the artist. It is from the artist and his transcendental realizations that the reader or viewer learns to distinguish the genuine from the pinchbeck. The artist is also dependent on the report from his five senses to actualize his ideas. So Cummings found spiritualities in "facts" and celebrated them in his poems of love and compassion. The significance that Cummings assigned to "failure" is further evident in a sonnet from *Is 5*, "if i have made, my lady, intricate/imperfect various things . . ." And a study of the Foreword to *Is 5* will reveal affirmations of the themes of *Him*: that the poet knows he is "competing" with reality and therefore "failure" is predestined. What is increasingly noticeable in the play and in the volumes of poems that follow it is the changing concept of love and the frank presentation of the artist's self-doubt. He insists on finding out who he is before he can be either artist or lover. Cummings' belief that the artist's total attentiveness to an object or subject should result in simultaneity for his audience — which was also the aim of the Imagist movement in poetry and of Cubism in painting — was not completely realizable. He therefore began to think of art as a series of mirrors reflecting the "object" in various lights and not as the thing-in-itself. So, with a sense of the "awful responsibility" of the poet, he regarded his extraordinary successes in putting on the page a flying bird, a grasshopper, a falling leaf as "failures" and called himself a nonhero.

The falling leaf poem is the first of the *95 Poems*. It is not a complete sentence and there are only four words. The form has the narrowness of a needle. In a time when novels tell no story and music is not melodic — relatively speaking — this pictogram brings new insights, which have been perceptively set forth by Norman Friedman and Barry A. Marks in their critical studies of Cummings; their lead is followed here.

l(a

le
af
fa

ll

s)
one
l

iness

Each of the first four lines has but one consonant and one
vowel: two *l*'s, three *a*'s, one *e*, and two *f*'s. This suggests the
fluttering pattern of a falling leaf. The next line, treated as a
stanza, is a double *l*, extending meaning as the reader waits for
the necessary completion. The poem ends on a shifting note which
accentuates the import of "alone," "one," and "oneliness" (de-
fined as "own").

The mind of the reader seizes the two ideas: loneliness and the
parenthetical interjection of the fall of a leaf. In splitting "loneli-
ness" Cummings shows by variations on a word blurred by indis-
criminate use that it is, as Marks noted, "quite a singular word."
Cummings strips the sheath from the ordinary, and the extraordi-
nary is revealed. The "le/af/fa/ll" involves both sound and
visual values; the musical relation echoes the meaning emerging
from "le" and "af."

The *l* in "leaf" repeats the first *l* in "loneliness" and helps the
reader keep in mind simultaneously the material inside and out-
side the parentheses. His old typewriter played an important role
here in Cummings' idea of form as it affects thought: in the first
line *l* can be either the digit "one" or the letter "el." A parenthe-
sis separating it from *a* suggests that while the idea of doubling
up on "oneness" is attractive, it is not plausible. Following the
trail of the parenthesis, the reader discovers a "verse" that rein-
forces the necessity that *l* be "el" in the fourth stanza. The word
"one" and an apparent digit reflect back to the initial *l* and in
their interplay the digit vanishes into the letter.

The reader is pleased with his success in working out the
"puzzle"; casually he has participated in the dance of the poet's
mind. Then he arrives at the last line, "iness." The isolation and
the desolation of the individual, the I alone with the I, be it a leaf
or a man, have been established. Forgotten are the secondary ideas
of oneness with the universe or the intimations of autumn: the
reader now knows he has misunderstood the form if he accepted
it as a needle stitching together all created things. However, as
Henry James asserted by implication in *The Wings of the Dove*,
the tragic element is art and art is delight. Yet another idea is

added to the possibles of interpretation: man's unhappy isolation
comes from self-loving activities and trivial goals. Self-forgetful-
ness is the reward of the disciplined athlete and of the artist, with
the result an unblemished performance. The ever-evolving de-
vices of Cummings are a witness to his profoundly moral nature
in conflict with an imperfect world, and to his vision that it
could be perfected.

The "puzzle" of the following lines from *No Thanks* is simi-
larly rewarding to the reader willing to work it out:

r-p-o-p-h-e-s-s-a-g-r
          who

a)s w(e loo)k
upnowgath
     PPEGORHRASS
                  eringint(o-
aThe):l
   eA
    !p:
  s   a

The poet, through spacings of word and letter and the unortho-
dox use of capitals, presents a grasshopper living in his muscles.
At first he is invisible, coming from the grass to us only in the
sounds reverberating from earth or pebbles. But as Lloyd Frank-
enberg pointed out in his study of modern poetry, *Pleasure
Dome*: "These sounds — some soft, some loud, some intermit-
tent — are rearrangements of his name; just as he rearranges
himself to rub forewing and hind leg together. Then he 'leaps!'
clear so that we see him, 'arriving to become, rearrangingly, grass-
hopper.'" The reader has been, briefly, the grasshopper and that
has extended his capacity for being alive. Note that in this poem
Cummings used a device resembling Cubistic painting: "r-p-o-p-h-
e-s-s-a-g-r" and "PPEGORHRASS" and ".gRrEaPsPhOs" (which
appears after the lines quoted above) record the "realization" of
experiences that he wished to share with his readers.

In other poems which demonstrate his delight in the natural
world, Cummings often used mimicry. Cummings had a talent
like that of the Greek comic playwright Aristophanes, who in his
oft-quoted line "Brekekekéx koáx koáx" sought to reproduce the

sound of frogs. A similar mimicry is found in such unlikely Cummings poems as the colloquial "buncha hardboil guys from duh A.C. fulla" (*ViVa*) and "joggle i think will do it although the glad" (*Tulips and Chimneys*). In a punning poem, "applaws)" (*One Times One*), the "paw" is a kind of mimicry and a reminder that fundamentally we are animals.

Another aspect of the "creaturely" life that interested Cummings is to be found in his poems about horses, those animals now vanishing from sight, except in parades or circuses. In the lines below from a poem in *No Thanks* the scene is set by "crazily seething of this/ raving city screamingly street." What opens the windows to be "sharp holes in dark places" is the light from flowers. And what do the "whichs" and "small its," the half-alive, half-asleep people see?

> what a proud dreamhorse pulling(smoothloomingly)through
> (stepp)this(ing)crazily seething of this
> raving city screamingly street wonderful
>
> flowers And o the Light thrown by Them opens
>
> sharp holes in dark places paints eyes touches hands with new-
> ness and these startled whats are a(piercing clothes thoughts kiss
> -ing wishes bodies)squirm-of-frightened shy are whichs small
> its hungry for Is for Love Spring thirsty for happens
> only and beautiful

Through the raucous sounds of a city street a horse is pulling a load of flowers. In that setting his movements have a grace such as is found in dreams. The horse establishes his reality as we watch him "stepp . . . ing" — the poet has plowed with horses his family's fields; he has watched milk wagons in the city. However, as Lloyd Frankenberg has suggested, the horse, "whose feet almost walk air," brings to mind Pegasus. That wingèd steed of the Muses is associated in legend with Hippocrene, the fountain of inspiration, which supposedly sprang from the earth at a blow from his forehoof. In one legend the Greek hero Bellerophon, with the aid of Pegasus, slew the Chimaera, a ravaging beast. Then he tried to fly to heaven, thereby offending the gods, and fell to earth. A poet is often trying to fly and often he fails. So we come back to the name that Cummings gave himself, "non-hero."

In another city sonnet, from *And* ("my sonnet is A light goes on in"), we meet the dray horses that sleep upstairs in a tenement stable. "Ears win-/ k funny stable. In the morning they go out in pairs." Implied in the poet's words is the ancient horse sacrifice to the sun, to encourage the sun to rise again. So the sonnet comes to a climax on a line of life and beauty: "They pull the morning out of the night." There is the same fidelity to sensory perception in poems that include references to rain: "the rain's/ pearls singly-whispering" (from "the moon is hiding in," *Tulips and Chimneys*) and "i have found what you are like/ the rain" (*And*).

The opening lines of an early poem, from *Tulips and Chimneys*, show both Cummings' delight in the natural world and his ability to respond freshly to it:

> stinging
> gold swarms
> upon the spires
> silver
>
> chants the litanies the
> great bells are ringing with rose
> the lewd fat bells

The poet avoided the obvious ideas that cluster around the subject of sunset: the timeworn meanings of silver and gold are freshened by the adroit combination of "stinging" and "swarms"; sound and image suggest the flight of a young queen and the creation of a new hive. "Spires" is echoed later in the poem in the phrase "a tall wind," and the poem concludes with an image of a dreamy sea. In an experiment Laura Riding and Robert Graves converted the pattern of this poem, the last part of which imitates a retreating wave, into conventional stanzas and concluded, rightly, that in the process the significance as well as the poetry was lost.

Informed critics, among them Barry A. Marks and the poet William Carlos Williams, have directed attention to "nonsun blob a" as probably the most difficult of Cummings' poems and yet as one containing very useful clues for the reader. It has a regularity of stanza, an Elizabethan tone, and a simplicity that might place it among the poet's charming verses for children. However, it offers a severe challenge to the mind: to put away old habits of associative thinking and to examine each stanza, line by line and word by word, for the relationships the poet has evoked. It also sums up Cummings' innovations and ideas to a remarkable degree. The emphasis Cummings himself placed upon it is evident in its position as the opening poem of the volume *One Times One.*

> nonsun blob a
> cold to
> skylessness
> sticking fire
>
> my are your
> are birds our all
> and one gone
> away the they
>
> leaf of ghosts some
> few creep there
> here or on
> unearth

Here the senses become elements of thought and the emotions are objectified to an extreme degree. The first stanza has neither verb nor expected sequences nor is it broken up to be reassembled, like an anagram. Each word compresses experiences from years of winter days; it is demanded of the reader that he be alert at all points so he may follow the clues in this celebration of bare, daunting specifics of a northern winter. Look at a winter sky: sunlessness is its chief characteristic but there is a gray waver, a "blob," sending out an almost invisible shine. The closing line, "sticking fire" — in which some critics observe a sexual connotation — brings into focus a dumb fear of being lost in a glacial world and paradoxically suggests all the physical and moral efforts to bring life-giving warmth to man, from Prometheus to nuclear industrial activities.

As we move on to a consideration of the second stanza, an

observation made by Marks in his *E. E. Cummings* is especially illuminating. He noted: "the words of the first two lines . . . form two mathematical equations. One says, 'my + your = our.' The other, based on the phonetic pun, 'our' and 'are,' says, 'my = your'; 'my + your = birds'; 'my + your + birds = all.'" Intimations of what concerned Cummings — that the nature of unity is love — occur in the merging of the possessive pronouns: "mine" into "yours" into "ours" into "all." This unity is felt on repeated readings of the poem. But a Cummings poem is always in motion; the second stanza ends with the unity destroyed, the bird flock scattered in quest of a vanished leader.

The "a" which ends the first line of the poem is significant for an understanding of the third stanza. In its isolation it is related to autumn leaves creeping like crippled birds on a cold earth as indifferent as the cold sky recorded in the third stanza. Unfriendliness deprives the earth of its nourishing function; therefore Cummings used the prefix *un-* to modify the word *earth*. What is to be made of a typical Cummings inversion: "leaf of ghosts"? A remnant of birds or leaves in the increasing cold is described in the first stanza; later, birds reduced to creeping are non-birds, and cold earth is heartless as cold sky; both environments when deprived of their function as givers and nourishers, and therefore of their reality, are also ghosts. What Henry James called "perception at the pitch of passion" is involved in this "circular" poem. The implication is that of Greek tragedy: the helplessness of the alive, be it leaf or bird or a man and a woman. Yet there is joy in the contemplation of the real: a sun so clouded it may have burned out centuries ago; the relationship between the afflicted birds, leaves, and lovers — and the reader of the poem. Cummings, keeping his agonies to himself, nearly always ends on a note of joy.

This poem in twelve lines anticipates the essence of the nine stanzas of a later poem, "rosetree,rosetree" (*95 Poems*). The last stanza of "rosetree,rosetree" tells us again what the poet believes and hopes for:

> lovetree!least the
> rose alive must three,must

> four and(to quite become
> nothing)five times,proclaim
> fate isn't fatal
> —a heart her each petal

The reader may wonder why this master of experimental form chose rhymed stanzas for this piece. It is another instance of Cummings' sensitivity to choice among the formalities — an Elizabethan song brimming with transcendental ideas although the rose is a literal rose in a sizzle of bees. Traditional form attracts simple ideas: tree-bird, mob-war, flower-death-love. In this poem it serves as a counterweight to the complex ideas of a mystic, the poet "dreaming-true." Norman Friedman in a reasoned study of 175 worksheets of "rosetree,rosetree," rescued by Marion Morehouse Cummings from the usual destruction of preliminary work, reveals Cummings as a craftsman perfecting his materials over a long period of time. Throughout the fifty-four lines of the poem — in the adjustment of negative to positive, the victory in the final stanza over darkness and fatality — the cerebral element is always in play.

A poem that relates to this one — by melodic form and a transformation of abstracts so that they are vivid images — is the remarkable "what if a much of a which of a wind" (*One Times One*). Its rhythm perhaps reflects the influence of a ballad (attributed to Thomas Campion) which begins with "What if a day or a month or a year." But there the similarity ends. In the Cummings poem we have a deeply felt comment on the plight of universal life — nature and man — communicated by pairs of opposites: "gives the truth to summer's lie"; "when skies are hanged and oceans drowned,/ the single secret will still be man." In this "song" there are combinations that are reminiscent of Cummings' intriguing phrase "the square root of minus one" which he employed in at least three different contexts, notably in the Introduction to his *Collected Poems* where he wrote: "Mostpeople have less in common with ourselves than the square-rootofminusone." When he says, "Blow soon to never and never to twice/(blow life to isn't:blow death to was)/ — all nothing's only our hugest home," he has made eloquent poetry of his abstract idea.

William Troy has commented that certain pages of Cummings' Russian travel journal, *Eimi*, are as good as all but the best of his poetry. Certainly there is a relation between the prose and poetry in theme and technique.

In *Eimi* Cummings' words are positioned logistically to establish the impact of viewing Lenin's tomb. Others had written, according to their political bias, of that tomb. Cummings presented what his senses reported: the smells and sounds of the never-ending line of humanity descending into the bowels of the earth to get a glimpse of the corpse of a small man with a small face, their Messiah — as secret in death as he was in life. Cummings had gone to Russia to find out what the socialistic experiment was doing to help man toward being more alive. He found men and women with "a willingness not to live, if only they were allowed not to die," in John Peale Bishop's words. In some circumstances apathy is a means of survival but for the poet this was too little — or so it seemed to the young man of Harvard and New Hampshire. Vivid, even gay, portraits of Russians lighten the record but the following passage — illustrative of his firming style, that "specialization of sensibility" — is what he understood at Lenin's tomb:

facefacefaceface
   hand-
       fin-
           claw
   foot-
       hoof
   (tovarich)
         es to number of numberlessness (un
-smiling)
with dirt's dirt dirty dirtier with others' dirt with dirt of themselves
dirtiest waitstand dirtily never smile shufflebudge dirty pausehalt
   Smilingless.

Francis Fergusson has referred to this passage as the beginning of "a sleepwalking death-rite." Cummings' deliberate abandonment of conventional syntax, which is based on an arrangement of thoughts and sensations already completed, makes the "instantaneous alone . . . his concern," as Troy put it, and he takes the reader into "an unworld of unmen lying in unsleep on an unbed of preternatural nullity."

Sensory awareness has been a dominant theme of Cummings' work discussed so far. A second primary theme in his work, both poetry and prose, is the integrity of the individual. The last lines of a sophisticated little poem about a Jewish tailor in Greenwich Village, "i say no world" (*50 Poems*), put his view succinctly: "unsellable not buyable alive/ one i say human being)one/ goldberger." Beginning with *The Enormous Room* and *Tulips and Chimneys*, Cummings celebrated individuals, perceiving the transcendental under the ephemeral disguise. Some of his poem-portraits focused on the famous: Buffalo Bill ("Buffalo Bill's/ defunct," *Tulips and Chimneys*), the tragicomic dancer Jimmy Savo ("so little he is," in "New Poems" of *Collected Poems*), Picasso ("Picasso/ you give us Things," *XLI Poems*). In others he turned a clear but sympathetic eye on burlesque queens, circus clowns, "niggers dancing," the Greenwich Village "Professor Seagull." He wrote too of bums — and caught the spirit of their search for a "self" even as they scoured the gutters for a cigarette butt.

It follows that anything threatening individuality would be the object of his hatred. War, for example:

> you know what i mean when
> the first guy drops you know
> everybody feels sick or
> when they throw in a few gas
> and the oh baby shrapnel
> or my feet getting dim freezing or
> up to your you know what in water or
> with the bugs crawling right all up
> all everywhere over you all . . .

In these lines from "lis/ -ten" (*Is 5*) Cummings conveys — through the agonized, almost hysterical, words of a soldier who was there — his deep-felt indignation against the senseless destruction of individuals. And the poet's skill transforms the ephemeral statistic of a newspaper battle account into transcendental man. The threats to the integrity of the individual posed by a mechanized society are many and pervasive. "Progress is a comfortable disease," commented Cummings in "pity this busy monster, manunkind" (*One Times One*), but a disease nonetheless. The attempts of man to identify with his inventions — to become the turbines and computers he developed — stir Cummings to remark: "A world of made/ is not a world of born." And so "when man determined to destroy/ himself he picked the was/ of shall and finding only why/ smashed it into because" ("when god decided to invent," *One Times One*).

In the morality *Santa Claus* Cummings speaks sharply against the blighting forces that keep a man from knowing his spontaneous self. "Knowledge has taken love out of the world/ and all the world is empty empty empty . . . joyless joyless joyless." The Child in the morality, however, can "truly see," as in Hans Christian Andersen's story "The Emperor's New Clothes." And when the Woman calls for death and Santa dressed as Death enters, she sees through the disguise because she looks with the eyes of the heart. Ironies of belief and unbelief are frequent in *Santa Claus*; the interchange of mask and costume is reminiscent of Shakespeare, and even more of the melodramatics of tent shows that toured the hinterland of the United States, and these again are related to the commedia dell'arte which began as skits performed on a wooden cart pulled by a donkey — to amuse Italian peasants. Cummings, writing to Allen Tate in 1946, said that the whole aim of *Santa Claus* was to make man remove his death mask, thereby becoming what he truly is: a human being.

In his concern to remove the death mask Cummings often employed satire. The satirist, it has been said, needs both irreverence and moral conviction. Cummings had both. His satire is like that of Swift; it comes from conviction that something is awry, as when he declared that this world is all aleak and "i'd rather learn from one bird how to sing/ than teach ten thousand stars how not to dance" ("New Poems," *Collected Poems*).

In the successful satires the penetration is trenchant, under-lined by a cheerful ribaldry. At other times his intention is mis-laid in a junk pile of name calling and irrelevant detail. Indigna-tion sometimes results in an absence of poetic statement and a series of stereotypes. As Philip Horton has noted, Cummings is at times guilty of bad puns and satires that miss their mark ("a myth is as good as a smile" from "little joe gould"; "obey says toc,submit says tic,/ Eternity's a Five Year Plan" from "Jehovah buried,Satan dead," both in *No Thanks*). However, in a notable example of the satiric, "A Foreword to Krazy" (1946; collected in *A Miscellany*), Cummings explained the symbolism of George Herriman's comic-strip characters and at the same time he defined his own position as a satirist. The cast is made up of Ignatz Mouse, a brick-throwing cynic, Offissa Pupp, a sentimental police-man-dog, and the heroine, "slightly resembling a child's drawing of a cat." On the political level Offissa Pupp represents the "will of socalled society" while Ignatz Mouse is the destructive element. The benevolent overdog and the malevolent undermouse, as Cummings saw it, misunderstood Krazy Kat. Not only is she a symbol of an ideal democracy but she is personal — she trans-forms the brick into a kiss; the senses aided by the spirit produce joy.

These ideas ran counter to those expressed in T. S. Eliot's essay "Tradition and the Individual Talent" which for so long after its publication made the personal in literature suspect. But the swing of the pendulum through the centuries from the formalized pro-saic (classic) to the formalized romantic is always rectifying the errors of critics. Today, such poets as John Berryman and Robert Lowell are carrying on experiments in the personal that Cum-mings would have found in his vein.

In two poems, "anyone lived in a pretty how town" and "my father moved through dooms of love" (both in *50 Poems*), Cum-mings very effectively worked the personal into a universal appli-cation. He used for one a contemplative narration of ideal lovers and for the other a portrait of the ideal man. The maturity of the poet's insights is displayed by his bold use of regular, rhymed stanzas to control a considered emotion and to weld it to his opinions, now sufficiently explored, of the social dilemma. The refrains are a charming blend of nursery rhyme ("sun moon stars rain" and "with up so floating many bells down") and sophisticated observation ("My father moved through theys of we").

Barry Marks has pointed out that as contemporary painters (like Juan Gris and Picasso) ambiguously employed a single curve for the neck of a vase and the edge of a guitar, so Cummings often deranged his syntax in order that a single word would both intensify a statement and question its validity; an example is the "how" in "anyone lived in a pretty how town." This word suggests, among other things, that the townspeople ask how and why about things from an emptiness of mind and an incapacity for simultaneity and the intuitive grasp. The direct vision of the painter-poet is similar to a child's delight in believing that a rain puddle is the ocean; it is a transcendental conception.

In the pretty how town "anyone" and "noone" are lovers; they live and love and die in a landscape of changing seasons, among children growing into adults and forgetting the realities and adults, "both little and small," without love or interest in life — from Cummings' penetrative view. The lively series of contrasts reinforces the ballad form; emotion and thought are strictly held to the development of the charade: "anyone" versus "someones," the individual opposed to the anxious status-seekers who "sowed their isn't" and "reaped their same." Children guessed the goodness of love between anyone and noone, because children are close to the intuitive life, but living things grow by imitation, so the children forgot as they imitated their "someones."

In the last line of the third stanza, "that noone loved him more by more," the word "noone" is emphasizing the public indifference as well as providing the identification of the "she" in the next stanza:

> when by now and tree by leaf
> she laughed his joy she cried his grief
> bird by snow and stir by still
> anyone's any was all to her

A compression of meanings is achieved in "when by now," "bird by snow," "tree by leaf," and they in turn are manipulated by repetitions suggested by later rhyme and alliteration: "all by all and deep by deep/ and more by more . . ." The climax of the ballad is in the line "and noone stooped to kiss his face." In the second to the last stanza the poet states the triumph of the individual way of life, as the lovers go hand in hand into eternity:

noone and anyone earth by april
wish by spirit and if by yes

Cummings' testament for his father, "my father moved through dooms of love," is a ballad only by stanza and innerly varied refrain; intertwined are seasonal references, as in "septembering arms of year extend" which gives individuality to the general term "harvest." It is heroic by virtue of lines that paraphrase the Prophets: "his anger was as right as rain/ his pity was as green as grain." The poem is distinguished by some fine couplets: "and should some why completely weep/ my father's fingers brought her sleep," and "if every friend became his foe/ he'd laugh and build a world with snow," which describes pretty accurately the poet himself. There is no narrative as such but the poem is held together by the feeling of compassion toward humble or unfortunate people.

In contrast to the abstract quality of "my father moved through dooms of love," a sequence of colorful details characterizes an early poem for Cummings' mother, "if there are any heavens" (*ViVa*). The opening lines establish clearly the heroic light in which Cummings viewed this woman who said of herself after a remarkable recovery from an automobile accident, "I'm tough":

if there are any heavens my mother will(all by herself)have
one. It will not be a pansy heaven nor
a fragile heaven of lilies-of-the-valley but
it will be a heaven of blackred roses

Cummings' virtuosity in the management of his mechanics may especially be noted in several poems revealing his intense concern with the individual. In one, the free-form poem beginning "5/ derbies-with-men-in-them" (*XLI Poems*), the reader is presented with a charade. With the poet he has entered a café that, like the Englishman's pub, seems more a social club than a restaurant: the customers play games such as backgammon and read and discuss the news while drinking coffee. Identity of place is established in the fourth stanza when one of the customers buys the Bawstinamereekin from a paperboy. But Cummings builds up an un-Yankee atmosphere with carefully chosen details: the men smoke Helmar cigarettes, one of them uses the word "effendi" and "swears in persian," two speak in Turkish, an Armenian record is played on the phonograph. This is, then, a Near Eastern café in Boston. Far from the feuds of the Old Country, proprietor and customers are united by homesickness. The men are not named; instead Cummings identifies them by lowercase letters:

> a has gold
> teeth b pink
> suspenders c
> reads Atlantis

And x beats y at backgammon. This device permits Cummings both to control his flood of feeling for the men and to stress their brotherhood. When two of them — the man with the gold teeth and the winner at backgammon — leave, Cummings says "exeunt ax"; and the coupled "by" follow. Cummings' characteristic use of space and capitals to underscore meaning is also to be found in this poem: "the pho/nographisrunn/ingd o w,   n" and then "stopS."

Capital letters (not meant to be pronounced) serve as an organizing and emphasizing device in "sonnet entitled how to run the world)" (*No Thanks*), which begins:

> A always don't there B being no such thing
> for C can't casts no shadow D drink and
>
> E eat of her voice in whose silence the music of spring
> lives F feel opens but shuts understand
> G gladly forget little having less
>
> with every least each most remembering
> H highest fly only the flag that's furled

Here we have a commentary on the existence of "mostpeople." This satire on the "unworld" employs the comparatives "less"

and "least" to emphasize the triviality and sterility of that world,
while the clause "in whose silence the music of spring/lives" indi-
cates what, for Cummings, is one of the symbols of the real world,
the transcendental world. There is a flash of mocking humor in
the repetition of the pedantic "entitled" in the ninth line of the
poem, "(sestet entitled grass is flesh . . ." but even this line has a
serious purpose: to reinforce the idea of a world where people
merely exist. It is followed by a richly thought-provoking state-
ment, "any dream/means more than sleep as more than know
means guess)," which prepares the way for the masterly conclud-
ing line, "children building this rainman out of snow." In this
poem Cummings uses for the most part simple words but com-
bines them so that the repetitions and contrasts of sound add a
fresh dimension to the theme and subtly contribute to the feeling
of empathy evoked for the individuals trapped in the "unworld."

Where in these two poems Cummings used, variously, lower-
case and capital letters as controlling devices, in "there are 6
doors" (*ViVa*), it is repetition of the phrase "next door" that
governs the orderly sequence. "Next door(but four)" lives a whore
with "a multitude of chins"; "next door/but three" a ghost
"Who screams Faintly" is the tenant and "next/Door but two"
a man and his wife who "throw silently things/Each at other."
Then Cummings tells what happens to some men who have been
jettisoned by society:

> ,next door but One
> a on Dirty bed Mangy from person Porous
> sits years its of self fee(bly
> Perpetually coughing And thickly spi)tting

Finally, "next door nobody/seems to live at present . . . or,bed-
bugs." The reader is left to ponder several kinds of waste of
human life. Emerson wrote in his essay "Self-Reliance," "This
one fact the world hates, that the soul *becomes*"; Cummings re-
corded in poem after poem instances of the world preventing the
action of the soul—but with the purpose of rousing the transcen-
dental spirit latent in his readers.

The individuals pictured in "mortals)" (*50 Poems*) are very
different from those in the rooms "next door" and so are the

technical devices used. Cummings here turns to highly skilled
acrobats and puts them into motion on the page:

mortals)

climbi
    ng i
    nto eachness begi
    n
dizzily
    swingthings
of speeds of
trapeze gush somersaults
open ing
      hes shes
&meet&
    swoop
      fully is are ex
            quisite theys of re
turn
  a
  n
  d
fall which now drop who all dreamlike

(im

"Eachness" is a critical word in this poem: as George Haines IV
has pointed out, the individuality of the performers is emphasized
by the separation of "climbi" and "begi" from the end letters
"ng" and "n"; the swinging of the trapeze is in the line repetition
"of speeds of." The reader discovering a similar pattern in
"&meet&" by this time is responding with a jump of his muscles,
as occurs in watching ballet or circus. As the "fully" continues
into "is are ex," movement has entered the area of the unknown;
the symbol *x* ("ex") is equal to the mystery of the encounters of
the "is" and "are," the "hes" and "shes." The use of "a/ n/ d"
permits visualization of the trapeze. The fortunate climax of
"who all dreamlike" brings together the specific skills and the
hovering mystery of art, whose function is to redeem what other-
wise would vanish from the earth like a dream. In another sense,

the acrobats are a congruent image since even the most skilled is in peril at every performance (mortals, Cummings called them) yet they are completely and happily themselves in the exercise of their art. From the final line to the first one in this "circular" poem — "im" plus "mortal" — the poet justifies his contention that precision makes motion which makes life, and that the "dark beginnings are his luminous ends."

Why did Cummings choose the symbol of acrobats for a metaphysical statement? He may have been inspired, as was Rilke, by "Les Saltimbanques" of Picasso. More likely, his enjoyment of folk amusements dictated the vehicle for his fundamental belief: mortals, by devotion to a skill, an art, become immortal.

Before leaving this aspect of Cummings' work, we may appropriately turn back to his prose to find a revealing conjunction of theme and technique. In *The Enormous Room* Cummings had used a phrase of John Bunyan's, the "Delectable Mountains," to refer to certain individuals — physically mistreated, spiritually mutilated, and yet triumphantly overcoming their situations. Of one example, whom he christened The Zulu, he said, "His angular anatomy expended and collected itself with an effortless spontaneity . . . But he was more. There are certain things in which one is unable to believe for the simple reason that he never ceases to feel them. Things of this sort — things which are always inside of us and in fact are us and which consequently will not be pushed off or away where we can begin thinking about them — are no longer things; they, and the us which they are, equals A Verb; an IS. The Zulu, then, I must perforce call an IS." Thus, using one of his typical devices, substitution of one part of speech for another, Cummings converted one way of seeing and of thinking into another to emphasize a theme that would be meshed in all of his writing. Whenever *is*, the verb, is turned into a noun, it becomes even more of a verb; it is dramatized, it gains — as Lloyd Frankenberg put it — the force of the colloquial "He *is* somebody." In other words, the quality of being becomes an active principle, the individual becomes a whole person, responding to the totality of experience.

A third major theme in Cummings' work, already touched upon, is the revelation of what it means *truly* to love. In his experiments with the idea of love Cummings assigned to the word the multiple connotations inherent in it: sexual, romantic, platonic. The most intense love, paradoxically, must function with the greatest objectivity; subjective impressions must be corrected by intent observation of objects, human or otherwise. Dante could write of his ideal Lady; Cummings addressed to a platonic vision a bawdy valentine that is revelatory of his stance toward life and art ("on the Madam's best april the," *Is 5*).

In the era following World War I and acceleration of industrial growth, disregard of an earlier generation's restraints on sex became a means of protesting against the increased restrictions of the national life. In literature, Sherwood Anderson, Ernest Hemingway, Eugene O'Neill, and Henry Miller emphasized the necessity for sexual freedom. Cummings participated in this critique of the dehumanizing forces dominating the modern scene. Frankly rejoicing in sexuality as a nourishing element in an integrated life, a bond between man and the cosmos, or satirizing customs based on habit and fear of public opinion, he wrote "O sweet spontaneous" (*Tulips and Chimneys*) and "she being Brand" (*Is 5*) and "i will be/ Moving in the Street of her" (*And*). A poem on Sally Rand, "out of a supermetamathical subpreincestures" (*No Thanks*), is not only a celebration of the fan dancer of the 1930s but also a transcendental view of the wonder of life. And it is a significant contrast to "raise the shade/ will youse dearie?" (*And*), a realistic piece exposing the joylessness in the pursuit of "pleasure."

Cummings eventually went "beyond sex as a critique of society and . . . beyond self-indulgence to self-discipline based on a new understanding of love," as Barry Marks put it. Cummings believed that morality depends on whether there is genuine giving on both sides. Sexuality is an ingredient of any I-you relationship, in the impersonal way that there is a trace of sugar in all vegetable and animal tissues, even if they taste salty or bitter. He illustrated insights into giving in a philosophical poem, "(will

you teach a/ wretch to live/ straighter than a needle)," and in a
comment on poverty that moves in nursery-rhyme couplets from
realistic deprivations to a more desperate psychological dilemma,
"if you can't eat you got to/ smoke and we ain't got/ nothing to
smoke" (both in *50 Poems*). And a poem (from *No Thanks*) with
neat stanzas to control his vehemence tells the reader from what
a distance the poet has come, smiling in a wry wisdom:

> be of love(a little)
> More careful
> Than of everything
> guard her perhaps only
> . . . .
>
> (Dare until a flower,
> understanding sizelessly sunlight
> Open what thousandth why and
> discover laughing)

Lloyd Frankenberg, in his introduction to a London reprint of
One Times One, said that, in effect, all of Cummings' poems were
love poems. A neat summation but then an "anatomy" of love is
also necessary. Conventional behavior in love is related to con-
ventional punctuation in prosody. And for a poet who lived on
the tips of not only his nerves but also his mind, love covers all
of existence: in one aspect it is involved with spit on the sidewalk
and in another with moonlight on the thighs of his lady; the
value of a thing or an experience is its revelation of an involve-
ment with life. Finally, in *95 Poems* and *73 Poems*, Cummings
came to a position whose simplicity may have surprised him: a
filial relation to the Divine. So this was what it meant, the witty
comment he made on his own struggles in *Is 5*:

> since feeling is first
> who pays any attention
> to the syntax of things
> will never wholly kiss you;
> . . . .
>
> for life's not a paragraph
>
> And death i think is no parenthesis

In his critical studies T. S. Eliot repeated his view that the entire output of certain writers constitutes a single work similar to an epic (*The Divine Comedy* or Williams' *Paterson*) and that individual pieces are endowed with meaning by other pieces and by the whole context of the work. This view may assist to an understanding of Cummings: fragmentation dissolves in the continuity of recurrent themes; interrelated images and symbols by their organizing force reflect and echo each other with cumulative effect. Cummings would have said it more specifically: in the here and now we can be happy and immortal if we use our wits and our will. Even if evil and death are the co-kings of this world, love is my king, and in serving him is my joy.

It is a leap into faith when a man casts off the customary motives of humanity and ventures to trust himself as taskmaster; he will need courage and vision "that a simple purpose may be to him as strong as iron necessity is to others" — so Emerson thought. From *Tulips and Chimneys* to *Poems 1923–1954* — a constellation of refracted and repeated images — to the posthumous *73 Poems*, Cummings led a succession of readers to accept his declaration: "I have no sentimentality at all. If you haven't got that, you're not afraid to write of love and death."

The metaphysical cord on which Cummings' sonnets are threaded was in evidence in the early "a connotation of infinity/ sharpens the temporal splendor of this night" (*Tulips and Chimneys*), in "put off your faces,Death:for day is over" (*ViVa*), and in "Love/ coins His most gradual gesture,/ and whittles life to eternity" ("it is so long since my heart has been with yours," *Is 5*). The efficacy of love in its multiple aspects pervades the notions of death until death becomes a gate to life. Dying is a verb as opposed to a deathly noun: "forgive us the sin of death." In another early poem, "somewhere i have never travelled,gladly beyond/ any experience" (*ViVa*), the abstraction "spring" is personified and its essential mystery is presented through the adverbs *skilfully, mysteriously, suddenly,* used as in the later poetry are *miraculous, illimitable, immeasurable*: adjectival aspects of natural phenomena capable of being perceived but incapable of being truly labeled or measured.

The concern of Cummings, even in his Sitwellian phase, with juxtaposed improbables — locomotives with roses — was an effort to get at the quintessence of an apparently trivial subject. Its mystery could be reached successfully only by the evolution of devices he had scrupulously crafted. In his war against formal "thinking" he was not against study or ideas; it was an opposition to the conformity which the accumulation of "knowledge" is inclined to impose. To discover the true nature of the world — to know it; to act in it; for the artist, to depict it — is the Cummings metaphysic, his politics, and his aesthetic. The world of cyclical process is for him a timeless world. He does not deny either the past or the future; rather he denies that hope or regret should warp the living moment. In this way he is related to Coleridge and to Blake (related doubly to the latter by reason of his sensitive drawings, such as the celebrated sketch of Charlie Chaplin). His eyes are fixed on fulfillment, consenting to the perpetuation of life through death as in "rosetree,rosetree." The individual rose dies that a hundred roses may be born; true lovers will be reborn into perfect love.

The antithesis between the false routine world and the true world is seen with icy clarity by a poet who feels mortality sitting on his shoulder. The result is a complexity of vision. That it should have cost so much to get there does not trouble the poet of transcendence; he is a compeer of all seekers, including a tramp on the highway. A poet's function is to embody in a poem the dynamics of nature (including his own response) which is primarily a mystery. Heightened awareness leads to a new dimension that leads into transcendentalism supported by specific detail: in "luminous tendril of celestial wish" (*Xaipe*), the cyclical moon is regarded as evidence of process leading to death and rebirth; the poet's humility is indicated by "teach disappearing also me the keen/illimitable secret of begin."

In *95 Poems* the poetic argument rises into an intense clarity. The affirmative transcending the negative as in "All lose,whole find" ("one's not half two," *One Times One*) and in "the most who die,the more we live" ("what if a much of a which of a wind," *One Times One*) has entered a final phase. The poet has now realized that the transcendental cannot abolish the "fact" of death but he proves the worth of the affirmative as the polarizing element of his philosophy. The former devices of making nouns into verbs and shifting the placement of antitheses are less in evidence; the reality of "appearances" is acknowledged: "now air is air and thing is thing:no bliss/ of heavenly earth beguiles our spirits,whose/ miraculously disenchanted eyes/ live the magnificent honesty of space." This is a reminder of the early "let's live suddenly without thinking/ under honest trees" (*And*). The poet, however, has come into the higher turn of the spiral of mystical development where the phenomenal world is transfigured and a tree is really understood.

In this volume Cummings has collected all of his phases: (1) look at what is happening around you; (2) the imagination is more real than reality; (3) the search for life and self brings you back to a transformed reality that is shared with a grasshopper on a flowering weed. As S. I. Hayakawa wrote in *Language in Thought and Action*, the only certainty and security is within the disciplined mind; so when Cummings says in "in time of daffodils(who know"

> and in a mystery to be
> (when time from time shall set us free)
> forgetting me,remember me

the troubadour is telling his lady to forget his life *in* time; to remember that his mortal love always looked toward lovers in immortality. Just so did his preoccupation with twilight reach beyond mist and the "dangerous first stars" to a world new to the senses.

Begin as you mean to go on. The English proverb may explain why the young Cummings was attracted to a statement of Keats: "I am certain of nothing but the holiness of the Heart's affections, and the truth of Imagination." The innovative devices that the young Cummings developed to implement this idea were a successful means of communication in the modern world. But the Cummings of *73 Poems* has traveled farther than that: into the realm of transcendence. The poet who said "—who'll solve the depths of horror to defend/a sunbeam's architecture with his life" ("no man, if men are gods," *One Times One*) has earned the right to explain time by timelessness. In total compassion he declares, in the last poem in *73 Poems*:

> (being forever born a foolishwise
> proudhumble citizen of ecstasies
> more steep than climb can time with all his years)
>
> he's free into the beauty of the truth;
>
> and strolls the axis of the universe
> —love. Each believing world denies, whereas
> your lover(looking through both life and death)
> timelessly celebrates the merciful
>
> wonder no world deny may or believe.

Growing from poem to poem — shedding skin after skin — Cummings emerges as really himself, and therefore as everyone: that is the true definition of transcendence. The artist's formalities have become clear as a washed windowpane, or the purity of a flower upturned to receive a heavenly dew — the canticles of a mystic.

MONROE K. SPEARS

Hart Crane

In "Words for Hart Crane" Robert Lowell called Crane *"Catullus redivivus"* and "the Shelley of my age"; in a *Paris Review* interview he said: "I think Crane is the great poet of that generation . . . Not only is it the tremendous power there, but he somehow got New York City: he was at the center of things in the way that no other poet was. All the chaos of his life missed getting sidetracked the way other poets' did, and he was less limited than any other poet of his generation. There was a fulness of experience . . ." As the major poet of a later generation, Lowell speaks with authority, and he expresses an opinion that seems to be increasingly prevalent.

In life and in poetry, Crane was intense, extreme, and uncompromising; he is as effective a flutterer of dovecotes as Catullus or Blake or Rimbaud. He challenges the imagination and compels judgment; no tepid response either to him or to what he stands for is possible. He was unquestionably a man of principle, whatever the merit of his principles. (His severest critic called him "a saint of the wrong religion.") Precisely what was wrong with these principles, aesthetic and religious, was defined early and very fully by several of our most brilliant critics. This was a necessary task, for certainly Crane was a dangerous model and an example various-

ly instructive. Forty years after his death, however, he has been
so disinfected by the passage of time that he is hardly likely to
spread any contagions, and it seems more profitable now to focus
attention on his achievement than on the nature and significance
of his failure. Allen Tate, the finest of the critics who defined
Crane's errors, recognized this in adding to his essay "Hart Crane"
an "Encomium Twenty Years Later" celebrating Crane as "a great
lyric poet" and "our twentieth-century poet as hero."

Crane has been the hero of many cults, on grounds often both
dubious and inconsistent. Homosexuals naturally canonized him
and made him their patron, as St. Hart the Homintern Martyr (to
adapt the title W. H. Auden once gave to Wilde). But Allen Tate,
his close friend, calls him "an extreme example of the *unwilling*
homosexual" and observes that he was never alienated in the sense
of rejecting the full human condition, any more than his poetry re-
jects the central tradition of the past. Patriots and optimists have
sometimes hailed him as the Pindar of machinery, the modern
Whitman who celebrates America and proves that our civilization
is no Waste Land but a triumphant Bridge. Crane did harbor such
aspirations, intermittently, but he was not taken in by them.
Social critics from Marxist to Beat have made Crane's "crack-
up," like that of F. Scott Fitzgerald, a type of the fate of the
writer in modern America. Crane does indeed exhibit all the pres-
sures of our civilization in their most extreme form, though he
also furnishes an almost embarrassingly obvious case history for
the psychological critic. Finally, Crane has been adulated by the
followers of all kinds of poetic unreason; much fake poetry has
been perpetrated in his name, and increasingly of late he has been
used as a stalking-horse by the Neo-Romantics. It is true that
Crane expounded and sometimes practiced a kind of irrational-
ism or mysticism, as we shall see; but it is also true that he was a
meticulous craftsman, seeking not to break with but to follow the
central tradition in poetry, and he strove to eliminate obscurity.

Crane's poetry has, then, provided the text for many sermons and
the ground for many controversies. The essential fact is, however,
that it is still alive as poetry, that it still speaks powerfully both to

readers encountering it for the first time and to those who go back to it. Its influence on Allen Tate, Robert Lowell, Dylan Thomas, and many lesser figures is plain. Now, some forty years after his suicide, we can say that his work survives all the contemporary disputes and passions, and that in spite of its small bulk and its obvious limitations and defects, it will remain among the permanent treasures of American poetry in the twentieth century.

Because Crane's life was spectacular and portentous, it tends to distract attention from his poetry. The biographical approach to the poetry is misleading; it gives chief prominence to Crane's personal disintegration and his unsuccessful attempt to create a myth. But these are not the central issues in his work, which, like all true poetry, has a life of its own apart from the poet. I shall therefore confine myself to a short biographical summary before considering the poetry.

Harold Hart Crane was born in 1899 in Ohio, into the midwestern small-town cultural milieu satirized by Sinclair Lewis and so many others. He was an only child and the product of a broken home; his childhood was dominated by the tension between his parents, who first separated in 1909, when Hart was ten, sending him to live with his maternal grandmother. His father, a hard-headed businessman highly successful in the manufacture of candy and in other enterprises, was remote from his son and showed him small understanding or sympathy. The mother enveloped and dominated him, turning him bitterly against the father and dragging him through all their quarrels (he said later that his childhood had been a "bloody battleground" for his parents' sex lives). This classic Oedipal situation was no doubt the basis of his homosexuality and his other psychological peculiarities. After quarrels, separations, and temporary reconciliations spanning Hart's childhood and early adolescence, the parents were finally divorced, and both later remarried. Hart had, of course, taken his mother's side throughout the quarrels — he had traveled with her through the West and to the Isle of Pines, south of Cuba — and after the divorce he symbolically truncated his name, using the maternal surname "Hart" as his first name and thus rejecting the father who had rejected him. In 1916, at the age of seventeen, he abandoned high school and went alone to New York to live. In this year he had published his first poem and prose piece (he had begun to write three years before), and he now committed himself irrevocably to poetry as a vocation.

Crane emerged from this background emotionally crippled, morbidly overstimulated, rootless, and unable ever to adjust to a "normal" pattern of living. Like most Americans, he cherished the notion of making quick money by writing a movie scenario or a popular story or novel; but aside from brief periods working in bookstores, in his father's factories and candy stores, and as a salesman, his closest approaches to success in earning a living were as an advertising copy writer — a profession chiefly dedicated to the debasement of language and the deception of the public. New York, citadel and symbol of the pressures toward rootlessness and alienation, was inevitably the place he would live most of the time, and partly in the underground world of the homosexual.

When Crane went to New York in 1916, one of the books he took with him was Mary Baker Eddy's *Science and Health with Key to the Scriptures*. Both his mother and grandmother were fervent advocates of Christian Science, and although Hart did not remain a believer in it as a religion for long, he remained convinced of its psychological efficacy. He wrote in 1919: "What it says in regard to mental and nervous ailments is absolutely true. It is only the total denial of the animal and organic world which I cannot swallow." His training in this faith, with the influence and example of the two people to whom he was closest, had a lasting effect on him. Born out of the union of American transcendentalism and American hypochondria, Christian Science holds that states of consciousness are the only reality, that matter is unreal, that all causation is mental and apparent evil the result of erring belief. Crane's predisposition to optimism and irrationalism and his later pseudo-mystical strivings for the "higher consciousness" undoubtedly owe much to this early background.

A similar and perhaps even more powerful influence in the formation of his aesthetic and religious attitudes was his early study of Plato. According to Philip Horton, Crane's earliest biographer, he underscored doubly with red ink the passages on the necessity of madness in a true poet, and the Platonic concept of a progression upward from earthly beauties in a search for absolute beauty became fundamental to his thought. Nietzsche, about whom Crane wrote an article as early as 1918, also played an important part in his development. Nietzsche's anti-philistinism, his exaltation of the artist, and his celebration of Dionysian joy appealed strongly to Crane and merged with other powerful currents. One such was the *Tertium Organum* (first published in the United States in 1920) of P. D. Ouspensky, a rhapsodic and pseudo-mystical work from which Crane took the phrase "higher consciousness," and which advocated the Dionysian type of mystical experience and the artist as guide to spiritual truth. Other currents in the mystical and pantheistic stream were the Bengali poet Rabindranath Tagore, whom Crane met in Cleveland in 1916, and such visionary and antirational poets as Blake, who exerted a powerful and continuing influence on Crane, and Rimbaud, whose disciple and heir Crane early came to consider himself.

Counterbalancing these powerful tendencies toward irrationalism, mysticism, and occultism was Crane's relation to his American literary heritage. When he was fifteen he spent several weeks at the establishment of Elbert Hubbard, a highly successful purveyor of culture and homely philosophy to the American public; as one of Crane's biographers, Brom Weber, puts it, he "capitalized upon the contradictory and confused American temper at the turn of the century by clothing materialism with an atmosphere of romance and culture." But, if he contributed to Crane's decision to go into advertising and his belief that he could somehow make money out of literature, he also helped to acquaint Crane with the classic American poets. Crane recognized early, at a time when it was by no means the truism it is now, that the great American writers were Whitman, Melville, Dickinson, and James, with Poe as progenitor and type. (He seems not to have been aware of Hawthorne.) Through Mrs. William Vaughn Moody, who be-

friended him, he became acquainted with some of the new writ-
ers and the "little magazines" that were their chief media of pub-
lication; and he also knew the older generation of writers such as
Sherwood Anderson, Lindsay, Masters, and Sandburg.

Though Crane was from the beginning intensely aware of the
new movements and the emerging writers, and though Pound and
Eliot were soon to become his chief mentors, it is curious and inter-
esting that the dominant influences on his early poetry (roughly
1916–20) were Swinburne, the early Yeats, and especially Wilde,
Dowson, and the other "Decadents." *Bruno's Weekly* and *Bruno's
Bohemia* frequently reprinted the works of Dowson and Wilde and
praised Wilde's life and writings; Crane's first poem, called "C 33"
(Wilde's designation in Reading Gaol), appeared in the former in
1916 and his "Carmen de Boheme" in the latter two years later;
both are, as the titles suggest, *fin de siècle* in spirit and conven-
tional in form. Crane's first published prose, a letter to *The Pagan*
(1916), reveals the way ninetyish aestheticism and the "new" co-
existed harmoniously in the literary awareness of the time. He
said, "I am interested in your magazine as a new and distinctive
chord in the present American Renaissance of literature and art.
Let me praise your September cover; it has some suggestion of the
exoticism and richness of Wilde's poems." New York in the win-
ter of 1916–17 was especially exciting, not only because of the
war, but because the literary "American Renaissance" of which
Crane spoke was at its height. Since the founding of *Poetry* by
Harriet Monroe in 1912 numerous "little magazines" had been
established and many anthologies, as well as volumes by in-
dividual poets, had appeared. There had been much agitation
about Imagism, with Amy Lowell taking over the movement
from Ezra Pound. In 1917 Pound transferred his allegiance from
Poetry to the *Little Review*, which had just moved from Chicago
to New York; thenceforth the *Little Review* followed his cos-
mopolitan aim of bringing together the best English and French
writers with the best of the Americans — a program cultivated by
the *Dial* also after 1920. Other magazines, notably *The Seven Arts*,
had a more nationalistic emphasis.

These magazines, and numerous others with such names as *The Egoist, Blast, The Modern School, The Modernist*, were the main agents of Crane's education. His chief teachers in the years during which he would have been attending a college or university, in the normal course of affairs were Pound and Eliot, with Pound first dominating (as early as 1917) and then, a year or two later, Eliot most decisively. Both as critics and as poets, they form his taste, stimulate and provoke him, and teach him the craft of poetry. It is through them that he discovers the Elizabethans and Metaphysicals (special enthusiasms being Donne, Marlowe, and Webster), Dante (whom he did not, however, study intensively until 1930), and most overwhelmingly the French poets from Baudelaire on.

By 1921, Crane had achieved full poetic maturity, finding his own voice, style, and themes; and in the same year he broke decisively with his father. From his first departure for New York in 1916 until this time, he had felt the "curse of sundered parentage" with particular virulence. He had returned to Cleveland and had lived in Akron and Washington, D.C., for varying periods in response to pleas from his mother or offers of work in various capacities (all humble—clerk, salesman, supervisor) in his father's candy business. The year 1921 did not mark the achievement of any sort of stability, emotional or economic, but it may be said to signal the end of the process of education and definition of himself as poet and as person.

The external events of the rest of his life require little space to describe. In the single decade remaining to him, he tried with small success to find a satisfactory means of support in advertising or other hackwork. The increasing disorder of his personal life, dominated by alcoholism and homosexuality, made the various forms of temporary patronage he finally received of little use to him. The chief of these were a grant from the banker Otto Kahn in 1925 and a Guggenheim fellowship in 1931, though he also served briefly as traveling secretary to a wealthy stockbroker and enjoyed the extended hospitality of Harry and Caresse Crosby in Paris. His first volume, *White Buildings*, was published (after many delays and difficulties) in 1926. In the same year he made another stay on the Isle of Pines, writing there many of the poems

collected as *Key West: An Island Sheaf* and published post-
humously, and much of *The Bridge*. Late in 1928 he sailed for
Europe, spending the first half of 1929 mostly in Paris, where he
found society all too congenial to his vices. The Crosbys did,
however, provide him with the stimulus to finish *The Bridge* —
which Crane had begun in 1923 and worked on at intervals since
— by undertaking to print it at their Black Sun Press in Paris; it
was published both there and in New York in 1930. In 1931 he
went to Mexico on his Guggenheim fellowship, projecting an
epic on the conquest of Mexico; but in spite of devoted efforts
by several people to help him — Hans Zinsser, the famous bac-
teriologist; Katherine Anne Porter, his neighbor in Mexico; and
Peggy Baird, former wife of Malcolm Cowley, with whom he lived
for a time in a last approach to heterosexual love — he was able to
do little writing. Quarrelsome, drunk much of the time, alternating
between manic exhilaration and suicidal depression, he had little
control of himself and was frequently on, and sometimes across, the
border of insanity. He did produce one last poem as good as any-
thing he ever wrote, "The Broken Tower," in February–March
1932. A month later he leaped from the stern of the ship taking
him from Mexico to the United States, acting out the symbolism
of many of his poems by drowning in the Caribbean. A final sym-
bolic touch was added to the story when his mother died in 1947
and her ashes were scattered, according to her directions, from
Brooklyn Bridge.

Crane's talent was astonishing indeed to survive the extreme dis-
order of his life and all the other forces inimical to it and enable
him in spite of everything to produce poetry of lasting value. But
Crane was by no means passive, a mere vessel; his attitude to-
ward his poetry was much more conservative and shrewd and dis-
ciplined than the sensational outlines of his life would sug-
gest. His constant effort was to educate himself poetically, to
discipline his gifts, to establish a valid relation to tradition. He
was rarely taken in by fads or extremists, and his critical com-
ments show great penetration. His letters, collected in 1952, seem
to me the most impressive since Keats's, and fully worthy of

comparison to them; they are profoundly moving human documents, colorful, penetrating, often humorous, and rich in moral insight (unexpected as this quality might seem). The letters reveal much about the nature of our civilization in that crucial period 1916–32, and the symptomatic aspect of Crane's career; they also have the special human interest and pathos of portraying the artist who dies young and as victim. (He wrote in 1922, "I shall do my best work later on when I am about 35 or 40.")

The challenge of Crane's poetry called forth from several of our best critics essays that remain classics. Such are Allen Tate's crucial pieces, R. P. Blackmur's explorations of how Crane's language works, and Yvor Winters' definitions of how Crane was misled by the "American religion" of Whitman and Emerson. Full-length studies of Crane's poetry and his life have likewise been of high caliber. Philip Horton's biography of 1937 is exceptionally readable without sacrifice of thoroughness and accuracy. Brom Weber's study, a decade later, presented much further information; Weber also skillfully edited Crane's letters. L. S. Dembo's study (1960) of *The Bridge* is an impressive Neo-Romantic interpretation. The books (both 1963) by Samuel Hazo and Vincent Quinn are useful brief introductions. In the last few years there has been a resurgence of interest in Crane, manifested in a new edition of the poems, with selected letters and prose, edited by Brom Weber (1966), a reprint of the letters (1965), full-length critical studies of the poetry by R. W. B. Lewis (1967), H. A. Leibowitz (1968), and R. W. Butterfield (1969), and a massive critical biography by John Unterecker which won the National Book Award in 1969.

To turn now to specific discussion of the poetry. Of the twenty-eight poems in *White Buildings*, all but two were written in 1920–25, and most of them in the latter part of that period. (The two Crane chose to preserve from the large number he had produced before 1920 were "North Labrador" and "In Shadow.") They are all mature work, and an approach in terms of development and chronology is not very revealing. Perhaps the best way is to begin with some poems about the nature of poetry and the poet.

"Chaplinesque" is an early and relatively simple presentation of one aspect of the situation of the poet.

> We make our meek adjustments,
> Contented with such random consolations
> As the wind deposits
> In slithered and too ample pockets.

> For we can still love the world, who find
> A famished kitten on the step, and know
> Recesses for it from the fury of the street,
> Or warm torn elbow coverts.

It was inspired by Chaplin's *The Kid,* and Crane explained his intentions in several letters: "I am moved to put Chaplin with the poets [of today]; hence the 'we.' . . . Poetry, the human feelings, 'the kitten,' is so crowded out of the humdrum, rushing, mechanical scramble of today that the man who would preserve them must duck and camouflage for dear life to keep them or keep himself from annihilation. . . . I feel that I have captured the arrested climaxes and evasive victories of his gestures in words, somehow . . . I have made that 'infinitely gentle, infinitely suffering thing' of Eliot's into the symbol of the kitten."

The Romantic irony of the clown-poet figure and the tone and language of this poem suggest the French Symbolists, whom Crane had been studying; he had recently translated three poems by Laforgue. But the poem also illustrates a more distinctive and lasting influence: that of the graphic arts. Fundamental to Crane's aesthetic was the similarity between poetry and painting (and such related graphic arts as photography). Painting was, from early adolescence, almost as important to him as poetry, and he surrounded himself with prints as well as books. When he went to New York in 1916, Carl Schmitt, a young painter, went over Crane's work, giving him the benefit of the painter's sensitive response to rhythm and movement. They agreed, according to Horton, that Crane ". . . should compose a certain number of poems a week simply as technical exercises with the purpose of breaking down formal patterns. These he would bring to his critic as he wrote them, and the two would read them over together, Schmitt illustrating with pencil on paper the rising and falling of cadences, the dramatic effect of caesural breaks, and the general movement of the poem as a whole. . . . Surprisingly enough, this conscious experimentation with verse forms did not lead him, as it might well have done during those flourishing days of *vers libre*, to abandon meter and rhyme." Both Schmitt and Crane also composed nonsense verses in which meaning played no part; the main purpose was to exploit the sounds of words and letters as if they were musical notes.

After his return to Cleveland, Crane became friendly with a group of painters who further stimulated his interest in the art and taught him much about it. His closest friend among them was William Sommers, whom he celebrated in "Sunday Morning Apples"; in this poem the "Beloved apples of seasonable madness" are transfigured by art in a Dionysiac metamorphosis, poised "full and ready for explosion." Specific paintings by El Greco and Joseph Stella provided part of the inspiration for *The Bridge*, and the analogy with painting seemed to be constantly in Crane's mind. As Horton puts it, his attitude toward his poems "was primarily plastic. . . . Crane intended these poems not as descriptions of experience that could be *read about*, but as immediate experiences that the reader could *have* . . ."

In replying to a friend's request for an explanation of "Black Tambourine," Crane said, "The value of the poem is only, to me, in what a painter would call its 'tactile' quality, — an entirely aesthetic feature. A propagandist for either side of the Negro question could find anything he wanted to in it. My only declaration in it is that I find the Negro (in the popular mind) sentimentally or brutally 'placed' in this midkingdom, etc." This remark is especially interesting because Crane is denying any intentional concern with a social and moral value that is certainly in the poem. Crane is, of course, right when he says that it is a "bundle of insinuations, suggestions," remote from propaganda; but its imaginative apprehension of the Negro's plight is not a purely aesthetic phenomenon:

The interests of a black man in a cellar

> Mark tardy judgment on the world's closed door.
> Gnats toss in the shadow of a bottle,
> And a roach spans a crevice in the floor.
>
> Æsop, driven to pondering, found
> Heaven with the tortoise and the hare . . .

In the light of later events, readers now can hardly avoid calling the poem prophetic, though its prophecy is not the vision of a seer but the best kind of social consciousness and moral perceptiveness. (It was written in 1921.) The Negro in the cellar (driven underground, pushed out of sight) regards the "world's closed door." His situation keeps him dirty and drives him to drink (at least this is one interpretation of the bottle and the roach). The second stanza considers Aesop, who perhaps would not have pondered had he not been a slave, and notes that he counseled patience in his fable of the tortoise and the hare; he "found Heaven" with them in the sense that he achieved literary immortality, but the "Fox brush and sow ear" on his grave suggest ironically that his solution was not complete. Aesop is appropriate here also because so many of the Uncle Remus stories derive from him, and the images of the ancient and the modern slaves fuse: both wise, both counseling resignation and patience ("Uncle Toms" in contemporary language), and both dead — i.e., the situation has changed. The "mingling incantations" suggests both the remains of primitive superstition and the singing of Negroes. The last stanza puts explicitly the dilemma of the Negro, wandering forlorn between his recent past in America, symbolized by the tambourine of the minstrel show, when he could be regarded merely as a clown, a stock figure of fun, and his savage and primitive origins in Africa, symbolized by the "carcass quick with flies." But the day of the minstrel show is past; the tambourine is stuck on the wall, and the Negro has been closed up in the cellar. The poem has a poise and taut restraint that are remarkable, and an intensity of perception not inferior to the more obviously emotional later poems.

"Praise for an Urn" is an elegy for Ernest Nelson, at whose funeral in December 1921 Crane, with Sommers, had been a pallbearer. Nelson was a Norwegian who had come to the United States at fifteen, gone to art school and done some good paintings and written some good poems, but then been forced to go into lithography to make a living. Crane called him "One of the best-read people I ever met, wonderful kindliness and tolerance and a true Nietzschean. He was one of many broken against the stupidity of American life . . ." The funeral, Crane said, was "tremendous, especially the finale at the crematorium . . . That funeral was one of the few beautiful things that have happened to me in Cleveland." I have quoted these remarks from Crane's letters because they reveal the feelings that went into the poem and contrast with its poise and restraint; they also clarify some of its allusions.

> It was a kind and northern face
> That mingled in such exile guise
> The everlasting eyes of Pierrot
> And, of Gargantua, the laughter. . . .

In this first stanza, "exile" is richly ambiguous: the Mediterranean qualities of Pierrot and Gargantua lived, in exile, in Nelson's "northern" face, and Pierrot, the pathetic clown, and Gargantua, who laughed at the serious world, counterbalance each other nicely. Further, Nelson was himself in exile both from his original Norwegian home and from the world of art, as he worked in his Cleveland lithography factory. His thoughts (in the second stanza) passed on to Crane were "inheritances" — tradition in the literal sense — but in a world where traditions are increasingly precarious, "Delicate riders of the storm," and Crane hopes to pass them on in turn. The third stanza describes shared experiences in which they discussed such traditions (and perhaps more personal kinds of immortality also); but the clock of the fourth contradicts this, with its insistent comment reminding of death. Survival even in memory is dubious in the penultimate stanza, and the last bids an ironic and resigned farewell to the friend's ashes and to the elegy ("these well-meant idioms"); both will be scattered and lost in the smoky spring of the typical modern suburbs.

These two poems in quatrains exhibit a moral and aesthetic poise as well as a moral penetration and awareness that are not often found in Crane's later work. The major poems of the next few years follow a new line and method of composition. A letter to his good friend Gorham Munson points the direction. He had had a mystical experience in a dentist's chair — an anesthetic revelation: ". . . under the influence of aether and *amnesia* my mind spiraled to a kind of seventh heaven of consciousness and egoistic dance among the seven spheres — and something like an objective voice kept saying to me — 'You have the higher consciousness — you have the higher consciousness. This is something that very few have. This is what is called genius' . . . A happiness, ecstatic such as I have known only twice in 'inspirations' came over me. I felt the two worlds. And at once. . . . O Gorham, I have known moments in eternity."

The essence of Crane's later poetic may be found in "The Wine Menagerie." The title indicates very precisely the whole theme of the poem. "Menagerie" suggests both a collection of wild animals and, etymologically, a household; hence it evokes immediately the central image of the contents of the mind as wild animals. (Yeats's "Circus Animals' Desertion" uses a very similar metaphor.) "Wine" suggests that the menagerie exists (or, perhaps, that the animals become wild) only through the stimulus and release of alcohol. When "wine redeems the sight," then a "leopard ranging always in the brow / Asserts a vision in the slumbering gaze." The lying reality of everyday ("glozening decanters that reflect the street" as the poet sits in a bar) is transcended; the poet sees "New thresholds, new anatomies! Wine talons / Build freedom up about me . . ." But the whole experience is viewed with romantic irony: the wild animals are dangerous to the poet, and the world not really transcended: "Ruddy, the tooth implicit of the world / Has followed you." The poet is betrayed, his head separated from his body like those of Holofernes and John the Baptist; and he is as ineffectual as the puppet Petrushka's valentine. This is, of course, the notion of the poet as visionary and seer, capable of a higher consciousness, a divine madness, which

Crane took primarily from Blake and Rimbaud (who provide the epigraphs for two of his three volumes) and ultimately from Plato and Nietzsche. Crane, notoriously, often strove to achieve this condition through the stimulus both of alcohol and of a phonograph playing loudly and repetitiously.

In "General Aims and Theories," he described his poetic theory at some length. The core of this essay is Crane's insistence that he is not an impressionist, but an "absolutist." The impressionist, he says, "is interesting as far as he goes — but his goal has been reached when he has succeeded in projecting certain selected factual details into his reader's consciousness. He is really not interested in the *causes* (metaphysical) of his materials, their emotional derivations or their utmost spiritual consequences. A kind of retinal registration is enough, along with a certain psychological stimulation. And this is also true of your realist . . . and to a certain extent of the classicist . . . Blake meant these differences when he wrote:

> We are led to believe in a lie
> When we see *with* not *through* the eye."

The absolutist, however — and the predecessors Crane cites are Donne, Blake, Baudelaire, and Rimbaud — hopes to "go *through* the combined materials of the poem, using our 'real' world somewhat as a spring-board, and to give the poem *as a whole* an orbit or predetermined direction of its own." Such a poem aims at freedom from the personalities of both poet and reader, and is "at least a stab at a truth"; hence it may be called "absolute." Crane then suggests the kind of truth such poetry attempts to embody: "Its evocation will not be toward decoration or amusement, but rather toward a state of consciousness, an 'innocence' (Blake) or absolute beauty. In this condition there may be discoverable under new forms certain spiritual illuminations, shining with a morality essentialized from experience directly, and not from previous precepts or preconceptions. It is as though a poem gave the reader as he left it a single, new *word*, never before spoken and impossible to actually enunciate, but self-evident as an active principle in the reader's consciousness henceforward." As to technique, Crane says that the "terms of expression" employed are often selected less for their logical or literal than for their associational meanings: "Via this and their metaphorical inter-relationships, the entire construction of the poem is raised on the organic principle of a 'logic of metaphor,' which antedates our so-called pure logic, and which is the genetic basis of all speech, hence consciousness and thought-extension."

He then goes on to explain and defend the difficulty of his poems in terms of these principles, speaking of the "implicit emotional dynamics of the materials used" and the "organic impact on the imagination" of the poem; the poet's business, he says, is the "conquest of consciousness." In a letter to Harriet Monroe, he put it more plainly: "as a poet I may very possibly be more interested in the so-called illogical impingements of the connotations of words on the consciousness (and their combinations and interplay in metaphor on this basis) than I am interested in the preservation of their logically rigid significations at the cost of limiting my subject matter and perceptions involved in the poem." And in the essay "Modern Poetry," he casts further light on his notion of poetic truth: "poetic prophecy in the case of the seer has nothing to do with factual prediction or with futurity. It is a peculiar type of perception, capable of apprehending some absolute and timeless concept of the imagination with astounding clarity and conviction."

We may now consider some of the poems in *White Buildings* that follow and exemplify this poetic. "Recitative" begins:

> Regard the capture here, O Janus-faced,
> As double as the hands that twist this glass.
> Such eyes at search or rest you cannot see;
> Reciting pain or glee, how can you bear!

It is so very difficult that even Allen Tate had trouble with it, and Crane wrote an apologetic explanation to him: "Imagine the poet, say, on a platform speaking it. The audience is one half of Humanity, Man (in the sense of Blake) and the poet the other. ALSO, the poet sees himself in the audience as in a mirror. ALSO, the audience sees itself, in part, in the poet. Against this paradoxical DUALITY is posed the UNITY . . . in the last verse. In another sense, the poet is *talking to himself* all the way through the poem, and there are, as too often in my poems, other reflexes and symbolisms in the poem, also, which it would be silly to write here . . ." As usual in explaining his own poems, Crane begins here by describing the dramatic situation, and his comments, as always, are convincing and helpful; but they are far from resolving the difficulties of the poem. The situation itself is so ambiguous, with so many alternative interpretations (as Crane indicates), that visualizing it is not much help. The fourth stanza is the source of the title of the volume:

Look steadily — how the wind feasts and spins
The brain's disk shivered against lust. Then watch
While darkness, like an ape's face, falls away,
And gradually white buildings answer day.

The white buildings, contrasted with darkness and the ape's face, are embodiments of the Ideal, testaments of the Word; they are, specifically, poems of the sort Crane is writing. They are also, of course, New York skyscrapers transfigured by the dawn light. It is worth noting that the redemption takes place although — or perhaps because — the brain is unable to control lust. The next two stanzas describe the magnificence and isolation of the skyscrapers, and urge: "leave the tower" for the bridge — abandon isolation for unity. The final stanza evokes unity in the image of "All hours clapped dense into a single stride" in the sound of "alternating bells." Crane called the poem "a confession," and certainly the contrast between the violent dualisms and the final vision of unity is characteristic; the images of the Bridge and the Tower also anticipate strikingly the use Crane was to make of them in later poems.

"Passage" is another difficult and visionary poem. Biographically, it probably derives from the feeling of refreshment Crane experienced in spending the summer of 1925 in the country. This is, however, very little help. The poem is about the experience of vision, of "higher consciousness," which is for Crane synonymous with the writing of poetry; it is in this respect like "The Wine Me-

nagerie," though the perspective here is autobiographical, through
time and distance, rather than a closeup as there of the physio-
logical aids and the experience itself. The title suggests a voyage,
as often in Crane, and perhaps also the anthropologist's *rite de
passage*, a farewell to childhood. The first four stanzas describe
the experience of the visionary voyage, promising "an improved
infancy" — i.e., a rebirth, a return to innocence. Memory, de-
scribed scornfully in the second stanza, is left behind. The feeling
is of heightened life, of unity with nature, and the voyage almost
reaches its goal (the valleys are in sight); but the wind dies,
the vision fails, through time and smoke (the evil in man's heart?
"chimney-sooted heart of man"), as so often ("a too well-known
biography"). The speaker returns to the ravine where he left Mem-
ory, and finds a thief beneath the "opening laurel," holding the
poet's book. (The laurel is opening because the poet is beginning
to gain some reputation; the thief is presumably Memory, or per-
haps the Intellect — those faculties, at any rate, that the poet as
visionary has abandoned.) After a brief dialogue, Memory closes
the book (perhaps in sign of reconciliation), and there is a further
visionary experience: History (the sand from the Ptolemies) and
Time (the serpent) bring consciousness of past and future (un-
paced beaches), and there are further incommunicable revelations
("What fountains . . . speeches?") which overstrain Memory. One
meaning (and here, as in much of the preceding, I follow Dem-
bo) would seem to be that Memory is accepted as part of the vi-
sionary experience, necessary to it in its mature form, as opposed
to the simpler childish form described in the first four stanzas. The
poem is evocative of Rimbaud, though very much Crane's own;
it has a peculiar intensity, a haunting quality that is remarkable.

"Paraphrase" describes a different kind of vision. It had its incep-
tion, according to Horton, in Crane's experience of waking from
a drunken sleep into the bright morning light and thinking him-
self dead. The first two stanzas evoke such an experience: "One
rushing from the bed at night" finds, more or less reassuringly, the
"record wedged in his soul" of the regular and dependable alterna-
tions of life in its various cycles of light and dark, sleeping and

waking, expansion and contraction, and the like. The "steady winking beat between / Systole, diastole" suggests such devices as the cardiograph which attest and observe the regularity of the life processes; the tone is clinical. The following phrase, "spokes-of-a-wheel," however, suggests the hysterical and terrifying quality of the experience, as these processes seem speeded up in panic until the alternations blur and seem to reverse, like the spokes of a rapidly revolving wheel. The second stanza represents the sleeper's nightmarish experience with ironic detachment: to the sleeper death has seemed a physical force or object trying to get in between the sheets and immobilize his fingers and toes ("integers of life" suggests also the integrity and unity of body and soul that constitutes life). The last two stanzas evoke that inevitable morning when the experience will be real and not illusory, when the sleeper will really (in the language of folk humor) wake up to find himself dead. However "desperate" the light, however systematically morning floods the pillow, until it is like an "antarctic blaze" of whiteness, it "shall not rouse" the sleeper, whose head will only post "a white paraphrase" among the "bruised roses" of the wallpaper. The word "paraphrase" suggests, together with the "record" of the first stanza, an analogy between the inadequacy as descriptions of natural processes of records such as the cardiogram and the inadequacy of the dead body as equivalent of the living man who was an "integer," a unity. In the simplest terms, the dead body is a paraphrase (with the connotations both of "translation" and of "explanation") and a poor one, of the living man.

Of course I should not insist on any exclusive validity for this reading, though I hope it is convincing enough to demonstrate, at least, that the poem is not centrally obscure. It is difficult, but with a tension and power inseparable from the difficulty. The comparatively regular four-stress lines arranged in quatrains with only an approximation to rhyme in each stanza until the last, when "paraphrase" emerges as a full rhyme to "blaze," produce an effect of climactic intensity.

"Possessions," which follows in *White Buildings*, returns to the visionary theme with its characteristic obscurity. The situation would seem to be that the poet is embarking on a new (homosexual) affair, driven by his lust, and almost sure that this affair will turn out like all the others, but going on nevertheless with his tormented seeking. The first stanza contrasts the rain, which has direction, and the key, which finds its proper lock and turns its bolts, with the poet's "undirected" condition and his phallic "fixed stone of lust" which is no key. The second stanza recites the total of such past experiences. The third places the poet specifically in Greenwich Village, apprehensive beyond words, inspecting his lust, and "turning on smoked forking spires" — the image is apparently of being roasted as on a turnspit over the "city's stubborn lives, desires." The last stanza changes the metaphor to the poet as gored by the horns of lust (as bullfighter or simple victim?); he who "bleeding dies" after such goring achieves nothing but "piteous admissions" to make up a "record of rage and partial appetites." But in spite of all there is the final affirmation:

> The pure possession, the inclusive cloud
> Whose heart is fire shall come, — the white wind raze
> All but bright stones wherein our smiling plays.

The word "possession" has, of course, the double sense of amorous consummation, with the pure one to wash away all the preceding impure (in the sense both of unchaste and of adulterated) experiences, and the supernatural or diabolical sense of being possessed by another spirit and personality; there is perhaps also the third sense of possessions as merely the physical things one owns. The pure possession, when it comes, will be a guiding force like the biblical pillar of fire by night and pillar of cloud by day, with the myth rationalized to mean that the heart of the cloud must be fire — or, to put it crudely, that passion is the only guide. When the state of possession, of ecstasy (in the etymological sense) is complete (for "partial appetites" are worthless), then the troublesome and archaic stone of lust will be transformed into "bright stones wherein our smiling plays." But one serious difficulty with the poem is that the logical and rhetorical relation of the last three lines to the rest of the poem is not clear. Perhaps the "pure possession" is death — its fiery and destructive force suggests this — and the "bright stones" of the last line are seen only after the purgation of death, as the kind of automatic resurrection or guaranteed paradise suggested in many other poems. But the primary suggestion would seem to be a contrast between those who die through failure to achieve complete appetites, pure possessions, and those who do achieve them and therefore do not die. The poem seems to me, however, far less effective than "Paraphrase," partly because of this central ambiguity.

I have thought it better to present reasonably detailed accounts of those poems in *White Buildings* that seem to me central to Crane's achievement than to attempt to mention all of them, though this has meant omitting, for instance, "Repose of Rivers," Crane's most magical example of incantation and control of sound. Something must be said briefly, however, of "At Melville's Tomb." Crane placed it immediately before the series of "Voyages" at the end of the volume, and it forms a kind of prelude to them, introducing the Voyage symbol which had been implicit in many of the preceding poems. Crane wrote a famous letter (reprinted in Horton's appendix) to Harriet Monroe, editor of *Poetry*, explaining the poem and defending it against her objections; the letter is too long to quote, but may be recommended as containing Crane's detailed explications of some of his most intricate images. The poem seems to me notable, however, as a tribute to Melville and an introduction to "Voyages" rather than as an achievement in its own right.

"Voyages" is, in my judgment, Crane's best long poem. The first section was written in 1921 and an early version of the sixth in 1923, all the rest in 1924–25. Some of the literary inspiration came from the poems of Samuel Greenberg, which Crane had read in manuscript (Greenberg had died in 1916 at the age of twenty-three); but the principal inspiration was Crane's affair with an imaginative and sensitive sailor-lover. As Horton says, "Possibly no other writer but Melville has ever been able to express the mysteries and terrors of the sea with such eloquence and imagination . . ." and this is probably part of the explanation of Eugene O'Neill's enthusiasm for Crane's poetry.

The first section, written much earlier than the others, is much less ambitious. Crane originally called it "The Bottom of the Sea Is Cruel" and, in a letter, "Poster" (saying deprecatingly, "There is nothing more profound in it than a 'stop, look and listen' sign"); the latter title is indicative of its attractive simplicity. The contrast of the children's innocence and gaiety and the mystery, the cruelty and terror, the lightning and thunder of the sea (in the depths beyond the "fresh ruffles" of the surf) is almost Wordsworthian. Its sense of the sea's fatal attraction, which will render the warning to the children futile, foreshadows the theme of the rest of the poem. Compared to the other sections, it is minor art; but it forms an effective introduction to the sequence.

Section II is the most widely anthologized and admired part of the poem; Winters called it "one of the most powerful and one of the most nearly perfect poems of the last two hundred years." Rhetorically, this section would seem to be a counterstatement to the first: the sea is cruel, "And yet" it exempts lovers from its cruelty, regarding them with special favor and sympathy. The sea is a "great wink of eternity" — the wink as sign of complicity and secrets shared only with lovers. (The image also suggests, perhaps, wink as lapse of attention, and hence the sea as escape from time.) Her vast belly bending moonward (and the connotation is not only of the tides but the moon as patron of lovers) is "Laughing the wrapt inflections of our love" — and on one level the image is of the sea as a fat old woman, a bawd or go-between for lovers (like Juliet's nurse), laughing at their raptures while encouraging them and participating in them. This connotation is qualified by the preceding image of the sea as "Samite sheeted and processioned" — the Lady of the Lake and other exalted or mysterious ladies in Arthurian legend wore white samite (often with gold thread), and these qualities of remoteness, legendary and ritualistic and awesome, are attributed to the sea.

The dominant image of the second stanza is of the sea as Judge, terrible and severe to all but lovers: "The sceptred terror of whose sessions rends . . . All but the pieties of lovers' hands." The next stanza explores this partiality of the sea to lovers: as the undersea bells of the sunken cathedral answer and correspond to the stars reflected on the surface of the sea, so "Adagios of islands" complete the "dark confessions" spelled by her veins. Crane explained the former phrase in "General Aims and Theories": ". . . the reference is to the motion of a boat through islands clustered thickly, the rhythm of the motion, etc. And it seems a much more direct and creative statement than any more logical employment of words such as 'coasting slowly through the islands,' besides ushering in a whole world of music." Presumably the meaning is that the rhythm of the blood in the lover's veins (and "O my Prodigal" addresses Crane's lover directly for the first time) echoes and corresponds to the sea's rhythm (as the stars and bells have echoed each other above). The dark confession is, then, that the sea is like the lover's feelings; her veins are like his veins.

The next stanza draws a kind of conclusion: since the sea (or love) is in time ("her turning shoulders wind the hours"), the lovers should commit themselves to time and "Hasten, while they are true," for "sleep, death, desire" (and the equation of all three is highly significant) are all as much in time, as transient, as "one floating flower." The magnificent last stanza is a prayer (to vague and pantheistic deities of sky and sea — clear Seasons and minstrel galleons) that the lovers may be allowed enough time and committed fully enough to it, and granted enough sense of wonder ("Bind us in time . . . and awe"), to penetrate the secret — which will mean death. Being bequeathed to an "earthly shore" would mean, presumably, abandoning the life of passion and remaining alive. The grave is a "vortex" which will reveal the sea's depths and secrets and hence answer (provide the only fulfillment of) the "seal's wide spindrift gaze toward paradise." (The last image suggests the equation of sea and death once more: spindrift is windblown spray, hence sea united with air, as the seal is a sea creature which breathes air and has humanoid eyes.) Crane is not asking to live long enough to learn the secret, as some commentators have said, but to remain in the element of the sea — i.e., the passionate life, or love — until he learns the secret through dying.

The third section continues the exploration of the blood relation ("Infinite consanguinity") between the sea and time-bound love and death; in a sense it develops and explains the somewhat cryptic images of the last stanza of the preceding section. The first image is of the relation between sea and sky (the otherworldly, the paradisal) imagined as together supporting the lover's body as "tendered theme." But death is also present in the "reliquary hands" of the sea. The second stanza presents the dramatic climax or resolution: the poet therefore will commit himself, immerse himself in the destructive element (there is no echo of Conrad, but the theme is closely parallel), in the faith that death "Presumes no carnage, but this single change, — . . . The silken skilled transmemberment of song" — a sea change like that in *The Tempest*, which Crane called the "crown of all the Western world," or like Eliot's "Death by Water," but without any of Eliot's dual possibilities of outcome or supernatural significance; this is a purely secular baptism into passion, with its closest parallel Wagner's "Liebestod." The fusion is complete in the last line, where "love" is both the lover and the sea (the exaltation of poetry and the state of being in love): "Permit me voyage, love, into your hands."

Sections ii and iii seem to me the best parts of the poem. The chief point I shall hope to establish concerning the remaining parts is that the poem constitutes a genuine sequence and unity. In iv, the lovers are separated and the sea (which literally separates them) is imagined as the element that unites them (for love is a voyage upon this element, this passionate state of being) and conveys the poet's love through song; he has a vision of reunion after suffering (after being lost in "fatal tides" the "islands" will be found through the spiritual geography of the lover — "Blue latitudes and levels of your eyes") when the final mysteries ("secret oar and petals of all love") will be revealed.

The fifth section, however, presents a sad contrast. The lovers are now physically united once more, but the harmony is broken and love is dead. Waking past midnight, "lonely" though his lover is with him, the poet uses images of hardness, coldness, brittleness to suggest the broken relation. One image seems to be, proleptically, of a bridge with broken cables ("The cables of our sleep so swiftly filed, / Already hang, shred ends from remembered stars"). Moonlight is "deaf," tyrannous, inexorable as the tide, in contrast to the sympathetic moon of II. (The suggestion is also, of course, that this outcome is as inevitable as the tides.) The sky, instead of being mysteriously consanguine with the sea, is a "godless cleft . . . Where nothing turns but dead sands flashing" (the dead and meaningless moon). The lovers part, unable to communicate; as the sailor-lover leaves, the poet accepts the separation (even though he cannot understand it) and bids him farewell in a moving stanza.

The sixth and last section presents the poet's affirmation, in spite of everything, of his continued commitment to the sea (in all its meanings). Though he is "derelict and blinded," he continues to believe in the bond between sea and sky ("O rivers mingling toward the sky") and in the possibility of reaching the harbor which is as rare as the phoenix; though "thy waves rear / More savage than the death of kings" he still awaits "Some splintered garland for the seer." The second half of the poem describes the vision of reaching this harbor of resurrection and fulfillment. Belle Isle, "white echo of the oar" of love's mystery imagined at the end of IV, will contain the "lounged goddess" and will be found through the "imaged Word" (which will, presumably, correspond to "Creation's blithe and petalled word" once thundered to the "lounged goddess" of the island). It will transcend time, hold "Hushed willows anchored"; it will eliminate all betrayals and partings, making love perfect: "It is the unbetrayable reply / Whose accent no farewell can know." The amorous vision and the poetic vision, then, are one; the perfect Word (to which the perfect poem can be reduced) will also redeem love.

I have postponed discussion of "For the Marriage of Faustus and Helen," Crane's first long poem (written in 1922–23), because it seems best to consider it in relation to *The Bridge*, to which it is precursor and parallel. It is a very ambitious performance indeed, similar in intention to Joyce's *Ulysses* and Eliot's *Waste Land* in suggesting a fusion of present and past, a "bridge between so-called classic experience and . . . our seething, confused cosmos of today," in Crane's words. Of *The Waste Land*, Crane said, "After this perfection of death — nothing is possible in motion but a resurrection of some kind"; and this he hoped that his poem would provide. He described his plan thus in a letter: "Almost every symbol of current significance is matched by a correlative, suggested or actually stated, 'of ancient days.' Helen, the symbol of this abstract 'sense of beauty,' Faustus the symbol of myself, the poetic or imaginative man of all times. . . . Part II . . . begins with *catharsis,* the acceptance of tragedy through destruction . . . It is Dionysian in its attitude, the creator and the eternal destroyer dance arm in arm . . ." Actually, the Faustus-Helen symbolism is of very limited validity, not going far beyond the title (Crane seems not to have known Goethe's *Faust*; Marlowe was his only source), and the structural parallels between past and present are flimsy indeed. Though there are several fine passages, the poem seems to me of interest chiefly for the full embodiment of Crane's visionary theme in the last part: the fourth dimension, the mystical "lone eye," the Dionysian acceptance and transcendence of war, tragedy, and death. It was written not long after his mystical, or anesthetic, revelation in the dentist's chair and his commitment to the visionary poetic, with the Rimbaudian program of intoxication and derangement of the senses.

The Bridge was begun in 1923 as an attempt to carry further the kind of interpretation of modern life and its relation to the past that Crane had made in "For the Marriage of Faustus and Helen." The greater part of it was written during the visit to the Isle of Pines in 1926; but Crane was constantly occupied with the project, revising and adding to it, until its publication in 1930. Crane thought of it as his magnum opus, his poetic testament; he spoke of it as an epic like the *Aeneid,* planned like the Sistine Chapel, embodying the Myth of America, and refuting Eliot's pessimistic

Waste Land to provide an affirmative interpretation of modern civilization. These rash and grandiose claims were demolished promptly and definitively by Allen Tate and Yvor Winters when the poem appeared. We may begin, therefore, by granting that *The Bridge* is not the Great American Epic, or any kind of epic, and that it is not a mature or responsible interpretation of American history or of the modern world. What kind of poem is it, then, and what kind of interest does it have now, after several decades?

In his highly persuasive exegesis, Dembo calls it "a romantic lyric given epic implications" and defines its theme as "the exiled poet's quest for a logos in which the Absolute that he has known in his imagination will be made intelligible to the world. . . . Crane tried to find in the history of American society some evidence that this society was capable of a psychological experience essentially identical with the poet's ecstatic apprehension of the Ideal as Beauty. The narrator in *The Bridge* thus journeys to a mythic Indian past that represents 'the childhood of the continent,' becomes an Indian himself, and marries Pocahontas in a ritual fire dance. Having thus learned the Word, attained the guerdon of the goddess, he returns to his own time . . . Although he now sees Pocahontas not as a fertile goddess, but as a sterile prostitute, the poet keeps his faith and concludes the poem with a hymn celebrating the Bridge as a modern embodiment of the Word."

The key Dembo finds in Nietzsche's theory of tragedy, which provided Crane "with a metaphysical argument with which to meet disillusion, whatever its source, and thus associated him not merely with Whitman, but with the whole tradition of optimism in nineteenth-century romantic literature." "Simply put, Crane accepted the proposition that resurrection always follows suffering and death. That is really the essence of what he took from Nietzsche." Except for the emphasis on Nietzsche, and the consistency and penetration of supporting analysis, Dembo's thesis is not new; Yvor Winters long ago observed that Emerson and Whitman taught a similar doctrine, and he argued that Crane merely put it into practice, following it to its logical end of suicide. For most of

us, Dembo's association of the doctrine with Nietzsche and the Di-
onysiac tradition makes it more palatable; but I cannot see that
it answers any of the objections of Winters and Tate. We are,
however, concerned primarily not with the intrinsic merits of the
doctrine, but with its effectiveness as theme of the poem. Conced-
ing it all possible efficacy as a unifying force, the unity of the
poem remains very loose indeed, and some parts remain very much
better than others.

The "Proem" begins with the image of the seagull in its poise
and freedom (its "inviolate curve," as in Hopkins' "Windhover,"
which Crane had certainly not yet read, suggesting a balance of
the forces of control and release). This image is contrasted with
that of the file clerk in his confined routine work, taken aloft only
by elevators, dreaming of sails, and with that of the denizens of
the cinema who hope for revelation there. The Bridge is then
evoked as a parallel to the seagull, uniting motion and stillness,
freedom and necessity; though, ironically, the madman commits
suicide by leaping from it. It is a symbol of the Divine, but its
rewards are mysterious: its accolade is anonymity, but it also shows
"vibrant reprieve and pardon." It is both harp and altar, threshold
of the future, prayer of the outcast, and cry of the lover; it con-
denses eternity and cradles night. "Only in darkness is thy shadow
clear" — and the poet, standing under it at night in winter and
in the symbolic darkness of suffering, prays to it to take the place
of his lost religious mythologies:

> Unto us lowliest sometime sweep, descend
> And of the curveship lend a myth to God.

The first section, "Ave Maria," is a monologue of Columbus as
he is returning from his first voyage. Columbus is, of course, the
poet-voyager, and Cathay is the terrestrial paradise, or the Abso-
lute, or the Word. He praises God (and Crane notes that here the
rhythm changes from the earlier "waterswell" to a suggestion of
the "great *Te Deum* of the court, later held"), who "dost search /
Cruelly with love thy parable of man" in experiences of which this
voyage is a type, and testifies to awareness of His presence:
"Elohim, still I hear thy sounding heel!"

The second section, "Powhatan's Daughter," has five subdivisions. The basic symbol is Pocahontas as the mythical body of America to be explored and known, the past, the Absolute. "The Harbor Dawn" presents very beautifully the protagonist's vision of her, between sleeping and waking, in the modern city. In "Van Winkle" he merges with the legendary character from an older New York and takes the subway, which, in "The River," becomes the symbolically named "20th Century Limited" train; there is then the associated picture of the hobos, who with all their faults, "touch something like a key perhaps"; they remember the past and know the country: "They know a body under the wide rain." Both Tate and Winters consider "The River" the best part of *The Bridge*, with its description of the journey down the Mississippi as it appears both to the "Pullman breakfasters" on the modern train and to the hobos, who merge with the pioneers; there is no strained philosophy or symbolism, but a loving evocation of the country and the people, past and present, in concrete terms. "The Dance" follows, and is the climax of the section: the protagonist consummates his union with Pocahontas; he becomes Maquokeeta, an Indian, and is the sacrificial victim burned at the stake in a ritual death dance; he is then resurrected and symbolically united with Pocahontas, now become America. The poetry is intense and beautiful; but it is hard to forget Winters' comment: "one does not deal adequately with the subject of death and immortality by calling the soil Pocahontas, and by then writing a love poem to an imaginary maiden who bears the name of Pocahontas." With regard to the pantheism of the whole section, Winters remarked, "I believe that nothing save confusion can result from our mistaking the Mississippi Valley for God." The last part of the section, "Indiana," is a sentimental portrait of the pioneer woman; by common consent it is one of Crane's worst lapses.

"Cutty Sark," the third section, begins the loosely connected and generally less effective group that deal with the protagonist's effort to preserve his faith while living in a world that seems to deny the Ideal; it is this part that corresponds to Crane's description of the poem as an "epic of the modern consciousness." "Cut-

ty Sark" Crane described as a fantasy on the period of the whalers
and clipper ships, built on the plan of a fugue with two voices,
one that of the pianola, expressing the Atlantis or Eternity theme,
and the other that of the derelict sailor encountered in the South
Street dive. On the way home, the protagonist sees a phantom
regatta of clipper ships from Brooklyn Bridge; Crane uses the his-
torical names, and meant the arrangement on the page to be sig-
nificant: he called it a cartogram, and said "The 'ships' should
meet and pass in line and type—as well as in wind and mem-
ory . . ." (In this section particularly, Crane's description of his
intentions is more elaborate and more interesting than the
achieved result.) Some commentators who have puzzled about
the significance of the title seem not to have been aware that the
trademark of "Cutty Sark" whisky is a clipper ship.

"Cape Hatteras" Crane described as a "kind of ode to Whit-
man." It is also an ironic celebration of the airplane as embodi-
ment of the modern, its speed and its conquest of space. Man is
drunk with power and blind with pride— "the eagle dominates
our days" with its "wings imperious"; he neglects the past (the
recurrent symbols of the eagle for space and the serpent for time
here receive new emphasis) and the imaginative meaning of in-
finity. His technological triumphs have led only to more destruc-
tive war, and Crane evokes the dogfights of World War I. But the
Falcon-Ace has "a Sanskrit charge / To conjugate infinity's dim
marge"— in Dembo's interpretation, "to plumb beneath death to
resurrection and thereby . . . define the Word." War is justified
in that beyond it lies resurrection and a new understanding of the
Word; Whitman gives him a rebirth of faith through his vision
of the rebirth of the slain.

"Three Songs" portrays three distortions of love in the modern
world, perversions of the ideal Pocahontas. The most effective of
them is "National Winter Garden," where the mythic dance is
reduced to a burlesque show. "Quaker Hill" pictures the corrup-
tion of the countryside by commercialism and philistinism: the
Quaker meeting house in Connecticut is now a weekend resort
called the New Avalon Hotel.

"The Tunnel" describes, literally, the subway ride under the river to get to the bridge; figuratively, as the epigraph from Blake suggests, the final descent into the abyss before the ascent. Thus it is a kind of Inferno, a descent into hell, into the dark winter night before morning.

> The phonographs of hades in the brain
> Are tunnels that re-wind themselves, and love
> A burnt match skating in a urinal . . .

The protagonist sees himself in Poe, the martyred poet. But he emerges, "like Lazarus," to stand by the East River and look at the harbor he has been under.

"Atlantis," the final section, Crane called "a sweeping dithyramb in which the Bridge becomes the symbol of consciousness spanning time and space." It is ironic that this, the most ecstatic section of the poem, was the first to be completed. "Atlantis" presents the imagined fulfillment of the quest and the end of tragedy: "Vision of the Voyage," Cathay, Belle Isle, as seen by the archetypal voyager and quester Jason; the vision is "Deity's glittering Pledge," "Answerer of all," and the "white, pervasive Paradigm" of Love; it is, of course, the Bridge apotheosized. Perhaps it is ultimately the poetic imagination. The poet prays, "Atlantis, — hold thy floating singer late!" The image is a pathetic one, since the singer is floating because Atlantis is not there, and the poem ends on an unanswered question.

Tate seems to me to put his finger on the trouble with the symbolism of *The Bridge*. He observes that the framework of symbol in "For the Marriage of Faustus and Helen" "is an abstraction empty of any knowable experience." Crane became dissatisfied both with its style and with the "literary" character of the symbolism, and so "set about the greater task of writing *The Bridge*." But the Bridge "differs from the Helen and Faust symbols only in its unliterary origin. I think Crane was deceived by this difference, and by the fact that Brooklyn Bridge is 'modern' and a fine piece of 'mechanics.' . . . The single symbolic image, in which the whole poem centers, is at one moment the actual Brooklyn Bridge; at another, it is any bridge or 'connection'; at still another, it is a philosophical pun and becomes the basis of a series of analogies. . . . Because the idea is variously metaphor, symbol, and analogy, it tends to make the poem static. The poet takes it up, only to be forced to put it down again *when the poetic image of the moment is exhausted.* The idea does not, in short, fill the poet's mind; it is the starting point for a series of short flights, or inventions connected only in analogy — which explains the merely personal passages, which are obscure, and the lapses into sentimentality."

Crane had intended "For the Marriage of Faustus and Helen" to be an answer to the pessimism of the school of Eliot, and *The Bridge* was to be an even more complete answer. But, Tate comments, "There was a fundamental mistake in Crane's diagnosis of Eliot's problem. Eliot's 'pessimism' grows out of an awareness of the decay of the individual consciousness and its fixed relations to the world; but Crane thought that it was due to something like pure 'orneryness,' an unwillingness 'to share with us the breath released,' the breath being a new kind of freedom that he identified emotionally with the age of the machine." And, he observes, "I think he knew that the structure of *The Bridge* was finally incoherent, and for that reason . . . he could no longer believe even in his lyrical powers; he could not return to the early work and take it up where he had left off. Far from 'refuting' Eliot, his whole career is a vindication of Eliot's major premise — that the integrity of the individual consciousness has broken down."

Key West: An Island Sheaf is a small volume of twenty-two poems that Crane left ready for publication at his death. (It was not issued separately but forms one section of the *Complete Poems.*) Most of them were written during or soon after his stay on the Isle of Pines in 1926; Waldo Frank accompanied him, and they stayed on the plantation belonging to Crane's maternal grandmother until it was wrecked by a hurricane. Some of the poems, however, were plainly written later, the last being "The Broken Tower," begun in Mexico only two months before Crane's suicide. Aside from being presumably Crane's choice of the best poems he had produced during these years (apart from *The Bridge*), the poems are unified by tropical imagery and feeling, the juxtaposition of fecundity and waste, beauty and death. Most of them are lower keyed, more "representational," and therefore more accessible than the poems of *White Buildings*; they are also more objectively personal and more varied in themes and techniques. Most critics have regarded these poems as exhibiting a great falling-off from the earlier volume, perhaps largely because Crane himself took this view — and certainly a primary motive for his suicide was his belief that "The Broken Tower" testified to the failure of his powers. But Crane was emphatically wrong about this poem, and he may therefore have been wrong about the whole trend. At any rate, it is possible to judge these poems by standards other than Crane's own "visionary" one, and to avoid equating them too closely with his personal agony and disintegration. Looked at thus independently, the poems in *Key West* and many of those labeled "Uncollected Poems" in the *Complete Poems* show a resemblance to the recent trend sometimes called "poetry of experience" — the direct and open-textured poetry, similarly related to personal crises, of Robert Lowell's *Life Studies* and W. D. Snodgrass' *Heart's Needle*, for example.

The title poem, "Key West," is a kind of farewell to the U.S.A. and to the modern civilization of which it is the most advanced embodiment.

> Because these millions reap a dead conclusion
> Need I presume the same fruit of my bone
> As draws them towards a doubly mocked confusion
> Of apish nightmares into steel-strung stone?

The "apish nightmares into steel-strung stone" is a negative counterpart to the lines in "Recitative"; in that poem, skyscrapers could be redeemed, at least metaphorically, when "darkness, like an ape's face, falls away / And gradually white buildings answer day." But now the apish nightmares remain, and are embodied in the skyscrapers. The poet's only recourse is to go to his tropical island, while knowing that he cannot escape the modern world.

"O Carib Isle!" is about death in the tropics. Nothing mourns

the dead: neither the "tarantula rattling at the lily's foot" nor
the other creatures. Against the pitiless violence of the scene the
poet can invoke only the fecundity of vegetation; but the wind
— the most violent force of all, as in tropical hurricanes —"that
knots itself in one great death — / Coils and withdraws. So sylla-
bles want breath." With no confidence in gainsaying death, the
poet therefore asks where and what the ruler of this kind of na-
ture is — the metaphor suggesting that He must be as bloodthirs-
ty as the legendary Captain Kidd. The last three stanzas show the
poet envisioning his own death in terms that are a kind of tropi-
cal equivalent of those of the *Divine Comedy*. He hopes that
he can die under the "fiery blossoms" of the poinciana so that
his "ghost" can ascend until "it meets the blue's comedian host."
What he fears is a slow and helpless death like those of the "huge
terrapin" overturned and spiked "Each daybreak on the wharf"—to
await slow evisceration; and, as he congeals, in the "satin and
vacant" afternoons, he fears that the tropics are making him like
the turtles. The shell (presumably both the shell of the poet as
turtle and the island itself) is a gift of Satan; a "carbonic amu-
let" created by cosmic violence, "the sun exploded in the sea."
    Only a few of the other poems in the volume can be mentioned.
"The Idiot" is a vivid, uncomplicated, and very powerful ren-
dering of an idiot boy whom Crane also describes in a letter: "When
I saw him next he was talking to a blue little kite high in the
afternoon. He is rendingly beautiful at times: I have encoun-
tered him in the road, talking again tout seul and examining peb-
bles and cinders and marble chips through the telescope of a twice-
opened tomato can." The poem describes the embarrassment and
ridicule he produces, with "squint lanterns in his head, and it's
likely / Fumbling his sex . . ."; it presents the kite and tin-can
telescope scene, and finally his song "Above all reason lifting";
the poet's "trespass vision shrinks to face his wrong." Quinn is
probably right in suggesting that Crane sees the idiot implicitly
as a distorted parallel to himself, a parody of the visionary poet,
similarly derided and rejected. It is not necessary to read the poem
in this way, but it helps to explain the moving quality it un-

doubtedly possesses. "Royal Palm" and "The Air Plant" — both in regular quatrains, like most of the poems in the volume — may be regarded as tropical "bridges," as Hazo suggests: the palm ascends to heaven and the air plant ("This tuft that thrives on saline nothingness") lives in air, welcoming hurricanes as well as breezes. Both poems are relatively simple, straightforward, and emblematic in technique; they are herbal equivalents of bestiaries like those of Marianne Moore, making the plants types of human qualities. "The Hurricane" evokes the power of an awesome divinity, its archaism suggesting the Old Testament god of the whirlwind. (There is an implicit parallel in several of these poems between the hurricane and the force of poetic inspiration.)

By common consent, the best poem in the volume, and one of Crane's greatest lyrics, is "The Broken Tower." Crane's letters give the background of the poem fully, and it is a very important and moving biographical document. Crane wrote it in February–March 1932, under the stimulus of his late and unexpected love affair with Peggy Baird. It was, of course, based on an actual experience of helping to ring the church bells at dawn in Taxco, Mexico. The poem testifies to his feeling of rebirth and integration both in what it says and in the fact of its existence, for it was the first poem Crane had been able to finish in two years. But the feeling of hope and confidence evaporated during the weeks of revision; the people to whom he sent the poem happened not to reply promptly; and Crane became convinced that the poem was a failure and that it proved his creative powers to be exhausted. This conviction was the basis of his despair in those fantastic final days in Mexico; with nowhere to go, feeling at a dead end, he alternated between drunken debauchery and paranoiac suspiciousness until the threats of suicide reached their inevitable conclusion. The poem can hardly be detached entirely from this biographical context — any more than can, say, the late sonnets of Keats or the "terrible sonnets" of Hopkins — or from the context of Crane's other poetry, and it derives added significance from the fact that it is a final triumphant affirmation of the visionary theme and a kind of poetic testament.

The basic image is the implicit identification of the utterance
of the church bells and the utterance of the poet; both are ex-
pressions and embodiments of vision and of divine love. The poet
himself is both the tower and the sexton within it, pulled up
and down in exultation and despair as the sexton is by his work
of pulling the bell ropes. (The images are inconsistent visually,
but not thematically; the poet is in both cases the agent and
vehicle of Poetry, which enslaves and destroys him.)

> The bells, I say, the bells break down their tower;
> And swing I know not where. Their tongues engrave
> Membrane through marrow, my long-scattered score
> Of broken intervals. . . . And I, their sexton slave!

The fifth stanza makes explicit the identification of the two kinds
of music — or perhaps it would be better to say, the substitution
of poetry for any other religion. The poet's dedication is religious:
he has become a poet ("entered the broken world," become a bro-
ken tower) for no other purpose than to "trace the visionary com-
pany of love," however fleeting its voice. The next stanza, how-
ever, voices doubt of the validity of the identification. "My word
I poured." But was it really divine, was it the Word? His blood
supplies no answer; but "she / Whose sweet mortality stirs latent
power" revives and reassures him so that he is "healed, original
now, and pure . . ." Although the biographical reference is clear
enough, in terms of the poem the "she" is also a psychic force,
a feminine part of the personality (although there is no evidence
that Crane ever read Jung, anyone who has can hardly avoid think-
ing of the Jungian *anima*) which brings about an integration
of the personality (the new tower built within, not stone, for "Not
stone can jacket heaven," but "slip of pebbles") and unites hu-
man and divine love. The tower in the last stanza becomes the
brazen tower of Danaë which Zeus entered in a golden shower,
thus uniting human and divine: "Unseals her earth, and lifts love
in its shower." Whether this psychological resolution of the ques-
tion of the status and origin of the vision seems satisfactory will
depend on the reader's convictions; in terms of imagery and tonal
climax, at least, it works brilliantly.

Many of Crane's poems raise the question of belief in a peculiarly urgent form. Not only do they proclaim allegiance to a "higher consciousness," a transcendent Vision attained through sexual passion or alcohol or art, but they exalt this dedication to ecstatic passion and death (with automatic resurrection) into a substitute religion, transferring to it the language and feeling of Christian devotion. This is particularly clear in the long poems, "For the Marriage of Faustus and Helen" and *The Bridge*. One's final judgment in this matter cannot be separated from one's religious and aesthetic beliefs. A number of able critics have recently asserted the claims of Neo-Romanticism in its various forms — Dionysiac ecstasy, vision, occultism, and mysticism — as against Eliotian classicism. My own view is that the formulations of Tate and Winters are still accurate: Crane was the "archetype of the modern American poet whose fundamental mistake lay in thinking that an irrational surrender of the intellect to the will would be the basis of a new morality" (Tate); "a poet of great genius, who ruined his life and his talent by living and writing as the two greatest religious teachers of our nation recommended" (Winters). Whether Crane took the doctrine primarily from Whitman and Emerson, as Winters thought, or from Nietzsche, as Dembo argues, makes no fundamental difference, nor does Quinn's attempt to make it respectable by associating it with Maritain's "creative intuition." Dembo's emphasis on the primacy of aesthetic reference in the doctrine — the poet seeking the absolute — makes it less repugnant; but it was more than aesthetic, it was the only religion Crane had. If we take it seriously as such, it is hard to see how it can be called (to use Eliot's criteria) a mature or coherent or responsible interpretation of the meaning of life and death. Aside from the odor of spilt religion, there is a feeling of strain in those poems in which the doctrine is presented explicitly, rather than as embodied in specific experience. This feeling, together with the ultimate incommunicability and obscurity of the doctrine in itself, is, I think, responsible for many of Crane's failures. Sometimes his linguistic effects — such as "adagios of islands" — seem not to correspond to any experience of poet or reader; they can be explained (as Crane brilliantly explained this one), but they still appear contrived and therefore ultimately mere tricks. Similarly, the symbolic structure of Crane's two long poems is abstract and "willed," standing for no real experience. Crane's "doctrine," then, is both shoddier and more dangerous than Yeats's "system"; and immensely less viable in poetry. Yeats's system enabled him to "hold reality and justice in a single thought"; Crane's allowed him too often to transcend, or to ignore, both.

Crane had no messianic ambitions, however, and it is unfair to him to overstress the "doctrine." In general, he seems to me most completely successful when he has a subject other than the pure visionary gospel, one that takes him outside himself and provides a dramatic situation. I have indicated by my choice of poems to discuss which I think are his best. After all possible reservations and subtractions have been made, there remain a substantial number of great lyrics, unique, splendid, and powerful; and these are enough. In the other poems — the minor successes and partial failures — there are unforgettable passages, images, phrases. Crane exploits the resources of the verbal medium to and sometimes beyond its limits; his language is always charged with meaning (to recall Pound's definition of poetry) and it never lacks excitement and challenge. At his best, he has a directness and immediacy, a haunting intensity and candor that are unlike anything else in English poetry.

SELECTED BIBLIOGRAPHIES

Selected Bibliographies

EMILY DICKINSON

Works

Poems of Emily Dickinson, edited by Mabel Loomis Todd and T. W. Higginson. Boston: Roberts Brothers, 1890.

Poems by Emily Dickinson, Second Series, edited by Mabel Loomis Todd and T. W. Higginson. Boston: Roberts Brothers, 1891.

Poems by Emily Dickinson, Third Series, edited by Mabel Loomis Todd. Boston: Roberts Brothers, 1896.

The Single Hound, edited by Martha Dickinson Bianchi. Boston: Little, Brown, 1914.

The Complete Poems of Emily Dickinson, edited by Martha Dickinson Bianchi and Alfred Leete Hampson. Boston: Little, Brown, 1924.

Further Poems of Emily Dickinson, edited by Martha Dickinson Bianchi and Alfred Leete Hampson. Boston: Little, Brown, 1929.

The Poems of Emily Dickinson, edited by Martha Dickinson Bianchi and Alfred Leete Hampson. Boston: Little, Brown, 1930.

Unpublished Poems of Emily Dickinson, edited by Martha Dickinson Bianchi and Alfred Leete Hampson. Boston: Little, Brown, 1935.

Poems by Emily Dickinson, edited by Martha Dickinson Bianchi and Alfred Leete Hampson. Boston: Little, Brown, 1937.

Ancestors' Brocades: The Literary Debut of Emily Dickinson by Millicent Todd Bingham. New York: Harper, 1945. (Contains some poems and letters published for the first time.)

Bolts of Melody: New Poems of Emily Dickinson, edited by Mabel Loomis Todd and Millicent Todd Bingham. New York: Harper, 1945.

The Poems of Emily Dickinson, edited by Thomas H. Johnson. 3 vols. Cambridge, Mass.: Harvard University Press, 1955.
The Complete Poems of Emily Dickinson, edited by Thomas H. Johnson. Boston: Little, Brown, 1960.
Final Harvest: Emily Dickinson's Poems, edited by Thomas H. Johnson. Boston: Little, Brown, 1961.

Letters

The Letters of Emily Dickinson, edited by Mabel Loomis Todd. 2 vols. Boston: Roberts Brothers, 1894.
The Life and Letters of Emily Dickinson, edited by Martha Dickinson Bianchi. Boston: Houghton Mifflin, 1924.
Letters of Emily Dickinson, edited by Mabel Loomis Todd. New York: Harper, 1931.
Emily Dickinson Face to Face: Unpublished Letters with Notes and Reminiscences, edited by Martha Dickinson Bianchi. Boston: Houghton Mifflin, 1932.
Emily Dickinson's Letters to Dr. and Mrs. Josiah Gilbert Holland, edited by Theodora Van Wagenen Ward. Cambridge, Mass.: Harvard University Press, 1951.
Emily Dickinson: A Revelation, by Millicent Todd Bingham. New York: Harper, 1954. (Contains letters published for the first time.)
The Letters of Emily Dickinson, edited by Thomas H. Johnson and Theodora Ward. 3 vols. Cambridge, Mass.: Harvard University Press, 1958.
The Years and Hours of Emily Dickinson, edited by Jay Leyda. 2 vols. New Haven, Conn.: Yale University Press, 1960.

Concordance

Rosenbaum, S. P., editor. *A Concordance to the Poems of Emily Dickinson.* Ithaca, N.Y.: Cornell University Press, 1964.

Biographical Studies

Higgins, David. *Portrait of Emily Dickinson: The Poet and Her Prose.* New Brunswick, N.J.: Rutgers University Press, 1967.
Johnson, Thomas H. *Emily Dickinson: An Interpretive Biography.* Cambridge, Mass.: Harvard University Press, 1955.
Ward, Theodora. *The Capsule of the Mind: Chapters in the Life of Emily Dickinson.* Cambridge, Mass.: Harvard University Press, 1961.
Whicher, George F. *This Was a Poet: A Critical Biography of Emily Dickinson.* New York: Scribner's, 1938.

Critical Studies

Anderson, Charles R. *Emily Dickinson's Poetry: Stairway of Surprise.* New York: Holt, Rinehart and Winston, 1960.
Blackmur, R. P. *Language as Gesture.* New York: Harcourt, Brace, 1952.

————. "Emily Dickinson's Notation," *Kenyon Review*, 18:224–37 (Spring 1956).

Cambon, Glauco. "Emily Dickinson and the Crisis of Self-Reliance," in Myron Simon and Thornton H. Parsons, editors, *Transcendentalism and Its Legacy*. Ann Arbor: University of Michigan Press, 1966.

Capps, Jack L. *Emily Dickinson's Reading 1836–1886*. Cambridge, Mass.: Harvard University Press, 1966.

Chase, Richard. *Emily Dickinson*. New York: Sloane, 1951.

Donoghue, Denis. *Connoisseurs of Chaos*. New York: Macmillan, 1965.

Franklin, R. W. *The Editing of Emily Dickinson: A Reconsideration*. Madison: University of Wisconsin Press, 1967.

Frye, Northrop. *Fables of Identity*. New York: Harcourt, Brace and World, 1963.

Gelpi, Albert J. *Emily Dickinson: The Mind of the Poet*. Cambridge, Mass.: Harvard University Press, 1965.

Griffith, Clark. *The Long Shadow: Emily Dickinson's Tragic Poetry*. Princeton, N.J.: Princeton University Press, 1964.

Pearce, Roy Harvey. *The Continuity of American Poetry*. Princeton, N.J.: Princeton University Press, 1961.

Poulet, Georges. *Studies in Human Time*, translated by Elliott Coleman. Baltimore: Johns Hopkins Press, 1956.

Ransom, John Crowe. "Emily Dickinson: A Poet Restored," *Perspectives USA*, 15:5–20 (Spring 1956).

Tate, Allen. *Collected Essays*. Denver: Alan Swallow, 1959.

Warren, Austin. "Emily Dickinson," *Sewanee Review*, 65:565–86 (Autumn 1957).

Wells, Henry W. *Introduction to Emily Dickinson*. Chicago: Packard, 1947.

Winters, Yvor. *Maule's Curse*. Norfolk, Conn.: New Directions, 1938.

————. *Forms of Discovery*. Denver: Alan Swallow, 1967.

EDWIN ARLINGTON ROBINSON

Principal Works

The Torrent and The Night Before. Cambridge, Mass.: Privately printed, 1896.

The Children of the Night. Boston: Badger, 1897.

Captain Craig. Boston and New York: Houghton Mifflin, 1902.

The Town Down the River. New York: Scribner's, 1910.

Van Zorn. New York: Macmillan, 1914. (Play.)

The Porcupine. New York: Macmillan, 1915. (Play.)

The Man against the Sky. New York: Macmillan, 1916.

Merlin. New York: Macmillan, 1917.

Lancelot. New York: Seltzer, 1920.

The Three Taverns. New York: Macmillan, 1920.

Avon's Harvest. New York: Macmillan, 1921.

Collected Poems. New York: Macmillan, 1921.

Roman Bartholow. New York: Macmillan, 1923.
The Man Who Died Twice. New York: Macmillan, 1924.
Dionysius in Doubt. New York: Macmillan, 1925.
Tristram. New York: Macmillan, 1927.
Sonnets 1889–1927. New York: Gaige, 1928.
Cavender's House. New York: Macmillan, 1929.
Collected Poems. New York: Macmillan, 1929.
The Glory of the Nightingales. New York: Macmillan, 1930.
Selected Poems. New York: Macmillan, 1931.
Matthias at the Door. New York: Macmillan, 1931.
Nicodemus. New York: Macmillan, 1932.
Talifer. New York: Macmillan, 1933.
Amaranth. New York: Macmillan, 1934.
King Jasper. New York: Macmillan, 1935.
Collected Poems. New York: Macmillan, 1937.

Letters

Letters of Edwin Arlington Robinson to Howard George Schmitt, edited by Carl J. Weber. Waterville, Maine: Colby College Library, 1943.
Selected Letters of Edwin Arlington Robinson, with an Introduction by Ridgely Torrence. New York: Macmillan, 1940.
Untriangulated Stars: Letters of Edwin Arlington Robinson to Harry de Forest Smith, edited by Denham Sutcliffe. Cambridge, Mass.: Harvard University Press, 1947.

Bibliographies

Hogan, Charles Beecher. *A Bibliography of Edwin Arlington Robinson.* New Haven, Conn.: Yale University Press, 1936.
Lippincott, Lillian. *A Bibliography of the Writings and Criticism of Edwin Arlington Robinson.* Boston: Faxton, 1937.

Critical and Biographical Studies

Barnard, Ellsworth. *Edwin Arlington Robinson: A Critical Study.* New York: Macmillan, 1952.
———. *Edwin Arlington Robinson: Centenary Essays.* Athens: University of Georgia Press, 1969.
Cary, Richard, ed. *Appreciation of E. A. Robinson.* Waterville, Maine: Colby College Press, 1969.
Coffin, R. P. T. *New Poetry of New England: Frost and Robinson.* Baltimore: Johns Hopkins Press, 1938.
Coxe, Louis. *Edwin Arlington Robinson: The Life of Poetry.* New York: Pegasus, 1969.
Fussell, Edwin S. *Edwin Arlington Robinson: The Literary Background of a Traditional Poet.* Berkeley: University of California Press, 1954.

Hagedorn, Hermann. *Edwin Arlington Robinson*. New York: Macmillan, 1938.
Kaplan, Estelle. *Philosophy in the Poetry of Edwin Arlington Robinson*. New York: Columbia University Press, 1940.
Murphy, Francis. *Edwin Arlington Robinson: A Collection of Critical Essays*. Englewood Cliffs, N.J.: Prentice-Hall, 1970.
Neff, Emery. *Edwin Arlington Robinson* (American Men of Letters Series). New York: Sloane, 1948.
Richards, Laura E. *E. A. R.* Cambridge, Mass.: Harvard University Press, 1936.
Robinson, W. R. *Edwin Arlington Robinson: A Poetry of the Act*. Cleveland: Press of Case Western Reserve University, 1967.
Smith, Chard Powers. *Where the Light Falls: A Portrait of Edwin Arlington Robinson*. New York: Macmillan, 1965.
Winters, Yvor. *Edwin Arlington Robinson* (The Makers of Modern Literature Series). Norfolk, Conn.: New Directions, 1946.

Articles

Hudson, Hoyt H. "Robinson and Praed," *Poetry*, 61:612–20 (February 1943).
Ransom, John Crowe. "Autumn of Poetry," *Southern Review*, 1:609–23 (Winter 1936).
Scott, Winfield T. " 'The Unaccredited Profession,' " *Poetry*, 50:150–54 (June 1937).
Stevick, Robert D. "Robinson and William James," *University of Kansas City Review*, 25:293–301 (June 1959).
Tate, Allen. "Again, O Ye Laurels," *New Republic*, 76:312–13 (October 25, 1933).
Zabel, Morton D. "Robinson: The Ironic Discipline," *Nation*, 145:222–23 (August 28, 1937).

MARIANNE MOORE

Works

POETRY

Poems. London: Egoist Press, 1921.
Marriage. New York: Manikin, Number Three, Monroe Wheeler, 1923.
Observations. New York: Dial Press, 1924.
Selected Poems. New York: Macmillan; London: Faber and Faber, 1935. (With an Introduction by T. S. Eliot.)
The Pangolin and Other Verse. London: Brendin Publishing Company, 1936.
What Are Years. New York: Macmillan, 1941.
Nevertheless. New York: Macmillan, 1944.
A Face. Cummington, Mass.: Cummington Press, 1949.
Collected Poems. New York: Macmillan; London: Faber and Faber, 1951.

The Fables of La Fontaine. New York: Viking, 1954. *Selected Fables of La Fontaine.* London: Faber and Faber, 1955. (Translation.)
Like a Bulwark. New York: Viking, 1956.
O to Be a Dragon. New York: Viking, 1959.
Complete Poems. New York: Viking, 1967.

PROSE

Predilections. New York: Viking, 1955; London: Faber and Faber, 1956. (Essays.)
The Ford correspondence. *New Yorker,* 33:140–46 (April 13, 1957). Reprinted by Pierpont Morgan Library, New York, 1958.
Puss in Boots, The Sleeping Beauty, and Cinderella, by Charles Perrault, adapted by Marianne Moore. New York: Macmillan, 1963.

READER

A Marianne Moore Reader. New York: Viking, 1961.

Bibliography

Sheehy, Eugene P., and Kenneth A. Lohf. *The Achievement of Marianne Moore: A Bibliography 1907–1957.* New York: New York Public Library, 1958.
Tate, Allen. *Sixty American Poets, 1896–1944.* Washington, D.C.: Library of Congress, 1954.

Critical and Biographical Studies

Auden, W. H. "Marianne Moore," *The Dyer's Hand and Other Essays.* New York: Random House, 1962.
Blackmur, R. P. "The Method of Marianne Moore," in *Language as Gesture.* New York: Harcourt, Brace, 1952.
Bogan, Louise. *Selected Criticism: Prose and Poetry.* New York: Noonday Press, 1955. Pp. 252–57.
Burke, Kenneth. "Motives and Motifs in the Poetry of Marianne Moore," *Accent,* 2:157–69 (Spring 1942).
———. "Likings of an Observationist," *Poetry,* 87:239–47 (January 1956).
Doolittle, Hilda (H. D.). "Marianne Moore," *Egoist,* 3 (no. 8):118–19 (August 1916).
Eliot, T. S. A review of *Marriage* and *Poems,* in *Dial,* 75:594–97 (December 1923).
Engle, Bernard E. *Marianne Moore.* New York: Twayne, 1964.
Frankenberg, Lloyd. "The Imaginary Garden," in *Pleasure Dome.* Boston: Houghton Mifflin, 1949. Pp. 119–50.
Gregory, Horace, and Marya Zaturenska. "Marianne Moore: The Genius of *The Dial,*" in *The History of American Poetry, 1900–1940.* New York: Harcourt, Brace, 1946. Pp. 317–25.

Hall, Donald. Interview, *Paris Review*, 7:41–66 (Winter 1961).

Hoffman, Frederick J. *The Twenties: American Writing in the Postwar Decade.* New York: Viking, 1955. Pp. 176–79, 260–61, and *passim.*

Jarrell, Randall. *Poetry and the Age.* New York: Knopf, 1953.

Kenner, Hugh. "Meditation and Enactment," *Poetry*, 102:109–15 (May 1963).

———. "Supreme in Her Abnormality," *Poetry*, 84:356–63 (September 1954).

Marianne Moore Issue, *Quarterly Review of Literature*, 4 (no. 2):121–223 (1948), edited by José Garcia Villa. (Contains essays by Elizabeth Bishop, Louise Bogan, Cleanth Brooks, George Dillon, Wallace Fowlie, Lloyd Frankenberg, Vivienne Koch, John Crowe Ransom, Wallace Stevens, John L. Sweeney, William Carlos Williams, T. C. Wilson.)

Nitchie, George W. *Marianne Moore.* New York: Columbia University Press, 1969.

Pound, Ezra. "Marianne Moore and Mina Loy," *Little Review*, 4:57–58 (March 1918). Reprinted in *The Little Review Anthology*, edited by Margaret Anderson. New York: Hermitage House, 1953. Pp. 188–89.

Sargeant, Winthrop. "Humility, Concentration and Gusto," *New Yorker*, 32:38–75 (February 16, 1957).

Tomlinson, Charles, comp. *Marianne Moore: A Collection of Critical Essays.* Englewood Cliffs, N.J.: Prentice-Hall, 1970.

Weatherhead, Kingsley A. *The Edge of the Image: Marianne Moore, William Carlos Williams, and Other Poets.* Seattle: University of Washington Press, 1967.

Williams, William Carlos. "Marianne Moore," *Dial*, 78:393–401 (May 1925).

Winters, Yvor. "Holiday and Day of Wrath," *Poetry*, 26:39–44 (April 1925).

———. *In Defense of Reason.* New York: Swallow Press and W. Morrow, 1947.

Zabel, Morton Dauwen. "A Literalist of the Imagination," *Poetry*, 47:326–36 (March 1936).

CONRAD AIKEN

Works

POETRY

Earth Triumphant and Other Tales in Verse. New York: Macmillan, 1914.

Turns and Movies and Other Tales in Verse. Boston: Houghton Mifflin; London: Constable, 1916.

The Jig of Forslin: A Symphony. Boston: Four Seas, 1916; London: Secker, 1921.

Nocturne of Remembered Spring and Other Poems. London: Secker, 1916; Boston: Four Seas, 1917.

The Charnel Rose; Senlin: A Biography; and Other Poems. Boston: Four Seas, 1918.

The House of Dust: A Symphony. Boston: Four Seas, 1920.

Punch: The Immortal Liar, Documents in His History. New York: Knopf; London: Secker, 1921.

Priapus and the Pool. Cambridge, Mass.: Dunster House, Harvard University, 1922.

The Pilgrimage of Festus. New York: Knopf, 1923; London: Secker, 1924.

Priapus and the Pool and Other Poems. New York: Boni and Liveright, 1925.

Prelude. New York: Random House, 1929.

Selected Poems. New York: Scribner's, 1929.

John Deth: A Metaphysical Legend, and Other Poems. New York: Scribner's, 1930.

The Coming Forth by Day of Osiris Jones. New York: Scribner's, 1931.

Preludes for Memnon. New York: Scribner's, 1931.

And in the Hanging Gardens. Baltimore: Garamond, 1933.

Landscape West of Eden. London: Dent, 1934; New York: Scribner's, 1935.

Time in the Rock; Preludes to Definition. New York: Scribner's, 1936.

And in the Human Heart. New York: Duell, Sloan, and Pearce, 1940.

Brownstone Eclogues and Other Poems. New York: Duell, Sloan, and Pearce, 1942.

The Soldier: A Poem. Norfolk, Conn.: New Directions, 1944.

The Kid. New York: Duell, Sloan, and Pearce, 1947.

Skylight One: Fifteen Poems. New York: Oxford University Press, 1949.

The Divine Pilgrim. Athens: University of Georgia Press, 1949.

Collected Poems. New York: Oxford University Press, 1953.

A Letter from Li Po and Other Poems. New York: Oxford University Press, 1955.

Sheepfold Hill: Fifteen Poems. New York: Sagamore Press, 1958.

Selected Poems. New York: Oxford University Press, 1961.

The Morning Song of Lord Zero. New York: Oxford University Press, 1963.

NOVELS

Blue Voyage. New York: Scribner's; London: Howe, 1927.

Great Circle. New York: Scribner's; London: Wishart, 1933.

King Coffin. New York: Scribner's; London: Dent, 1935.

A Heart for the Gods of Mexico. London: Secker, 1939.

Conversation: or, Pilgrim's Progress. New York: Duell, Sloan, and Pearce, 1940.

SHORT STORIES

Bring! Bring! and Other Stories. New York: Boni and Liveright; London: Secker, 1925.

Costumes by Eros. New York: Scribner's, 1928; London: Cape, 1929.

Among the Lost People. New York: Scribner's, 1934.

The Short Stories of Conrad Aiken. New York: Duell, Sloan, and Pearce, 1950.

Collected Short Stories. Cleveland, Ohio: World, 1960.

PLAY

Mr. Arcularis. Cambridge, Mass.: Harvard University Press, 1957.

CRITICISM AND OTHER PROSE

Scepticisms: Notes on Contemporary Poetry. New York: Knopf, 1919.
Foreword to *Two Wessex Tales* by Thomas Hardy. Boston: Four Seas, 1919.
Introduction to *Selected Poems of Emily Dickinson.* London: Cape, 1924.
Ushant: An Essay. New York and Boston: Duell, Sloan, and Pearce–Little,
   Brown, 1952.
A Reviewer's ABC: Collected Criticism, edited by Rufus A. Blanshard. New
   York: Meridian, 1958. Reprinted as *Collected Criticism.* New York: Oxford
   University Press, 1968.

Bibliographies

Stallman, R. W. "Annotated Checklist on Conrad Aiken: A Critical Study,"
   in *Wake 11,* edited by Seymour Lawrence. New York: Wake Editions, 1952.
Tate, Allen. *Sixty American Poets 1896–1944.* Washington, D.C.: Library of
   Congress, 1945.

Critical Studies

Hoffman, Frederick J. *Conrad Aiken.* New York: Twayne, 1962.
Lawrence, Seymour, editor. Conrad Aiken Number, *Wake 11.* New York: Wake
   Editions, 1952.
Lerner, Arthur. *Psychoanalytically Oriented Criticism of Three American
   Poets: Poe, Whitman, and Aiken.* Rutherford, N.J.: Fairleigh Dickinson Uni-
   versity Press, 1970.
Martin, Jay. *Conrad Aiken, A Life of His Art.* Princeton, N.J.: Princeton
   University Press, 1962.
Peterson, Houston. *The Melody of Chaos.* New York and Toronto: Longmans,
   Green, 1931.

Articles and Reviews

"Answer to the Sphinx," *Times Literary Supplement* (London), April 19, 1963,
   pp. 257–58.
Beach, Joseph Warren. "Conrad Aiken and T. S. Eliot: Echoes and Overtones,"
   PMLA, 69:753–62 (1954).
Benedetti, Anna. "Sinfonie in Versi," *Nuova Antologia,* 204:202–6 (January
   16, 1920).
Blackmur, Richard P. "Mr. Aiken's Second Wind," *New Republic,* 89:335
   (January 13, 1937).
Kunitz, Stanley. "The Poetry of Conrad Aiken," *Nation,* 133:393–94 (October
   14, 1931).
Moore, Marianne. "If a Man Die," *Hound and Horn,* 5:313–20 (January–
   March 1932).
Schwartz, Delmore. "Merry Go Round of Opinion," *New Republic,* 108:292–93
   (March 1, 1943).

Tate, Allen. "The Author of *John Deth*," *New Republic*, 68:265–66 (July 22, 1931).

———. "Conrad Aiken's Poetry," *Nation*, 122:38–39 (January 13, 1926).

Van Doren, Mark. "Effects in Verse," *Nation*, 112:86–87 (January 19, 1921).

Winters, Yvor. Review of *Selected Poems* in *Hound and Horn*, 3:454–61 (April–June 1930).

E. E. CUMMINGS

Works

For convenience of reference the capitalization of book titles in this essay follows conventional form rather than the typographical style of the title page in each book, which often reflected Cummings' own preference for lowercase letters.

Eight Harvard Poets: E. Estlin Cummings, S. Foster Damon, J. R. Dos Passos, Robert Hillyer, R. S. Mitchell, William A Norris, Dudley Poore, Cuthbert Wright. New York: Laurence J. Gomme, 1917. (Contains eight poems by Cummings.)

The Enormous Room. New York: Boni and Liveright, 1922.

Tulips and Chimneys. New York: Seltzer, 1923.

& (And). New York: Privately printed, 1925.

XLI Poems. New York: Dial Press, 1925.

Is 5. New York: Boni and Liveright, 1926.

Him. New York: Boni and Liveright, 1927.

Christmas Tree. New York: American Book Bindery, 1928.

[No title] New York: Covici, Friede, 1930.

CIOPW. New York: Covici, Friede, 1931.

W (ViVa). New York: Horace Liveright, 1931.

Eimi. New York: Covici, Friede, 1933.

No Thanks. New York: Golden Eagle Press, 1935.

Tom. New York: Arrow Editions, 1935.

1⁄20 (One Over Twenty). London: Roger Roughton, 1936.

Collected Poems. New York: Harcourt, Brace, 1938.

50 Poems. New York: Duell, Sloan and Pearce, 1940.

1 x 1 (One Times One). New York: Henry Holt, 1944.

Anthropos: The Future of Art. Mount Vernon, N.Y.: Golden Eagle Press, 1944.

Santa Claus: A Morality. New York: Henry Holt, 1946.

Puella Mea. Mount Vernon, N.Y.: Golden Eagle Press, 1949.

Xaipe. New York: Oxford University Press, 1950.

I: Six Nonlectures. Cambridge, Mass.: Harvard University Press, 1953.

Poems 1923–1954. New York: Harcourt, Brace, 1954.

E. E. Cummings: A Miscellany, edited by George J. Firmage. New York: Argophile Press, 1958.

95 Poems. New York: Harcourt, Brace, 1958.

100 Selected Poems. New York: Grove, 1959.

SELECTED BIBLIOGRAPHIES

Selected Poems 1923–1958. London: Faber and Faber, 1960.

Adventures in Value, with photographs by Marion Morehouse. New York: Harcourt, Brace and World, 1962.

73 Poems. New York: Harcourt, Brace and World, 1963.

E. E. Cummings: A Miscellany Revised, edited by George J. Firmage. New York: October House, 1965.

Letters

Selected Letters of E. E. Cummings, edited by F. W. Dupee and George Stade. New York: Harcourt, Brace and World, 1969.

Bibliographies

Firmage, George J. *E. E. Cummings: A Bibliography.* Middletown, Conn.: Wesleyan University Press, 1960.

Lauter, Paul. *E. E. Cummings: Index to First Lines and Bibliography of Works by and about the Poet.* Denver: Alan Swallow, 1955.

Critical Comments and Studies

Abel, Lionel. "Clown or Comic Poet?" *Nation,* 140:749–50 (June 26, 1935).

Baum, S. V. "E. E. Cummings: The Technique of Immediacy," *South Atlantic Quarterly,* 53:70–88 (January 1954).

———, editor. *EΣTI: E. E. Cummings and the Critics.* East Lansing: Michigan State University Press, 1962. (Good bibliography.)

Blackmur, R. P. "Notes on E. E. Cummings' Language," in *Language as Gesture.* New York: Harcourt, Brace, 1952. Pp. 317–40.

Bode, Carl. "E. E. Cummings and Exploded Verse," in *The Great Experiment in American Literature.* New York: Praeger, 1961. Pp. 79–100.

Breit, Harvey. "The Case for the Modern Poet," *New York Times Magazine,* November 3, 1946, pp. 20, 58, 60–61.

———. "Talk with E. E. Cummings," *New York Times Book Review,* December 31, 1950, p. 10.

Deutsch, Babette. *Poetry in Our Time.* New York: Henry Holt, 1952. Pp. 111–18.

Dickey, James. "E. E. Cummings," in *Babel to Byzantium: Poets and Poetry Now.* New York: Farrar, Straus and Giroux, 1968. Pp. 100–6.

Fergusson, Francis. "When We Were Very Young," *Kenyon Review,* 12:701–5 (Autumn 1950).

Frankenberg, Lloyd. *Pleasure Dome: On Reading Modern Poetry.* Boston: Houghton Mifflin, 1949. Pp. 157–94.

Friedman, Norman. *E. E. Cummings: The Art of His Poetry.* Baltimore: Johns Hopkins Press, 1960.

———. *E. E. Cummings: The Growth of a Writer.* Carbondale: Southern Illinois University Press, 1964.

Haines, George, IV. "::2:1 — The World and E. E. Cummings," *Sewanee Review,* 59:206–27 (Spring 1951).

Harvard Wake, No. 5 (Spring 1946). (A special Cummings number.)

Hollander, John. "Poetry Chronicle," *Partisan Review*, 26:142–43 (Winter 1959).

Honig, Edwin. " 'Proud of His Scientific Attitude,' " *Kenyon Review*, 17:484–90 (Summer 1955).

Horton, Philip, and Sherry Mangan. "Two Views of Cummings," *Partisan Review*, 4:58–63 (May 1938).

Marks, Barry A. *E. E. Cummings*. New York: Twayne, 1964.

Moore, Marianne. "People Stare Carefully," *Dial*, 80:49–52 (January 1926).

————. "One Times One," in *Predilections*. New York: Viking, 1955. Pp. 140–43.

Munson, Gorham B. "Syrinx," *Secession*, No. 5 (July 1923), pp. 2–11.

Norman, Charles. *E. E. Cummings: The Magic-Maker*. New York: Macmillan, 1958.

Riding, Laura, and Robert Graves. *A Survey of Modernist Poetry*. London: Heinemann, 1927. Pp. 9–34.

Shapiro, Karl. *Essay on Rime*. New York: Reynal and Hitchcock, 1945. Pp. 20–21.

Sitwell, Edith. *Aspects of Modern Poetry*. London: Duckworth, 1934. Pp. 251–57.

Spencer, Theodore. "Technique as Joy," *Harvard Wake*, No. 5 (Spring 1946), pp. 25–29.

Tate, Allen. "E. E. Cummings," in *Reactionary Essays on Poetry and Ideas*. New York: Scribner's, 1936. Pp. 228–33.

Time, September 14, 1962. (A full-page obituary.)

Troy, William. "Cummings's Non-land of Un-," *Nation*, 136:413 (April 12, 1933).

Voisin, Laurence. "Quelques poètes américains," *Europe: Revue Mensuelle*, 37:36–37 (February–March 1959).

Von Abele, Rudolph. " 'Only to Grow': Change in the Poetry of E. E. Cummings," *PMLA*, 70:913–33 (December 1955).

Wegner, Robert E. *The Poetry and Prose of E. E. Cummings*. New York: Harcourt, Brace and World, 1965.

Williams, William Carlos. "E. E. Cummings' Paintings and Poems," *Arts Digest*, 29:7–8 (December 1, 1954).

Wilson, Edmund. "*Him*," *New Republic*, 70:293–94 (November 2, 1927).

HART CRANE

Works

White Buildings: Poems by Hart Crane, with a Foreword by Allen Tate. New York: Boni and Liveright, 1926.

The Bridge. Paris: Black Sun Press; New York: Liveright, 1930.

The Collected Poems of Hart Crane, edited with an Introduction by Waldo Frank. New York: Liveright, 1933. (Includes the essay "Modern Poetry.")

The Complete Poems and Selected Letters and Prose of Hart Crane, edited with an Introduction and Notes by Brom Weber. New York: Liveright, 1966.

Letters

The Letters of Hart Crane, 1916–1932, edited by Brom Weber. New York: Hermitage House, 1952. Reprinted, Berkeley and Los Angeles: University of California Press, 1965.

Bibliography

Rowe, H. D. *Hart Crane: A Bibliography*. Denver: Alan Swallow, 1955.

Biographies

Brown, Susan Jenkins. *Robber Rocks: Letters and Memories of Hart Crane, 1923–1932*. Middletown, Conn.: Wesleyan University Press, 1969.

Horton, Philip. *Hart Crane: The Life of an American Poet*. New York: Norton, 1937. (Includes as appendixes an essay and several letters by Crane explaining his beliefs about poetry in general and his specific intentions in some of his own poems.)

Unterecker, John. *Voyager: A Life of Hart Crane*. New York: Farrar, Straus and Giroux, 1969.

Weber, Brom. *Hart Crane: A Biographical and Critical Study*. New York: Bodley Press, 1948. (Includes previously uncollected poetry and prose.)

Critical Studies

Butterfield, R. W. *The Broken Arc: A Study of Hart Crane*. Edinburgh: Oliver and Boyd, 1969.

Dembo, L. S. *Hart Crane's Sanskrit Charge: A Study of* The Bridge. Ithaca, N.Y.: Cornell University Press, 1960.

Hazo, Samuel. *Hart Crane: An Introduction and Interpretation*. New York: Barnes and Noble, 1963.

Leibowitz, Herbert A. *Hart Crane: An Introduction to the Poetry*. New York: Columbia University Press, 1968.

Lewis, R. W. B. *The Poetry of Hart Crane: A Critical Study*. Princeton. N.J.: Princeton University Press, 1967.

Quinn, Vincent. *Hart Crane*. New York: Twayne, 1963.

Articles and Parts of Books

Alvarez, Alfred. *Stewards of Excellence: Studies in Modern English and American Poets*. New York: Scribner's, 1958. Pp. 107–23.

Blackmur, R. P. *Form and Value in Modern Poetry*. Garden City, N.Y.: Doubleday Anchor Books, 1957. Pp. 269–85.

Cambon, Glauco. *The Inclusive Flame: Studies in American Poetry*. Bloomington: Indiana University Press, 1963. Pp. 120–82.

Dembo, L. S. "Hart Crane's Early Poetry," *University of Kansas City Review*, 27:181–87 (1961).

Frank, Waldo. *In the American Jungle*. New York: Farrar and Rinehart, 1937. Pp. 96–108.

Friar, Kimon, and J. M. Brinnin, editors. *Modern Poetry: American and British*. New York: Appleton-Century-Crofts, 1951. Pp. 449–56.

Friedman, Paul. "*The Bridge*: A Study in Symbolism," *Psychoanalytic Quarterly*, 21:49–80 (1952).

Gregory, Horace, and Marya Zaturenska. *A History of American Poetry: 1900–1940*. New York: Harcourt, Brace, 1946. Pp. 468–81.

Koretz, Gene. "Crane's 'Passage,'" *Explicator*, vol. 13, no. 8, item 47 (1955).

Matthiessen, F. O. "American Poetry, 1920–1940," *Sewanee Review*, 55:24–55 (1947).

Miller, James E., Jr., Karl Shapiro, and Bernice Slote. *Start with the Sun: Studies in Cosmic Poetry*. Lincoln: University of Nebraska Press, 1960. Pp. 137–65.

Rosenthal, M. L. *The Modern Poets: A Critical Introduction*. New York: Oxford University Press, 1960. Pp. 168–82.

Tate, Allen. *Collected Essays*. Denver: Alan Swallow, 1959. Pp. 225–37, 528–32.

Trachtenberg, Alan. *Brooklyn Bridge: Fact and Symbol*. New York: Oxford University Press, 1965. Pp. 143–65.

Vogler, Thomas A. "A New View of Hart Crane's Bridge," *Sewanee Review*, 73:381–408 (1965).

Waggoner, Hyatt Howe. *The Heel of Elohim: Science and Values in Modern American Poetry*. Norman: University of Oklahoma Press, 1950. Pp. 155–92.

Winters, Yvor. *In Defense of Reason*. New York: Swallow Press and W. Morrow, 1947. Pp. 575–603. (Same essay in *On Modern Poets*. New York: Meridian Books, 1959. Pp. 120–43.)

ABOUT THE AUTHORS

About the Authors

DENIS DONOGHUE is professor of modern English and American literature at University College, Dublin. He is the author of a number of books, including *Jonathan Swift, The Ordinary Universe, The Third Voice,* and *Connoisseurs of Chaos.*

LOUIS COXE is the Pierce Professor of English at Bowdoin College. He is the author of several volumes of poetry including *The Second Man and Other Poems, The Wilderness and Other Poems, The Middle Passage,* and *The Sea Faring and Other Poems.*

JEAN GARRIGUE has published a number of collections of her poetry, including *Country without Maps, A Waterwalk by the Villa d'Este, The Monument Rose,* and *The Ego and the Centaur.* She has taught at several colleges and universities.

REUEL DENNEY teaches at the University of Hawaii and at the East-West Center. His books, ranging from poetry to social criticism, include *The Lonely Crowd,* of which he is co-author.

EVE TRIEM's poetry has been published in the volumes *Parade of Doves* and *Poems* as well as in many magazines and anthology collections. A resident of Seattle, she has lectured on poetry from coast to coast.

251

Monroe K. Spears, Libbie Shearn Moody Professor of English at Rice University, was editor of the *Sewanee Review* from 1952 to 1961. He is the author of *The Poetry of W. H. Auden: The Disenchanted Island.*

INDEX

Index

Adams, Henry, 46, 47
Adventures in Value, 163
Aeneid, 220
Aeschylus, 168
"After great pain, a formal feeling comes," 31
Aiken, Anna, 123
Aiken, Conrad, 3, 6, 122, 132, 143, 155: as modernist, 5, 8; and Eliot, 7, 8, 153, 154; and Pound, 7, 8, 153, 154; as literary critic, 7, 139–40; psychoanalytic movement and, 8, 126, 128, 134–35, 138, 141, 142, 143; birth and early life of, 123; at Harvard University, 123, 126, 135; and Allen Tate, 123, 158; in New York City, 123; and England, 124; and family tragedy, 124, 136; poetic style of, 124–25, 146–47, 148, 149–50, 151, 152; literary influences on, 126, 127, 129, 130; use of music in poetry of, 126, 127, 138; and French Symbolists, 127; and impressionism, 127; poetic method of, 127–28; turns attention to fiction, 129–30; marriages and children of, 130; admired Henry James, 130; psychological fiction and, 130, 137, 138; and current forms of literature, 133; and Sigmund Freud, 135,

136, 153, 156; psychiatric interest of in his past, 136–37, 138; and characterology, 140, 153; and study of ethics, 141; relativism of, 142, 156; interest in "identity," 142, 145, 153; and psychological liberalism, 144; narrative poems of, 145, 146; figurative devices of, 147–48; critical assessment of, 151, 157, 158; liberalism of, 152; and humanism, 156; originality of, 157; and W. B. Yeats, 158
  WORKS: *And in the Hanging Gardens*, 148; *Anthropos*, 162; *Blue Voyage*, 8, 124, 131, 137; *Brownstone Eclogues*, 8, 151, 154; *The Charnel Rose*, 125, 138, 147; *Conversation*, 133; *The Divine Pilgrim*, 125, 126, 135; *Great Circle*, 131, 135, 136; *A Heart for the Gods of Mexico*, 133; *The House of Dust*, 125; *The Jig of Forslin*, 125, 126, 127, 138, 147, 153–54; *The Kid*, 145, 146; *King Coffin*, 132, 137; *A Letter from Li Po*, 156; *Mr. Arcularis*, 132, 137; *Nocturne of Remembered Spring*, 126; *Osiris Jones*, 142; *The Pilgrimage of Festus*, 125, 135, 138; *Preludes for Memnon*, 8, 142, 151, 152; *Punch*, 8, 138, 145; *Scepti-*

255